ENHANCING MOTIVATION

Change in the Classroom

ENHANCING MOTIVATION

Change

in the

Classroom

THE IRVINGTON SOCIAL RELATIONS SERIES

by

Richard deCharms

in collaboration with

Dennis J. Shea

Karl W. Jackson

Franziska Plimpton

Sharon Koenigs

Agusto Blasi

IRVINGTON PUBLISHERS, INC., New York
Distributed by HALSTED PRESS Division of
JOHN WILEY & SONS, New York

THE IRVINGTON SOCIAL RELATIONS SERIES

Distributed by HALSTED PRESS
A division of JOHN WILEY & SONS, New York

Library of Congress cataloging in publication information:

DeCharms, Richard.
  Enhancing motivation.

  Bibliography: p.
  Includes indexes.
  1. Motivation in education.   I. Shea, Dennis J.
II. Title.
LB1065.D27   370.15'4   75-38701
ISBN 0-470-01392-3

Book and Jacket design by Raymond Solomon

Printed in the United States of America

Preface and Acknowledgments

This book reports research that includes several areas of interest. It combines psychology and education, motivation and social psychology, experimental research and field observation. The audience that the book was written for includes students of both education and psychology, and I hope that it will be of interest to experienced teachers in the schools.

When the research was initiated in the mid-sixties, a large number of projects were trying to help ameliorate problems in the schools. Often the goal of such projects was to develop curriculum materials or to develop classroom techniques for teachers. Our goal was always quite different and stemmed from an interest in motivation theory. Our theory suggested that merely to provide teachers with materials or to try to tell them specifically what to do in their classrooms was to undermine their own motivation. So we set out to develop classroom exercises *with* rather than *for* teachers. Our goal was to work intensively with 15 to 20 teachers a year, thereby reaching more than 1200 children in the classrooms of these teachers over the life of the project. Our aim was to gain understanding of motivation in the classroom, rather than to develop specific procedures or materials to be packaged and disseminated.

At first we were intrigued by the question whether some of the basic findings of motivation derived from research on college students would hold with elementary school children. A first step, taken by Virginia Carpenter in her dissertation (Carpenter, 1967) that related achievement motivation to moderate risk taking in spelling and arithmetic exercises, reached the eyes of Mr. Arthur Singer who was then with the Carnegie Corporation of New York. Through his interest the grant that supported the major portion of the research was secured.

During the year between the time when Carpenter's results were clear and the Carnegie Grant began, I was fortunate to be granted a sabbatical by Washington University and was partially supported by the Achievement Motivation Training Project at Harvard University. Long discussions with Professor D.C. McClelland and his staff sparked my interest in motivation development and contributed in many ways to my thinking.

At Washington University the following year I found interest and enthusiasm for the project from a group of school administrators, notably Drs. Gerald Moeller and David Mahan, and Messrs. Clifford Evans and

v

William Pearson. Not only did they help with entrée into the schools, but also they contributed substantially with ideas.

During the project something in excess of 1200 children contributed their time and 35 to 40 teachers performed various activities to help in the development of motivation. A slightly larger number cooperated as we assessed the advancement of pupils in the absence of motivation training. The principals of the schools were cooperative in every way. We hope that even the control children gained something, if only the candy bars that we gave them in thanks for their efforts.

Each year, when we conducted the residential teacher training described in Chapter 4, Shri Manohar Nadkarni came from Harvard to act as principal trainer. It was always a delight and inspiration to work with him.

After the first year of the project one of the experimental teachers of that first year became one of our most valuable consultants and has helped every year since with teacher training and in other ways. Most of the teachers remember Bertha as both a delightful person and the "teacher" who treated them as a Pawn in the "Origin-Pawn Game" (see Chapter 4). We think of Mrs. Bertha Winningham as a major contributor to our better understanding of the teacher's role in the school, as a superlative teacher and as a warm and wonderful human being.

Meanwhile, at Washington University many brains and hands were at work. My colleagues in the Graduate Institute of Education have stimulated my thought in many ways. Special thanks are due to Professors Raymond Callahan and Arthur Wirth for help in the historical and philosophical contexts discussed in Chapters I and II. The University provided a small grant in 1971–72 that aided in writing the book.

To my doctoral students I cannot give enough credit. Ten of them wrote doctoral dissertations that were directly related to the project. They are acknowledged as collaborators on the title page. Many of them are co-authors of chapters in the book. Dr. Virginia Carpenter's dissertation, combined with earlier laboratory studies by Dr. Aharon Kuperman and Dr. Winnie J. Bridgeman, formed the basis for the Carnegie Proposal. Drs. Peter Rothenberg and Jane Landsbaum Brownstone contributed valuable data during the first year of the project. Dr. Dennis Shea's dissertation forms the major results of Chapter 6 and he and Karl Jackson collaborated on the difficult task of recording everything that happened as they participated in one week-long residential training session and then transforming their notes into Chapter 4.

Dr. Franziska Plimpton's work is evident in both Chapters 7 and 9. Simply put, her dissertation provided us with the most crucial measure of the whole project. Sharon Koenigs and Robert J. Hess contributed the Origin Climate Questionnaire discussed in Chapter 9.

Drs. Ina Coor, Janet Collins and Augusto Blasi stimulated our interest in ego development. Many discussions with them and with my colleague, Professor Jane Loevinger, resulted in several training units and the results reported in Chapter 10. Dr. Kelvin Ryals contributed to the discussion of ego development and moral development while conducting a parallel study of achievement motivation training.

The names of students and friends who helped collect, record and analyze data seem legion—Jay Noel, Lawrence Sondler, Nancy Sachar, Rusty Altheimer, Tedi Zweig, Mary Schatzkamer, Frances Shands, Marilyn Goodman and Wallette Lynch.

Knowles Dougherty, in addition to helping in the early theoretical formulations, discussed the project with school administrators. He then deserted us to start the Warehouse School in Boston, where I have been able to see some of our theoretical discussions take form in practical, day-to-day teaching of children seeking an alternative to the public school.

Another student who deserted us for Boston and Harvard was Karen Cohen, but not before she had served as scorer and then analyzed psychometrically the Plimpton measure (Chapter 7) on a small grant from the Office of Education, Number OEG-6-9-0090740-0078 (010).

Throughout the project Lola Latta was my secretary. Subsequent to her valiant efforts to keep things organized, Rebecca Lintz served as secretary and literary critic. Marny Muir suffered through the rewriting of every chapter as editorial consultant and secretary. In the past year this role has been assumed by Dorothy Altheimer along with all her other duties as executive secretary on a new grant.

It is impossible to express my thanks adequately to these people. I guess I am most grateful for the editorial and secretarial help, without which I am helpless.

Professor David C. McClelland has encouraged the work from its inception and has read the entire manuscript. His own work has been the inspiration throughout. I have also been inspired by Professor Fritz Heider and in recent years have been privileged to discuss some of the ideas contained herein with him.

Professor M. Brewster Smith read, encouraged and commented helpfully in the manuscript. Several thoughtful suggestions came from Dr. Samuel Ball of the Educational Testing Service, Princeton.

Scripta Publishing Company has granted permission to reprint several figures in the data chapters.

I have had much help and my hope is that the book will be helpful to others.

Richard deCharms

St. Louis, Missouri

Contents

Contents

Part 1

The Motivation Project

Chapter 1

Origins and Pawns at School

(R. deCharms)

A Pawn is the chessman of least value. The word is derived from the Old French *paon* or *peon,* meaning foot soldier. Figuratively, *Pawn* refers to a person who is pushed around by others, a person who is used to further the purposes of others. It is in this figurative sense that we shall use the term.

A person who is not pushed around by others but goes about seeking his own goals can be said to originate his own behavior. When a person is originating his own behavior, we shall say that he is acting as an *Origin*.

The research reported here started with the notion that people differ along a dimension from Origin to Pawn and that the basic concept underlying the dimension was relevant to motivation. A Pawn would be at most externally motivated, while an Origin would be internally motivated. Quite frankly, it seemed that to be an Origin was better than to be a Pawn.

We derived the Origin-Pawn dimension initially from motivation theory, but it seemed obvious that it could potentially be applied to educational problems. The child in the traditional classroom is most often a Pawn to the dictates of the teacher. If the child could be encouraged to originate his own learning behavior, then, it would seem, he could be more of an Origin in school.

This book can be seen in its psychological, educational and even broadly cultural context if it is seen as a history in microcosm of our discovery of the kernel of truth as well as the deceptive simplicity of our initial idea.

At the broadest level we had indeed picked an important problem, a problem that had ancient philosophical roots in discussions of freedom. Far from being simple, the problem was so complex that it seemed to be basic to certain paradoxes in our cultural heritage and it led us directly to a long-standing debate in education. In retrospect, we seem to have followed a well-worn path, starting with a simple dichotomy that led into a maze of finer distinctions.

In this first chapter we will try to sketch the psychological and educational territory leading to the conclusion that our point of departure had enough truth to support our research. In the last chapter we shall return to this most general level and attempt to generalize our welter of evidence to a more sophisticated approach to both motivation theory and educational practice.

PERSONAL CAUSATION AND THE ORIGIN-PAWN CONCEPT

Our position concerning motivation as we started the project was roughly as follows. Man at his best must be *active,* not *reactive*; he must strive rather than submit as a puppet. Man must author his own behavior, rather than have it dictated by authority. Man is not a pawn to the dictates of others; at his best man is the origin of his actions.

The objective antecedents of a person's behavior may be external events, but to the person *he* is the cause of his behavior when he decides to act from personal commitment. This is *personal causation* and it is our fundamental assumption about motivation. "Man's primary motivational propensity is to be effective in producing changes in his environment. Man strives to be a causal agent, to be the primary locus of causation for, or the Origin of, his behavior; he strives for personal causation" (deCharms, 1968, p. 269).

For ease of communication we adopted the terms *Origin* and *Pawn* to distinguish between two motivational states that are basic to personal causation. An Origin is a person who feels that he is in control of his fate; he feels that the cause for his behavior is within himself. A Pawn feels that he is pushed around, that someone else pulls the strings and he is the puppet. He feels the locus of causality for his behavior is external to himself. The motivational effects of these two personal states are extremely important. The Origin is positively motivated, optimistic, confident, accepting of challenge. The Pawn is negatively motivated, defensive,irresolute, avoidant of challenge. The Origin feels potent; the Pawn feels powerless (de-Charms, 1968).

The Origin-Pawn concept is not a motive, since it is not a descriptive name given to a class of goals. Rather, it is a feeling of purpose and commitment (or the lack of it) that can apply to any specific motive. To help a person to be an Origin is not to determine his goals but to help him develop commitment and purpose so that he can reach his own goals more effectively.

There are both theoretical and practical differences between Origins and Pawns. The most important theoretical distinction between these two polar aspects depends on how the person feels—a very personal reaction to his own capabilities. The most important practical aspects distinguishing between the Origin and the Pawn are the actions associated with feelings of commitment and competence (White, 1959) as opposed to aimlessness and powerlessness.

People are not always Origins, nor are they always Pawns. Some people are more characteristically one or the other and hence the concept applies to personal predispositions. In addition, situational constraints may interact with personal predispositions. *Situations* may induce more Origin or more Pawn feelings (deCharms, 1972). In some situations people are forced to act in predetermined ways by external circumstances. In other situations people are more free to choose for themselves and originate their own actions. The basic situational element is the relative amount of freedom in the situation.

Personal Concepts and Objective Behavior

Twentieth-century psychology has by-passed personal concepts such as meaning and purpose derived from experience. Since inquiry based on observed behavior can be verified by other observers, whereas personal reports of an individual's experience cannot, the nineteenth-century attempt at a systematic study of human consciousness has been replaced by the more objective study of behavior. Recent emphasis on predicting and controlling behavior (responses) by the manipulation of specific environmental events (stimuli) is the cornerstone of objective, stimulus-response psychology.

There is, however, no one-to-one relationship between stimuli and responses, because of variability in the organism's reactions to stimuli. The human being's personal experience elicited by the environmental events forms the crucial mediating link to explain why certain events produce specific behaviors in one individual and not in another. The intervening private events may include attributing meaning to the environmental events (a siren means danger), and arousal of purpose or motivation (a challenge means get to work).

From this point of view the stimulus-response chain includes a mediating link as follows:

Personal experience and interpretation

Antecedent environmental events   Consequent behavior

The critical element for explaining and predicting behavior is the intervening personal experience. In order to produce motivated behavior one must produce the experience of arousal, commitment and purpose. In the practical world of the school, the problem is to create conditions that will stimulate commitment and responsible choice felt to be originating from within the individual.

The conditions that promote commitment, internal choice and responsibility within a person, i.e., the conditions that encourage feeling and acting like an Origin, have four basic elements. The person should be encouraged to consider carefully his basic motives (self-study) in a warm atmosphere of acceptance by others in the group. The setting should help him to translate his motives into realistic short- and long-range goals (internal goal setting) and to plan realistic and concrete action to attain the goals (planning and goal-directed behavior). Finally, the setting should help him learn to accept responsibility for selected goals as well as for the success and failure of his attempts to reach them (personal responsibility).

If these conditions could be built into a training setting and experiences, they should induce increased commitment and purpose, greater personal responsibility, and higher motivation, all within a context of meaning to the life of the individual. Finally, the aroused motivation should result in more effective behavior, greater success in goal-attainment and hence greater satisfaction. This is what we mean by treating a person as an Origin and helping him to be an Origin and to be more effective in reaching his own goals. These conditions are what we have tried to create by the concrete experiences that we provided for the teachers (Chapter 4) and that we devised with the teachers for their students (Chapter 5).

Motives and Motivation

The concept of personal causation is different from more traditional motivational concepts. Still it has its roots in several more familiar concepts that helped the author formulate the original idea (deCharms, 1968). Let us review briefly the relation between personal causation and physical causation, motivation and the achievement motive.

First, the concept of cause itself is troublesome. One meaning of cause is a force or some other objective entity; another is cause as an inference made by an observer after a series of events. In the physical sciences, and especially mechanics, a cause is sometimes thought to be an external force impinging on an object and initiating a change. In the time-honored billiard ball example when the cue ball strikes another ball the explanation of the movement of the second ball comes from the laws of mechanics. The cue ball is said to *cause* the other ball to move because the cue ball makes a unique contribution to the motion of the other ball. But the concept of causation is much more complex than that even in mechanics, to say nothing of human behavior. Without reviewing the entire argument from deCharms (1968), suffice it to say that there appears to be no objectively demonstrable entity that we can point to and call a "cause." David Hume pointed this out long ago. Similarly, a motive is not something that can be completely objectified. Observation of the behavior of billard balls leads to an *inference* in the person about the cause. Similarly, the sight of a hard-working person leads us to infer motivation *because* we know that we feel motivated when we work like that. A motive is nothing more than that, it is not something out there, it is not a cluster of behaviors. A motive *is an inference that we make when we see a constellation of environmental conditions and individual behaviors*—an inference that helps us to understand the behavior in terms of an inferred goal. We make the motive inference easily, although not without error, because we all experience ourselves as a personal cause and assume that others do also.

We need no definition or precision when we personally experience motivation. Motivation as experience is immediate. When we attribute motivation to others, however, their direct experience is not available to us and we must infer it from observed behavior. Since behaviors are not motivation, nor are they perfectly related to motivation, inferences of motivation from observed behavior are imprecise. The term motivation carries much personal meaning for each of us, but as a scientific term it lacks precision of definition. Motivation is a global term used to encompass explanations for behavior. Specific motives are often identified in terms of the names of classes of goals, such as achievement motivation, the goal of which is success in competition with a standard of excellence,[1] or affiliation motivation, the goal of which is friendship.

Achievement Motivation

One of the specific motives about which much is known is the achievement motive. The goal of the motive is defined as "success in competition with a standard of excellence" (McClelland, Atkinson, Clark & Lowell, 1953). Research over the last twenty years has demonstrated that the man with strong achievement motivation is the entrepreneur, the man who is self-reliant, takes personal responsibility for his actions, calculates the risks involved and takes moderate risks, plans prudently, checks his progress, carefully uses his skills and is conservative of his time. Such a man appears internally motivated and seems to maximize his potential for personal causation.

Noting that these achievement characteristics were very helpful in becoming successful in business, McClelland and Winter (1969) designed training courses to help develop the achievement motive in businessmen. Subsequently, the achievement motivation courses have been adapted for use with high school boys (McClelland & Alschuler, 1971; and Alschuler, Tabor & McIntyre, 1970; Ryals, 1969). These training courses formed the immediate antecedent of the research reported in this book.

The influence of the theory of achievement motivation on our thinking about personal causation and the development of motivation is evident throughout the book. We have tried, however, to broaden our training using the concept of personal causation and, stressing the internal aspects, to make it more broadly applicable to school children. The result is a conception of motivation development that relies on the individual's personal ability to become committed through perceiving the meaning of his behavior in responsibly pursuing his purpose. In our view, achievement motivation training is less broad and in helping the individual evaluate his own excellence often relies on accountability to a superior.[2] Personal causation development does not restrict the goal to competition with a standard. It does provide internal choice of purpose followed by internal personal responsibility, not external accountability.

The internal-external dimension was clarified in our thinking by Heider's (1958a) distinction between personal and impersonal causality based on the central factor of intention. "If a person causes a change intentionally, then this intention of the person . . . is within a wide range of other conditions . . . the sufficient condition of the change. . . . The cause of the change is located in the person, and here, if anywhere, one can truly speak of a local cause; . . . " (Heider, 1958b, p. 29). The locus of causality can be said to be internal or external to a person and if a person experiences the locus of causality for an act to be within himself, then he experiences personal causation.

A related distinction is between intrinsic and extrinsic motivation. Behavior is often said to be extrinsically motivated when the goal of the behavior is something that is only arbitrarily tied to completion of the act. Thus, extrinsically motivated behavior, such as sitting through a dull lecture, is endured in order to reach a goal, such as a good grade. Intrinsically motivated behavior is behavior that cannot be placed in the extrinsic "in-order-to" category (Koch, 1956). Such behavior somehow "intrinsically" produces its own satisfaction. Although these twin concepts are imprecise, they carry a common-sense meaning that is persuasive.

In *Personal Causation* (deCharms, 1968) we said, "As a first approximation, we propose that whenever a person experiences himself to be the locus of causality for his own behavior (to be an Origin), he will consider himself to be intrinsically motivated. Conversely, when a person perceives the locus of causality for his behavior to be external to himself (that he is a Pawn), he will consider himself to be extrinsically motivated" (p. 328). This seems now to be overly simple. A person may desire a goal and willingly choose to engage in an odious activity to reach that goal and still feel that the activity is self-initiated, i.e., that he originated the activity. This is probably the case in much learning behavior in school even when the student desires the outcomes of learning. It is the context within which the activity is a meaningful step toward his purpose that renders the behavior freely chosen, although the action may provide no intrinsic satisfaction.

If we are right about personal causation being a basic predisposition, however, any activity that satisfies the condition of demonstrating a change effected by the actor ought to carry some intrinsic satisfaction in the realization that "I did it." The development of this feeling and of the anticipation "I can do it" is the development of personal causation.

Two other concepts currently in vogue in psychology deserve

mention here. They are attribution theory (cf. Kelley, 1967; Weiner, 1972) and Rotter's (1966) social learning theory. Attribution theory starts with Heider's (1958a) description of "the processes by which the individual makes attributions about his world—attributions of causes, dispositions, and inherent properties. . . . Equally important is the relevance of attribution theory to the *perception* of motivation, both in others and in one's self" (Kelley, 1967, pp. 192–93). The Origin-Pawn concept may be seen as a specific application of attribution of internal causality to oneself. We like to distinguish, however, between the *perception* of motivation and the *experience* of it, a distinction pointed out in another context by Malcolm (1964) that we shall return to in Chapter 7.

The Origin-Pawn distinction is often seen as synonymous with Rotter's concept of internal versus external control of reinforcements (Rotter, 1966). The distinction between the two orientations depends upon a definition of reinforcement. We shall postpone a discussion of this distinction until Chapter 6.

THE EDUCATIONAL CONTEXT

When we approached teachers with the Origin-Pawn concept, we found considerable enthusiasm for the basic distinction. They seemed to grasp the idea very quickly and see its application to the classroom. Often the initial enthusiasm seemed to stem from superficial understanding, however. Returning to her classroom after a session with us, one teacher who had formerly conducted a rather traditional class, asked her class to rearrange the neat rows into a circle and conduct their own class as a discussion. Her disappointment at the resulting chaos was soon converted into a healthy skepticism toward theory-based gimmicks.

More experienced teachers warned us that it was courting chaos to reduce control suddenly. Often such teachers were intrigued by the possibility of gradually developing "controls from within" the children themselves (Redl & Wineman, 1952). But this raised another issue. One teacher was especially concerned, since, as he said, developing motivation takes time and that time is taken away from teaching arithmetic, spelling or science. He was concerned that spending so much time on motivation units in class would erode the

effects of subject-matter teaching and deleteriously affect the results
of the standardized achievement testing at the end of the year.

In the first incident we recognized elements of the long-standing
debate concerning classroom organization and learning by discussion.
The psychological roots of this problem lie in the classic study of
authoritarian vs. democratic leadership styles (Lewin, Lippitt &
White, 1939) and in studies of dominative and integrative behavior in
children (Anderson, 1937, 1939). Since these classics, an enormous
literature has developed. Recent related classroom applications
include Thelen's (1960) concept of group investigation, Glasser's
(1969) classroom meeting model and the educational outgrowth of
Rogerian therapy as exemplified in *Freedom to Learn* (Rogers, 1969).
The original simple distinction between authoritarian vs. democratic
leadership has all but lost its meaning to the point where Anderson
can say *"The authoritarian-democratic construct provides an inadequate conceptualization of leadership behavior"* (Anderson, 1959, p.
212, italics in original). Still, these hazy distinctions form the intellectual backdrop for the current interest in open classrooms and alternative schools.

The concern of the second teacher mentioned above opened
another Pandora's Box that may be characterized as the subject-
matter vs. life-adjustment controversy. Obviously, this is not a completely separate issue from the first, but it may be seen as more of a
value issue and less amenable to empirical study. In this light it is not
as much a question of what empirically results from more or less
concentration on traditional subject matter as it is a question of what
is the goal of schooling.

The life-adjustment controversy has more distinctly educational
roots. Those who see emphasis on life-adjustment as the erosion of
the moral fibre of the country through "permissiveness," often lay
the blame at the door of John Dewey and progressive education.
Some of the more carefully considered treatises, however, are at
pains to point out that it is a mistaken view of Dewey's position if it is
"interpreted to mean allowing the child to do as he pleased, with a
resultant lack of direction" (Callahan, 1960, p. 138). Callahan quotes
Dewey's *Experience and Education* (1938) to the effect that to base
education on experience may entail more rather than less guidance
from adults than existed in traditional schools.

Wirth (1966) has made a careful analysis of Dewey's own application of his philosophy to education as seen in his design for and
initiation of the Chicago Laboratory School (Dewey, 1895, cited in
Wirth). "Contrary to a popular stereotype that Dewey wanted to

indulge children, it is clear that his goal was to create a reformed and vital liberal education, appropriate for a democratic society" (Wirth, 1966, p. 29).

It was Arthur Bestor (1955), however, who, while absolving Dewey and progressivism, most trenchantly hurled the epithet "life-adjustment" at the "Educationists." It was his *The Restoration of Learning* that drew the line between Dewey's progressive education and what Bestor called "regressive education" in the form of "life-adjustment." Bestor asked, "Is a good education undemocratic?" and accused administrators of public education with "a lowering of intellectual aims and of educational standards . . . as the proper adjustment to universal compulsory schooling" (p. 116). He claimed that Prosser (1951) and the Office of Education had sandwiched "life-adjustment training" between college preparation and vocational training. Life-adjustment was "to be condescendingly bestowed upon the remaining three-fifths of the population. . . . By definition it prepares students neither for systematic intellectual effort nor for 'desireable skilled occupations.'" (Bestor, 1955, p. 117).

The more recent history of this controversy includes the space-race of the late 1950's that stirred the scientific community to demand higher standards of scientific and mathematics training. In the 1960's the civil-rights movement began to take hold and desegregation led, among other things, to an enormous interest in "compensatory education" and "education for the disadvantaged." Some combination of disillusionment with science and a strong reaction to traditional schooling, especially among the college population, carried us into the present decade with its open classrooms and alternative schools.

This sketch of the educational climate sets the context. In addition it makes it abundantly evident that there are some deep-seated value conflicts involved. Either they are, in fact, inherent in the Origin-Pawn concept or at least they are raised consistently in discussions of the concept. Either way we can ill afford to ignore them.

Basic Cultural Values and the Origin-Pawn Concept

Democracy and Education. As Bestor (1955) has pointed out there is some question about how to reconcile universal compulsory education and the maintenance of high intellectual standards. At the height of the national search for talent spurred by the space-race,

John Gardner (1961) asked, "Can we be equal and excellent too?" A form of this controversy has flared recently in the wake of Jensen's (1969) discussion of "the failure of compensatory education" (p. 2) and the relationship between intelligence and academic achievement. We have no intention of entering that debate. It does seem, however, that the stress on IQ to the exclusion of other concepts was at first overdone, but as a result of that controversy it is becoming clear that other variables must be considered in educational policy making. Motivation seems a logical candidate and, although it is often discussed (see for instance Gardner, 1961), far less attention has been devoted to it than to intelligence in the classroom. Threads of evidence, such as Coleman's (1966) finding that feelings of control over the environment are related to achievement as well as to disadvantaged status, and Katz's (1968) findings relating achievement to self-concept in a complex way, as well as considerable evidence from the Rotter (1966) tradition, made the Origin-Pawn concept seem worthy of investigation.

If we accept the assumptions (*a*) that motivation is necessary for school performance and (*b*) that motives are learned (McClelland, 1965), then it seems reasonable that motivation can be gradually increased in school. Our project, however, did not set out to make education more democratic, nor did we consider our work compensatory. Further, we did not set out to compare low-income, inner-city school children with anyone else. If we have succeeded in producing changes in that population, we see it as a finding that can now be tested in other settings.

Reactions to Authority. Of more relevance possibly to being an Origin is the apparent paradox posed by the interaction between an adult authority figure and a student subordinate. The Origin-Pawn concept raises questions concerning this type of relationship immediately. It is often assumed, for instance, that in a dyadic interaction for one person to be an Origin the other must be a Pawn. Our own values lead us to suggest that in a cooperative (democratic) work group there may be division of labor and still each individual may originate his own behavior and at the same time treat others as Origins.

In the classroom, as elsewhere, the teacher is confronted with students' reactions to authority. It is not surprising in a country founded on the overthrow of a dominant British government that attitudes toward authority figures should be strong and ambivalent. As Wolfenstein and Leites (1950) have shown the American people are suspect of authorities. To be respected a person must achieve his status rather than have it ascribed to him. The Origin concept is rooted in the tradition of helping each child attain or achieve his own potential without dominance from authority.

Humanism vs. Humanitarianism. But how does a person of superior intelligence impart knowledge without imposing it and without condescending? Our democratic values seem opposed to assuming superiority of some over others. We are caught between ''all men are equal'' and some men are more knowledgeable than others. The humanitarian view seems to be that the schools bring out the potential of each child (life-adjustment). But this may entail intellectual compromise and the lowering of standards. The intellectual is apt to value humanism, as distinct from humanitarianism. As Babbitt defines the two, a humanitarian is ''A person who has sympathy for mankind in the lump, faith in its future progress, and desire to serve the great cause of this progress. . . . The poet Schiller, for instance, speaks as a humanitarian and not as a humanist when he would 'clasp the millions to his bosom,' and bestow 'a kiss upon the whole world.' The humanist is more selective in his caresses '' (Babbitt, 1908, p. 7). The humanist knows ''that what is wanted is not sympathy alone, nor again discipline and selection alone, but a disciplined and selective sympathy . . . The humanist . . . is interested in the perfecting of the individual'' (Babbitt, 1908, p. 8). Both the humanist goal of perfecting the individual and the humanitarian ideal of sympathy for mankind seem relevant to education. Babbitt warns of the extremes, however. ''Sympathy without selection becomes flabby, and a selection which is unsympathetic tends to grow disdainful'' (p. 8).

Meaning, Responsibility and Freedom. Throughout all of the above runs a thread that is at once another important cultural value and at the same time most closely related to the Origin-Pawn concept. That thread is the basic value of individual freedom. The relevance to the authoritarian-democratic studies is obvious when we recall that Kurt Lewin and several of the authors of *The Authoritarian Personality* (Adorno et al., 1950) came to this country to escape Nazi domination and to embrace freedom. Universal education is based on the tenet of democratic freedom. But the paradox arises when polar opposites such as progressive vs. traditional schools, life-adjustment vs. subject-matter or humanitarianism vs. humanism are equated with freedom vs. constraint. A classroom where no one takes the responsibility for learning results in chaos. Responsible direction both from the teacher and from within the students imparts meaning to learning.

''What all of us want is to be set free. The man who sinks his pickax into the ground wants that stroke to mean something. The convict's stroke is not the same as the prospector's, for the obvious reason that the prospector's stroke has meaning and the convict's stroke has none. It would be a mistake to think that the prison exists at the point where the convict's stroke is dealt. Prison is not a mere physical horror. It is using a pickax to no purpose that makes a prison; the horror resides in the failure to enlist all those who swing the pick in the community of mankind.

"We all yearn to escape from prison" (Saint-Éxupery, 1965, p. 155).

A school is a prison for those who can use it to no purpose, while others, even in the most prisonlike schools, sink their pickax to a purpose and find meaning. For a child to find meaning in school he should have a purpose for being there; he should want what the school has to offer; he should be motivated to learn. When he is committed to learning, he will come freely to school because school will have meaning for him. Freedom is the capacity to direct your own behavior, but directing your own behavior without regard to others can restrict their freedom. Therefore, self-directed behavior must be responsible behavior to contribute to freedom.

But "responsibility" may have a double meaning. When we use it in the phrase "personal responsibility," we will mean the internal state of conscience, of feeling responsible to self for thoughts and actions. The "double meaning" appears when the external state of *accountability* to someone else is implied. Compare the feeling of knowing you are right, either ethically or mathematically, because your solution has meaning for you within a broad context of moral or mathematical propositions—compare such an internal feeling, based on commitment to the propositions—with the feeling of being right because an external authority says so. That is the difference between "personal responsibility" as we shall use it and external accountability.

Internal standards are a part of the meaning structure within the person that result from commitment and purpose. A person who is committed is a motivated person. To help a child to develop such standards and to become a committed person with multiple but clearly defined purposes is to help him to originate his own behavior. If the teacher can develop commitment and motivation, the development of necessary skills and knowledge will follow smoothly as the child demands them. Motivation development will contribute to intellectual development and not be at the expense of time devoted to "subject matter."

Commitment gives meaning to actions. Commitment and meaning

cannot flourish without freedom, but lack of constraint does not create commitment. *"The freedom of the subjective person to do as he pleases is overruled by the freedom of the responsible person to act as he must"* (Polanyi, 1958, p. 309). This book is an exploration of commitment and freedom: How meaning, commitment and purpose can be developed in the lives of children in school.

THE PROJECT

In 1965 we had some evidence from laboratory studies to support the Origin-Pawn concept. DeCharms, Carpenter and Kuperman (1965) found the Origin-Pawn variable to be important in the perception of other persons. Kuperman (1966) demonstrated that subjects enjoyed working as Origins and were more satisfied with their productions than those working as Pawns. DeCharms, Dougherty and Wurtz (deCharms, 1968) repeated Kuperman's findings and extended them to behavioral measures of preference for Origin productions and even to greater recall after a month of the Origin versus the Pawn productions. Whether these laboratory findings could be put to use in a real setting was the question that stimulated the project to be described here.

The initial plan was simple. A group of teachers would be trained in motivation enhancing techniques with special emphasis on treating students as Origins. Techniques developed by the trained teachers would be used by them in their classrooms and we would try to assess the effects on the motivation and achievement of the students by comparing them with a comparable group of students who did not have trained teachers or motivation enhancing exercises in the classroom.

The resulting project extended over four years. A group of children were followed from the end of the fifth grade until they completed the eighth grade. Although the plan was simple, the ultimate design became complex as teachers and students were shifted by the school district from class to class and school to school. Chapter 2 presents in detail a combined history and design of the project.

The teachers and students all came from one large inner-city school district. The characteristics of the people and the district are presented in Chapter 3. Chapter 4 describes in detail the teacher training and Chapter 5 describes the classroom units devised and used by the teachers. Both the teachers' and the students' training concentrated on four major overlapping concepts: development of (*a*) the self-concept, (*b*) achievement motivation, (*c*) realistic goal setting, and (*d*) Origin behavior.

Results of the project appear in descriptions of observations and in measures of motivation and school behavior. Chapter 7, for instance, presents a description of specific children who showed either Origin or Pawn behavior and presents the results of an instrument designed to measure the Origin-Pawn variable in trained and untrained children. Chapter 6 presents similar evidence for measures of achievement motivation and goal setting behavior. The effects of the training on academic achievement, grades and other school behavior appear in Chapter 8. In Chapter 9 the classroom as a whole is considered and trained classrooms are compared with untrained as seen through observations and reports of the students. Chapter 10 discusses the concept of ego development (Loevinger & Wessler, 1970) and motivation development. In a final chapter we try to bring together all of the results and discuss their meaning for a theory of motivation and for education.

Notes

1. In a personal communication Professor McClelland has suggested that the goal of achievement motivation is *efficiency* or more literally improvement in performance and that this must be distinguished from "success" in terms of recognition, which is the goal of the power motive.

2. In the same communication cited above, Professor McClelland has taken exception to our use of accountability here. He suggests that, although he would agree that achievement motivation training is narrower than personal causation training, he would emphasize that achievement training stresses improving relative to a standard of performance which may be personally or socially defined. We do not mean to suggest that achievement motivation training relies *entirely* on accountability to a superior. Rather, such training seems to give equal weight to striving for personal standards and standards set by others. Too often in the educational setting, at least, standards, excellence and efficiency are all imposed by superiors and hence reduce rather than enhance feelings of personal causation.

Chapter 2

Design of the Motivation Project

(R. deCharms)

ENTRÉE INTO THE SCHOOL DISTRICT

At 9:00 o'clock on the morning of March 18, 1966, the project director
had an appointment with Mr. Eaton, the District Superintendent. Mr.
Eaton had been suggested by a member of the city superintendent's
staff because he was known by the top administrators to be concerned
about motivation. He had recently become Superintendent in a newly
outlined district. He was selected for the job probably because of his
leadership qualities and his apparent desire to strike out anew in a
district that comprised a section of the city that had been in rapid
transition from a white to a black neighborhood over the past ten
years.

Mr. Eaton's office was in a large, gracious old house, typical of
that section of the city, that had been converted into the district reading clinic and administrative offices. The goal of the first meeting was
to describe the project and to invite Mr. Eaton and his assistant to
participate in a short, three-day training session similar to that which
would be provided for the teachers in the project. Mr. Eaton and his
assistant agreed to fly to Boston for the training session to be held by
Dr. McClelland in the Department of Social Relations at Harvard (a
capsule version of the one described in Chapter 4 of this book).

After the training session, Mr. Eaton became enthusiastic about the training and sought and obtained approval by the city superintendent's office.

From that moment on the cooperation that we received in the district was beyond our hopes. We like to think that it was because we tried in every way to work with the administrators and teachers on problems that were important to them and tried always to consider their goals while conducting the study. We tried to do everything possible to treat each individual from superintendent to pupil as an Origin.

Early in the discussions with Mr. Eaton he encouraged us to innovate from the very outset. Whereas we had planned to observe conditions as they were at first, he said, "We can't wait around for you to study longitudinal trends as they exist. What can you do now to try to shake things up and change things?" He emboldened us to take seriously the dictum, "If you think you understand something—try to change it."

With Mr. Eaton's help the motivation project was designed to be a longitudinal field experiment comparing students of trained and untrained teachers over three years, starting in fifth grade. We could not dictate the placement of students and teachers, but close cooperation was sought so that the project's goals included both research objectives and concrete benefits for the school district, the teachers and the students.

Our major premise made it impossible for us to maintain complete control over the situation. Nevertheless, it was possible to take advantage of district policies and still maintain an experimental design. This was one of the basic challenges: to maintain the integrity of our major premise, to treat individuals as Origins, and at the same time to conduct a field experiment from which we could derive data on treated and untreated samples leading to scientifically based conclusions.

THE DESIGN

The project continued for four years, starting with premeasurement of the children at the end of their fifth grade and continuing until the end of their eighth grade.

Fifth Grade Year

During the children's fifth grade year the project accomplished three things: (*a*) entrée into the district was gained through careful discussions with and training of the District Superintendent; (*b*) motivation and academic achievement data were collected on all of the fifth grade children in the district: eleven schools and thirty-two classrooms, approximately 1200 children; and (*c*) sixteen teachers were trained.

The experimental teachers were selected at random from the thirty-two who were to teach the tested children in the sixth grade (see Technical Note 2.1 for details). The other sixteen teachers, the control group, were comparable in age, sex and years of experience with the experimental teachers so that they and their students would give us a comparison group of children who experienced only the standard sixth grade curriculum.

During their spring vacation (1967) the sixteen experimental teachers participated in a five-day residential training workshop. Much of the workshop this first year was identical to that used with businessmen in India and the U.S. (McClelland & Winter, 1969). For the first time, however, the Origin-Pawn concept was incorporated into the training. This was also one of the first complete training sessions ever conducted for teachers and was the first to include women. Near the end of the training week considerable time was allotted to discussion of the school setting, the teachers' problems and possible ways to introduce the Origin concept into the classroom. A detailed description of the training appears in Chapter 4 below.

Sixth Grade Year

The sixth grade year was also devoted to three major activities: (*a*) an intensive effort to develop four classroom exercises in cooperation with fifteen trained teachers, nine of whom used the units in their sixth grade classrooms was of major importance; (*b*) data were collected at the end of the year on all the sixth grade children in the district; (*c*) sixteen seventh grade teachers were trained in preparation for the following year.

As a result of changes in teaching assignments beyond our control, only nine of the sixteen trained teachers were assigned to teach sixth grade. One teacher had entered management training, three were teaching other grades, two had moved to special classrooms and one had become a curriculum supervisor. All fifteen teachers who remained in the district helped to develop motivation training procedures for classroom use. Nine of these used the procedures with sixth grade classes and became the primary source of data. The other six applied the techniques in fifth, seventh or eighth grades or special classrooms. Data from these non-sixth grade classrooms were incomplete (i.e., no data were available from the pre-training year and no relevant controls were available), so these classrooms were not considered in data analysis (Technical Note 2.2).

The experimental design for this project year may be seen in Figure 2.1 under "Sixth Grade." It is basically an experimental–control comparison.

At the beginning of the school year the experimental teachers formed a contract with the research staff to attend scheduled meetings approximately once a month, to develop and vote on classroom exercises and to attempt to use in their classrooms all procedures so developed. In return, they were to be paid a nominal sum at the end of the year. Although the payment was important to them and within a range commensurate with their salaries, it was small enough to be only a minor incentive, particularly after they became involved.

At the monthly meetings the staff and teachers concentrated on four basic concepts that were inherent in past motivation change projects (McClelland, 1965); i.e.: (*a*) self-study and evaluation of personal motives, (*b*) achievement motivation, (*c*) goal-setting and (*d*) the Origin-Pawn concept. All of these had been stressed in the teacher training so that the teachers were familiar with them. The rationale behind choosing these particular concepts and more detail about the concepts are presented in Chapter 4.

Our first aim, in keeping with treating the teachers as Origins, was to encourage the teachers to take as much initiative as possible in developing classroom procedures. The early meetings were frustrating to the research staff, who were caught between trying to tell the teachers what to do and waiting for them to make proposals. The former was obviously contrary to our whole Origin orientation, the latter resulted in very little progress. A genuine cooperation began to develop, however, and it soon became evident that the teachers did not have time to initiate complete proposals. The research staff began presenting first approximations of classroom techniques that the teachers eagerly began to mold and reform. After such sessions, the research team produced the final form of the classroom technique, prepared necessary instructions and forms and, either at the next meeting or by visiting each teacher in school, obtained the teacher's

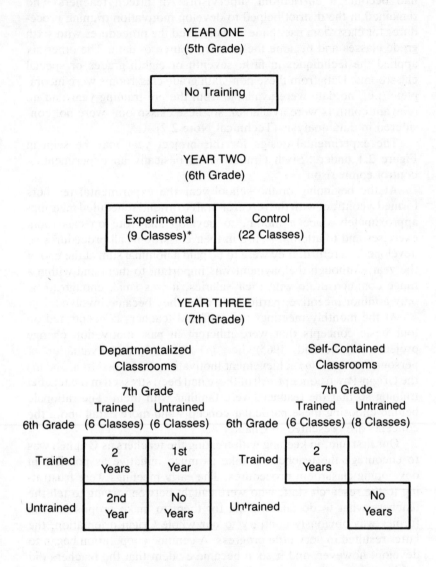

Fig. 2.1

**Summary of Design of Trained and Untrained Classes
Over Three Years of the Project**

*Of 16 trained teachers 7 were reassigned to other grades.

approval of the technique. Finally, the schedule for implementation of the technique in the classroom was arranged.

The concrete results of these teacher-staff sessions were four classroom units dubbed for the children: (a) "The Real Me," (b) "Stories of Achievement," (c) "The Spelling Game" and (d) "The Origin Manual." These are described in detail in Chapter 5. Each unit had specific instructions. Each teacher, however, was encouraged to present the material in a way best fitted to her class. Deviations from instructions usually were in the direction of doing more than was agreed upon rather than less.

A less concrete result of the planning sessions that may have been even more important than the classroom exercises was the commitment of the teachers to implement the basic ideas through the techniques which they helped to create. It is our impression that having the teachers themselves work on the classroom techniques produced a commitment and enthusiasm that may have been the critical element in making them successful.

Seventh Grade Year

Three major things were accomplished during this year of the project: (a) two classroom exercises were developed and used in the seventh grade classrooms; (b) data were collected at the end of the year on all seventh grade children; (c) thirty-two new seventh and eighth grade teachers were trained for the following year. Although these are essentially the accomplishments of the sixth grade year, there were two major differences. The number of classroom exercises was reduced and the experimental design was altered as a result of teacher and pupil placements.

Approximately one-half of the children in the district transferred from their sixth grade school to a large "middle" school containing only seventh and eighth grades. Fortunately for our design, approximately one-half of the children who entered the middle school had been experimentals and the other half controls. Anticipating this mixing of trained and untrained students, we had selected approximately one-half of the seventh grade teachers in the middle school for training.

The organization within the middle school further complicated our design. First, children were assigned to their classes according to their achievement test scores, and as it turned out, every seventh grade classroom in the middle school was composed of some experi-

mental (sixth grade) and some control children. As a result, by the
end of the seventh grade, we had some children with two years of
training (sixth and seventh), some with only one year of training
(either sixth or seventh grade) and some with no training. We turned
this situation to our advantage, since it gave us a chance to compare
children who had only sixth grade training with children who had only
seventh grade training. In addition, of course, we could still compare
the children who had training both years with children who had no
training.

The second organizational complicator was that the middle school
was a departmentalized school, whereas their sixth grade schools had
self-contained classrooms. In the self-contained classrooms children
have one teacher all day for all the academic subjects. In the departmentalized school the teachers taught "blocks" of the basic subjects.
Each child had a block teacher in his home room in the morning. In
the afternoon the child went to another block teacher and his morning
block teacher received another group of children. Consequently, each
block teacher had two groups of children and had to use the training
techniques with each group. As not all block teachers were trained,
the children experienced less than a full day with a trained teacher.
We anticipated that the training would be less effective in these
departmentalized classrooms.

The middle school accounted for approximately one-half of the
project children. Fortunately, the situation was much simpler for the
other half who did not change schools. Their schools maintained the
self-contained classrooms essentially intact from sixth to seventh
grade. By training seventh grade teachers who received previously
trained classes the result was that all children were trained both years
or neither year. The experimental children's contact with the trained
teacher was maximal, since the teacher only had to teach one group of
children. We anticipated that the training under these conditions
would have more powerful effects on the children than in the middle
school.

To summarize, by the end of the third year we were forced to
divide our sample into two groups to be called the self-contained
group, who stayed in their sixth grade schools, and the departmentalized group, who transferred to a middle school. The self-contained
group consisted of two groups of children: (*a*) those who had been
trained both years (grades six and seven) and (*b*) those who had been
trained neither year. All of these children studied with the same
(trained or untrained) teacher all day every day. The departmentalized group consisted of four types of children: (*a*) those trained in

both sixth and seventh grades, (*b*) those trained in sixth grade only, (*c*) those trained in seventh grade only and (*d*) those who were never trained. These experimentals experienced a motivation-trained teacher only one-half of each day. Figure 2.1 displays this design under the heading "Year Three (7th Grade)."

Only two classroom exercises were developed and used in the seventh grade. They embodied the self-concept and the Origin concept. Achievement motivation was dropped completely, although goal setting was included in the seventh grade Origin Manual. The units developed were called the "Person Perception Unit" and the "Origin Manual" and they are described in Chapter 5.

Eighth Grade Year

The last year of the project was primarily a follow-up year. No new classroom exercises were developed. A minimal amount of training occurred in the classes. The major accomplishments of the year were (*a*) the development of the Origin Classroom Climate Questionnaire (see Chapter 9) and (*b*) final measurement at the end of the year.

Comparisons of classrooms of trained and untrained teachers and the development of new classroom exercises were hampered by the introduction into the middle school of a large federally supported program to prevent dropouts. There were advantages and disadvantages for the motivation project. On the plus side, the teacher training was financed by the Dropout Program. As a result teacher training for the eighth grade year was expanded in an attempt to include all of the teachers in the middle school in both seventh and eighth grades. It appeared that the school district was taking over the motivation project and the university staff would gradually move entirely to a consulting role.

The disadvantages of losing even more control of the situation had to be molded again into the design. Hopes to develop and use more classroom units were dashed early, when it became clear that the Dropout Program, designed primarily to utilize the teachers as counselors, was too demanding of the teachers' time. As a result, no motivation exercises were developed and although a person perception unit was offered to the teachers, it was only used in a few classrooms. At mid-year each teacher was given a manual for achievement-motivation training (Alschuler, Tabor & McIntyre, 1969). The commitment and enthusiasm of teacher-developed exercises was lacking, however, and the manual was never used by any teacher.

In short, the classroom exercises played a minor role during the last year of the project, when the students were in the eighth grade. It was, however, possible to conceive of the eighth grade year as one in which both previously trained and untrained children were taught by both trained and untrained teachers, but in which the teachers did not develop or use classroom motivation exercises. This was possible for two reasons. First, although we had tried to train all of the teachers at the middle school, a few had escaped us and could form a control group, although from the point of view of randomization they were a poor control. Second, we discovered that some previously trained teachers in other self-contained classroom schools were teaching eighth grade this year and could be compared with untrained teachers in self-contained classroom schools. For the first time we had trained teachers who were not formally using motivation classroom procedures designed by them and the project.

The design for the last year, consequently, consisted of separate analyses of departmentalized classrooms from the middle school and self-contained classrooms from the other schools as in the seventh grade design. This time both of these analyses could be divided two ways: (*a*) into students with trained or untrained teachers and (*b*) into previously trained or not trained students. There are, unfortunately, weaknesses in assuming that these factors occurred completely independently of each other, as well as problems concerning the appropriateness of the control groups in some cases. These problems will be discussed when the data are presented (Chapter 8), so that any conclusions can be appropriately interpreted.

During this last year, an Origin Classroom Climate Questionnaire was developed (see Chapter 9). It was administered in all of the classrooms in the middle school to determine whether the students in fact perceived a difference in treatment at the hands of trained teachers as compared to untrained teachers. In addition, the Origin Climate Questionnaire was administered to the classrooms of teachers in other schools who had been trained during the first years of the project and who were now teaching seventh or eighth grade. The classes of comparable untrained teachers were also investigated to provide a comparison.

A glance back at Figure 2.1 gives the overview for years one, two and three. Each year the design increased in complexity and in potentiality of yielding more information. Year four, the follow-up, is not shown in Figure 2.1.

Technical Note 2.1

The thirty-two sixth grade teachers were divided equally into experimental and control teachers by the technique of blocking (Campbell & Stanley, 1963) where matching the groups on sex, age and years of teaching experience was used as an adjunct to randomization. This randomized block design made the sampling unit the teacher and her classroom. Wherever possible in data analysis we used the classroom as the sampling unit. The strict randomization used to select teachers for training was partially affected by subsequent teaching assignments that were beyond our control, a fact that must be borne in mind in evaluating statistical results.

Technical Note 2.2

Untrained teachers who taught in the schools with trained teachers were potentially influenced by close contact with trained teachers and hence did not represent a good control comparison with trained teachers. Consequently, data from classrooms of untrained teachers who might have been contaminated by trained teachers were treated separately from data from teachers in control schools. The control classrooms were divided into potentially contaminated controls and uncontaminated controls.

If contamination takes place, the untrained teachers may learn some of the desired techniques from the trained teachers. This effect could have practical utility. Perhaps it would be possible to train only some of the teachers from a school and benefit all of them. There were some indications that this in fact occurred. For instance, on all four subscales of the Iowa Test of Basic Skills the mean grade placement scores were slightly higher for the contaminated control children than for the pure control children at the end of sixth grade. As a result the contaminated controls fell between the pure control means (the lowest means on all four subscales) and the experimental means (the highest). The differences between the two control groups were not significant, however.

Chapter 3

The Cast of Characters

(R. deCharms)

The subjects in an experiment can often be adequately described for scientific purposes by presenting statistics concerning the average age, socio-economic status and other group characteristics. For several reasons a more detailed description of the people in the motivation project is necessary. First, the teachers constituted the primary contact with the children, but we had very little statistical data on the teachers. It is important to know whether these teachers formed a special group or whether we could expect our procedures to work with any group. Second, the teachers all played the same role and in the teachers' role there appeared to be considerable conformity to middle-class dress and modes of behavior. Yet as individuals the teachers showed a wide diversity of behaviors and interests. It was obvious that the children were sensitive to these differences in personalities.

As for the children the primary data tell us about their scores on various tests, but we also have other sources of information to round out the picture with their stated interests, hobbies, etc. This chapter is intended to introduce the reader to the people in the project and to the district in which they lived and worked.

THE SCHOOL DISTRICT

In the decade preceding initiation of the motivation project a large urban redevelopment effort had displaced many residents (mostly black) from an area near the center of the city. Many of these families moved into the residential area served by the school district where the motivation project was conducted. The schools in this area were consequently overcrowded. Attempts were made to relieve over-crowding by busing, erecting temporary buildings, planning new buildings and redistricting. Created in 1963 as a response to the increase in population, the school district had twenty-one elementary schools (many of which were branch schools housing only the lower grades and hence not included in the motivation project) and one high school. Mr. Eaton, who had previously been principal of an elementary school in another district, was appointed the first superintendent of the new district in July, 1964, and helped with its original organization. The purpose of establishing the new district with its own superintendent was to move the superintendent out of the center city and into the community that was being served by the schools. The parents responded favorably to the change by seeking interaction with the school administration to improve the school system.

By 1966 the district had one new school and another was dedicated in 1968. Busing was almost entirely eliminated before the motivation project started, but many temporary structures erected on playgrounds were still in use for classrooms. The average class had between thirty and forty pupils.

THE TEACHERS

"The Teacher"—a Role to Play and Defend

Compared to Montessori and Summerhill, the schools in which these teachers work seem traditional, reactionary, even authoritarian. Each person seems more often a Pawn than an Origin; the teachers seem to be more disciplinarians than learning facilitators. For instance, one of them, Mrs. K., apparently could not tolerate a child chewing gum. Strict penalties were imposed against it. Mr. M. developed a reputation as a disciplinarian among the children, who referred to him and his methods of physical punishment as "Here come da judge."

Many of the disciplinary techniques resulted from the role the teachers often found themselves forced to play in the theatre that was school. Discipline must be maintained before any learning can occur. The teacher must keep her class quiet so as not to disturb others. The pressures to conform were enormous and the young teacher soon learned that she was always on stage and her behavior was constantly under observation by more experienced teachers and the principal.

Within the classroom the teacher may have been much freer to innovate than she realized. Nevertheless, the teachers felt strongly that innovation was not appreciated. The surveillance that they felt showed itself in subtle ways. For example, in an exercise designed to help the children to express themselves freely, the teachers (in the Stories of Achievement Unit described in Chapter 5) encouraged the children to write quickly, ignoring spelling, punctuation and such technical aspects as might interfere with free expression. Using their own criteria the children selected one "Story of the Week" and it was posted on the bulletin board. Some teachers were hesitant to display the papers and were concerned that the principal would see this specimen of poor grammar. Because of their own fear of authority, they would help the child to rewrite the story before it was displayed.

Some of the fear of being perceived as non-professional—as not playing the prescribed teacher role—must have been allayed by our attempts to have the motivation project accepted by the principals. At one meeting, an enthusiastic principal told his colleagues, "The other day when I passed Mrs. C.'s room some of the children were out in the hall throwing erasers at a waste basket. I was about to intervene when I thought 'that must be part of that crazy motivation project.'" In fact, of course, Mrs. C. had devised a goal setting task like the ring toss game used in the teachers' training (see Chapter 4) and the principal allowed her to violate norms that he would not have done otherwise.

The general image that these teachers project (in the schools *as teachers*) is that of being the traditional dispenser of the birch rod and the prescribed curriculum, usually in that order. To see them all as disciplinarians is, of course, overly simple. There were wide variations to which the children were very sensitive. Most teachers tempered their discipline with a personal touch and the discipline was apparently most often accepted by the children as necessary but not completely arbitrary.

The Teachers as People—Everything from Flutes to Horses

The varied talents of the teachers were impressive and the variation of the personalities despite the teacher role obviously made them unique individuals in front of the class. The men almost invariably held other jobs, often in the evening. One played several instruments in popular orchestras and disappeared occasionally during the teacher training to practice his flute in secret. One of his ambitions was to play in a symphony orchestra. One man's amateur passion was flying and he managed to bring this into his teaching. He organized a student flying club and took some of the children up in a small plane.

Mrs. Worthington had studied modern dance with Katherine Dunham. Mr. H. had an interest in radio and announcing. And Mrs. B. and Mrs. I. revealed with some delight and embarrassment that they often indulged in their passion for betting on the horses. Mrs. B had a farm in the country to which she took children from the inner city and she hoped to obtain horses for them to ride.

Banister Shoes and Middle-class Values

Observing the on-guard, on-stage behavior of these teachers may well support one's stereotypes of teachers. Invariably, they present themselves at school immaculately dressed. During one discussion, the teachers were talking about the goals of their students. They kept saying that the boys all wanted Banister shoes. Finally, one of the staff asked, "What are Banister shoes?" One of the ladies looked around at people's feet and said, "Well, Mr. B. has on a pair and so does Mr. S." Mr. B. and Mr. S. looked embarrassedly at their feet, as did the rest of the group. Both had on quite new, highly polished, expensive shoes, one pair made of alligator.

Does this desire to have expensive clothes, cars and other things indicate a difference between the teachers and their pupils, who are from humble, often crumbling homes? Do these teachers, who have recently climbed the social ladder, see the children as threats to their secure position in the middle class? We rarely heard any hint of such rejection among the teachers. A suggestion to remove the worst children from school was made in a brainstorming session and immediately rejected. One of the very reasons for wearing good clothes is to show the children what is possible to achieve with hard work and education.

The teachers described themselves in personal statements and interviews. Many of the older teachers struggled to travel north when very young. Often when they got there they were completely alone. "I was born some 54 years ago in a small country town. My mother died when I was one and a half years old. I was reared by my aunt, who was quite religious. I finished grade school in this small country town and came to the city, where I finished high school after a long hard struggle all alone . . ." After college "I held positions as teacher, principal and coach. When the schools were integrated my teachers and my staff were all fired. I was sent to another city to teach, but I had the wrong color of skin."

Another man of comparable age wrote in his personal statement: "In retrospect I have had a very humble beginning. I was born in (a southern state) in the rural area. My parents were very poor, but honest and hard working. There were twelve children in our family. My father taught school in the rural areas . . . I learned early to fend for myself." In fact, he came to the city at a very early age all alone on a freight train because he had heard that they gave books to high school students.

Many of the younger teachers have been in the city all their lives: "Born and raised in the ghetto, I only felt secure in the ghetto because white American society made me feel ashamed of my own blackness." And many have parents who were teachers. "I was a child who struggled against becoming what her mother and sisters were before her—a teacher. But who even as a child wanted to teach."

The theme of rising pride in blackness is very evident in these personal histories, as is the strong commitment to help others by teaching. "I'm a person dedicated to helping the poor as much as I possibly can. That is one reason I'm teaching school, because you always get a chance to help someone." Home life and children are almost always warmly mentioned. Parental families are often large, their own children usually number about three or four. Typically they are the farthest advanced educationally of their siblings, since they all have college degrees and many have graduate work or master's degrees. "For as long as I could remember my father had been telling me, 'Get yourself an education so you won't have to work hard like me and your mother.' It must have done some good. I was the first person in my family to attend and complete college. It took some doing but I made it."

The city where these teachers work is fortunate in that it has had a black teachers' college for many years that has developed a large group of dedicated teachers—not the best trained in the world, perhaps, but drawn from the most able, intelligent and motivated individuals of the black community, a group of teachers who have survived and even thrived in the face of incredible odds. This group of teachers was not specially selected. They are a random sample of all the teachers teaching one grade in the district.

THE CHILDREN

Gerald's Day Begins

Gerald woke up cold and bleary eyed. The TV had been on until 2 A.M. the night before and he had watched and dozed from his cot in the corner of the small living room where he and his kid brother slept. His two older sisters slept in the back bedroom in the old wrought iron bed like the one in the other bedroom where mother and father and the baby slept. The one-story house was small and very much like all the others crowded onto the block. When the neighbors "fussed," you could hear them. In front of the house was a small plot of grass that Gerald was supposed to keep neat; in back was an alley. Gerald's parents wanted to keep their yard neater than any other on the block.

As he dozed in bed Gerald thought of the fun he had had that afternoon in an abandoned car. His mother had said that the city was trying to get rid of the abandoned cars on the streets, but there was still one in their block and he passed several on his way to school— broken windows, no wheels, but you could pretend to drive one.

Gerald's father worked at the city incinerator, sometimes on the day shift and sometimes the night shift. In order to keep the job which he had had for five years he had to work either shift that they told him to work. He also worked for people out in the suburbs, painting, cleaning and gardening. He had recently bought a secondhand pickup truck and set up a hauling business, but he wasn't doing too well. Gerald didn't see his father much during the week. He was always working, except on Sunday morning, when they all went to church.

This morning it was cold and Gerald's mother was trying to get the kids off to school. She fussed at Gerald to comb his hair and keep his clothes neat. He was hungry, but there wasn't much left in the cereal box when the girls were through and only a little cold milk. His corduroy jacket was missing a button when he put it on over his Tshirt and his mother looked up from feeding the baby and scolded him for losing it. Then she told him to hurry and not be late to school, because he had to get an education.

As he started out of the house he broke the ice on a puddle and got his sneakers wet. Two blocks down the street he crossed Big Street, where they had once caught the bus to go downtown to a baseball game. On the other side of Big Street were big houses. Shirley, one of the kids in his class, lived in one of them with her mother, grand-mother, and aunt and her brothers and sisters and cousins. Shirley's father went to Chicago a long time ago and she doesn't remember him. Gerald always thought that Shirley's house was a mansion. The stained glass around the big front door, the marble fireplaces and the tall ceilings seemed so beautiful in the summer. But Shirley said they can't keep it warm and the roof in the back leaks into her bedroom sometimes. Many big houses on her block are abandoned and all boarded up after the kids broke the windows. Gerald's mother had told him never to go into them. Way over near the big park there were even bigger houses, where rich people lived. Gerald had seen the houses from the bus, but the children who lived there didn't go to his school.

Parents' Occupations and Houses

This snapshot of two children and their houses results from inter-views and visits to the district. Rothenberg (1968) attempted to mea-sure the social class of the people in the district in two ways. Having chosen a sample of 100 boys from two schools that represented areas with both the highest- and lowest-income families, he asked each boy to write down his parent's (or guardian's) occupation. When the response was unclear ("works for 'Big' Corporation"), Rothenberg interviewed the child and the teacher and checked school records until he was able to classify the results. In addition, he and a co-worker went to each boy's house and viewed it from the street. Each house was classified on a scale according to its appearance and state of physical repair.

Rothenberg's two measures resulted from the Index of Social Characteristics (Warner et al.; 1960). Rothenberg used Warner's rating scale for occupations and adapted the house-type scale.

Despite the limitations of the data (small sample collected for specific children), we can gain a general idea of the occupations of the children's parents and of the houses they lived in.

Typical sixth graders in class (photo by Richard W. Levine)

About one-fourth of the boys' parents held occupations in War-ner's lowest category—manual workers, odd-job men, janitors, scrubwomen, etc. The largest group (43%) held occupations of semi-skilled workers, such as watchmen, taxi and truck drivers and gas station attendants, Warner's next-to-lowest class. About a third were above the largest group and had occupations such as store clerks, beauty operators, cooks, bartenders, policemen and firemen. A few were more skilled—plumbers, carpenters or social workers. One boy reported that his father was a doctor and thereby fell into the highest class (professionals) on the Warner scale.

The data on the boys' houses in Rothenberg's sample give a similar picture. About one-third of the group lived in houses described as "run-down but not severely deteriorated or beyond repair" (Roth-enberg, 1968, p. 196). Another third lived in houses in noticeably better repair. Only a few (about one in twenty) lived in houses described as "obviously deteriorated, badly in need of repair . . . unclean to the point of being unhealthy and unsafe" (Rothenberg, 1968, p. 196). (The proportion of these may have risen in the district since these data were obtained when the boys were in fifth grade.) About one of the houses in ten was described as "neat, clean, and obviously well cared for . . . mostly one-family houses, but not necessarily large" (Rothenberg, 1968, p. 196).

In general these data give a picture of a district that has a mixture of the lower and lower-middle classes with almost no professionals and few "white collar workers." This is not the lowest income "slum" area in the city, although it has recently become a "ghetto" in the sense that it is almost entirely black and that it is still difficult for the residents to move out of it.

What Are the Children Like?

The children who live in this area may be more clearly understood through the results of interviews. Shea (1969) interviewed 200 sixth grade boys and girls as part of his study. From his data we know several things about the children. More than half of them live with both parents and rather large families. (Families average five or six children per family. One child in 100 is an only child; a few have eleven or twelve siblings.) About one child in three has no father at home and lives with mother or with a grandmother, sister or aunt. Many of the mothers receive financial help from the government in the form of Aid to Dependent Children.

Unlike the older teachers, many of whom had come to the city from the country, about 75% of these children have lived in this city all their lives. Those who have moved here come almost equally from southern states or other large midwestern cities with large black communities.

Although the majority of the children grew up in the city, four out of five have traveled out of it, in most cases to visit relatives. Travel was usually to southern states or large midwestern cities. A few children had been to California, fewer to New York and a couple to Mexico. One reported being in Germany when his father was in the army.

Within the city the boys were given more freedom to leave their neighborhood by parents than girls. Equal numbers of boys and girls (25%) reported that they walk. The boys predominantly rode the bus and a few rode bicycles, while more girls traveled in cars and none reported leaving their neighborhood on bicycles. As might be expected more boys than girls said they went places alone, but this was only 35% even of the boys.

Where do they go in the metropolitan area? Almost all of them reported visiting the major tourist attractions downtown or having visited the sports stadium. Only about one-half of the boys and sixty percent of the girls reported having been to the largest, almost entirely white, suburb.

Seventy-five percent of both boys and girls reported that their parents gave them an allowance. They almost all supplemented this by working. Nearly 90% of the boys reported that they earned some of their own money, while 70% of the girls did. Less than 10% of those who earned money said that they gave it to their family. The typical jobs for girls were baby-sitting and housework; for boys, yard work and housework. Although a few sold papers, the paper route is dying out, having been taken over by adults with trucks. The shoe shine boy only appeared once in this sample.

What Do They Think About?

If I had three wishes . . .

"I'd wish I had all the money in the world. And I wish I had all the bikes, candy, and skates. And I wish that I was a million air and would by mostly all the 1968 cars. I would have all the clothes and shoes from every story in the world. And every time I be on my way to school I would have something to eat every recess we go out. I would have a big house about the size of a castle. And I would have skating rings and swimming pools inside my house thats the size of a castle."

"My first wish would be; if I was in colleage now to study subjects like Science, Machine, and instrumental music.

"My second wish would be; Out of (school) at age of 16, making music, and teaching the people to play a instrment.

"My third and last wish would be; A professinal instrmenter who know how to play a instrment better than anyone else."

The dominant theme in the personal statements written by the children in "The Real Me" Input (see Chapter 5) was the desire for nice things, wealth and big houses. Many children wanted to pass in school and to get an education, but only a few mentioned concrete goals such as being a "professinal instrmenter" or a "professional artist" or doctor. Some wished for peace and no hungry children in the world and for untroubled family life.

The perfect family was described by them as one that stays together and doesn't fight; they keep a clean house and yard and neat clothes.

"The only way you will have a perfect (family) you will have to do the wright things you are suppose to do. If you want a perfect family keep your house clean. Never bright all your neighbors in the house. If you do they mite through candy on the floor. Are they mite have grease on there hand and on the wall."

"The perfect family would be people who wouldn't have fight, and the father would bring his check home. And he would rember the bills or something he said to the children.

"He'd have a nice home a nice job. And his children would have good home training. And he could aford the thing that him and his family wanted. His children would have good grades in school."

As might be expected the children report successes in school and sports. "My greatest success" for one boy was building a go-cart, for a girl making a dress that her grandmother helped her finish after she had failed several times.

The written personal statements were usually touchingly candid and showed a wide range of writing and verbal skills. The average level of skill was reflective of the fact that in general these children were behind the national norms on academic achievement and the average intelligence quotient was approximately 93.

THE RESEARCH STAFF

The core of the staff each year was a group of graduate students who were working on doctoral dissertations related to the project. The four years of the project produced ten doctoral dissertations directly related to the project. In keeping with treating these graduate students as Origins, the project and the book have both been molded around some of their interests.

Each year the most senior graduate student served as an organizer and helped train more junior members of the staff. Three different people served in this role. Their most difficult task was organizing the spring testing, when the battery of measures was administered to all the children of the district in the relevant grade. To do this they recruited a core of five or six people each year (whenever possible experienced teachers) and trained them for about a week to insure standardization of administration. Elaborate schedules were devised with the schools in order to visit each classroom twice for two half-day sessions each spring. The testing was conducted starting in April and arranged to occur immediately before the school district administered its own academic achievement tests.

Several undergraduate and graduate students worked in their early training on scoring, coding and analyzing data. Over the years the number of people involved at all levels was approximately twenty. Because of the composition of the university's student body, all of these were white.

The major contact with the children, of course, was through the teachers, all of whom were black. The potential difficulties of white staff working with black teachers were, we think, minimized by the fact that the major staff people always attended the week-long teacher training sessions before each year. Each year (after the first) previously trained teachers served on the staff as assistant trainers. Before these residential sessions were over, many of the barriers between staff and teachers were lowered and many friendships had developed. The shared experiences of working, eating and playing together tended to produce a cohesive group.

CONCLUSION

In summary it is safe to say that the primary subjects of the experiment, the children, were low-income children from lower- and lower-middle-class homes. They lived in a deteriorating neighborhood that constituted a ghetto but was not the worst "slum" in the city.

It is unfortunate, perhaps, that we have less objective data on the teachers. To test them was to threaten them and treat them as Pawns. The resourcefulness and dedication of these teachers was impressive and, in retrospect, it is not surprising when one considers that they had risen almost to the top of the achievement ladder available to them in the segregated America of the 1950's and early 1960's. They far surpassed our initial expectations, but do not appear to be different from the rest of the teachers in the district.

Chapter 4

Motivation Development Training with Teachers

(Dennis J. Shea and Karl W. Jackson)

The major goal of the motivation training for the teachers was to treat them as Origins. This goal derived from our major thesis that Origin behavior is more meaningful than Pawn behavior (Chapter 1). To treat the teachers as Origins and hence help develop their motivation, we tried to help them (a) to understand their own motives through self-study and hence to understand others better, (b) to choose realistic goals for themselves in dealing with students, (c) to develop concrete plans for reaching their goals in the classroom and (d) to consider how they could tell whether they were reaching their goals. The two major aspects of the training are taking personal responsibility and planning concrete action. Rather than allow the teachers to do as they wished, to treat them as Origins we had to help them to be more responsible and more effective in influencing students.

The first steps toward these goals that were taken in the workshop were to engage the teachers in self-study, to convey some understanding of basic motives and to develop for them an understanding of the Origin concept. The context within which such goals may be reached is extremely important. Self-study can best be pursued in a climate of acceptance and trust. Such a climate only develops over time in close association with others. A subgoal of the training, therefore, was to develop group cohesion and solidarity, a feeling of group spirit. Living and working together for many hours a day is indispensable in accelerating the formation of personal bonds that result in a cohesive group.

The residential setting is not merely conducive to group cohesion; it is essential to presenting the Origin concept of responsibility. To be an Origin is to pursue personal goals and personal change in the context of other people pursuing their goals. The responsibility is to reveal one's self, to learn from others. At the same time one must learn to assert oneself but not treat others as Pawns. Thus, to learn the full import of the Origin concept one must experience it in the social context.

To be able to concentrate on one's own motives in interaction with others it is important, at first, to confine the interaction to a small group of acquaintances and to exclude family members and all of the attendant demands of family life. In a small group of acquaintances one can tentatively try out new behaviors without completely committing one's self. This temporary "not for real" atmosphere encourages the first hesitant steps toward change. Movement toward confronting the real world can progress slowly at first but must accelerate near the end of the week of the workshop.

The motivation workshop which is described in this chapter was led by a staff member whose major task was to help the group develop trust with each other, to stimulate discussion, to handle possible conflict and to take major responsibility for supplying activities to meet the needs of the group. The members of the staff included university professors and graduate students in human motivation who were to work with the teachers during the school year. After the first year of the project, the staff included teachers from the district who had participated in previous workshops.

The description of the activities of the workshop is neither an "operational definition" of motivation training, nor is it meant to be a cookbook for potential workshop leaders. While we have tried to describe carefully what we did, we certainly cannot present either a complete analysis of what went on or what each input meant to particular group members. Every workshop was slightly different and each input affected individuals in a different manner.

The application of the Origin concept to practical concerns in the classroom was the ultimate aim of the training in the workshop. The activities of the first half of the week can be categorized under

Table 4.1 – Summary of the Inputs in the Motivation Development Workshop Categorized by Major Concepts or Subgoals

Self-Study	Basic Social Motives	Origin-Pawn Concept	Group Solidarity	School Problems	Goal-Setting Problem Resolution
Test of Imagination (#1)	#1				
Who am I? (#2)	#2		#2		
Ring Toss (#3)	#3		#3		#3
	Block-Stacking (#5)	#5	#5		
#6	Measuring achievement motivation (#6)		#6		
			#7	Dramatic presentation (#7)	
#8		Blindfold game (#8)			
#9	Power role plays (#9)	#9			
#10	Family control role play (#10)	#10			

Business game (#11)

Party (# 12)

Measuring power motivation (#13)

Lunchroom role play (#14)

Origin-Pawn game (#15)

Leadership game (#16)

School problems (#17)

Brainstorming (#18)

Teachers as experts (#19)

Planning manual (#20)

Sharing goals (#21)

#11   #11   #11

#13

#14   #14

#15   #15   #15   #15

#16

#17   #17

#18   #18

#19   #19

#20

#21   #21   #21

concepts of learning from (*a*) *self study,* about (*b*) *basic motives* and (*c*) the *Origin-Pawn concept.* As the week progressed, the group developed (*d*) *group solidarity* as they (*e*) identified *school problems* and became engaged in (*f*) *goal setting* for problem resolution.

Table 4.1 presents the six basic concepts at the head of columns, and the activities or inputs of the training session are placed in the most appropriate column. In several cases an input embodies more than one concept, so that the input number is included under other columns.

The rest of this chapter is devoted to a chronological description of the activities of the workshop.

DAY 1: MONDAY

Input 1: The Test of Imagination

After some brief introductions, the staff presented the first exercise. The participants were asked to respond to a series of six pictures by writing imaginative stories. The participants wrote for five minutes in response to each picture projected on a screen. The pictures were adapted from Murray's (1943) Thematic Apperception Test (TAT). The following questions were used as guidelines:

1. What is happening? Who are the people?
2. What has led up to this situation? What has happened in the past?
3. What is being thought? What is wanted? By whom?
4. What will happen? What will be done?

After the stories were written, the participants were asked to keep them for later use (see Input 6 on measuring achievement motivation, where the stories were analyzed for individual motives). One of the staff then told the participants what they might expect in the coming week. He told them that the workshop was designed to help individuals answer four basic questions: (*a*) What are my own motives? (*b*) How can I increase my motivation? (*c*) What are the motives of others? and (*d*) How can I help others to be "more motivated?" The staff did not have any "magic techniques," but felt strongly that motivation could be increased and that self-understanding was a key to dealing with the four questions.

Input 2: Who Am I?

To begin the process of self-understanding the staff member asked each participant to write an essay in response to the question, "Who Am I?" The teachers wrote for approximately one half hour.

After a break for lunch, the entire group reassembled in a lounge area where chairs were formed in a circle. Personal name tags were available for each person. The entire afternoon was spent in a discussion of the "Who Am I?" question as each individual was encouraged to express something about himself. Content of the discussion included goals, values, life styles, conflicts, hobbies, concerns, etc. The staff encouraged free expression of personal feelings by revealing some of their own more private thoughts without dominating the discussion.

Input 3: The Ring Toss Game

The group discussion continued after dinner and by early evening the discussion, which began slowly, was more animated, as the group felt more comfortable in its setting. Meanwhile, each participant was asked to come individually to an outside hall. There he met one of the staff, who had set up a ring toss game—a peg set up at one end of the hall with three-foot distances marked off from it. The staff member gave the following instructions:

> This is the ring toss game. The object of this game is to put two of these four rings on the peg. You may stand at any distance you want to throw the rings, but you must throw all four from the same distance (from 3, 6, 9, 12, 15, 18, or 21 feet).

Each member of the group participated in the ring toss game in the isolation of the hall, while the staff member recorded the individual's chosen distance and success or failure in tossing the four rings.

When the "Who Am I?" discussion reached a stopping point, the ring toss game was repeated, but this time each participant acted in full view of the whole group. The instructions were the same as in the previous individual condition.

Finally, the group played the game for a third time with the directions slightly changed. The members were told that they had to pay ten cents to play the game. If they succeeded in putting two of the four rings on the peg, they could win money, the payoff being a function of the distance from which their rings were thrown. The payoff odds were:

Money Invested	Distance from Peg	Return (if successful)
$.10	3 feet	$ .10
.10	6 feet	.15
.10	9 feet	.25
.10	12 feet	1.00
.10	15 feet	2.50
.10	18 feet	5.00
.10	21 feet	10.00

Following the three versions of the ring toss game, a general discussion centered at first around a chalkboard that displayed the choice of distance and number of successful rings for each participant in each condition. Successful and unsuccessful players reported why they chose a particular distance and how they felt upon succeeding or failing. Differences between the alone, group and money conditions were discussed. Finally, participants were led to discuss more general motivational problems from the point of view of goal setting, the factors of skill and luck, and what appeared to be realistic goal setting.

The ring toss game was the first of many experiential units which provided data about the individuals from their own motivated behavior. It demonstrated individual strategies in a goal-setting situation, as some members went for a "sure thing," others took calculated risks and still others attempted almost impossible tasks. In addition the game demonstrated how different individuals used information about their performance in setting new goals. Later in the workshop this information became increasingly meaningful to the group.

Monday Evening

The official part of the training ended at about 10:30 P.M., following the discussion of the ring toss game. After that, and following the structured activities on Tuesday and Thursday evenings, the participants usually relaxed, went out for refreshments and engaged in informal conversation, often in a party atmosphere. The importance of these "after session" sessions should not be underestimated. Each workshop day was long and quite intense, and the participants and staff needed some time to unwind and relax. In addition, the informal, partylike atmosphere, while a break from the more structured sessions, provided additional time for sharing of concerns and development of group cohesion.

Summary of Monday

By Monday evening, some of the most important objectives of the workshop were coming into focus. First of all, as each participant (including the staff) began to express something about himself, anxiety about self-study was reduced and group cohesion began to form. While the written exercise stimulated thought, the group discussion made it more comfortable to share aspirations and self-doubts. As the week progressed the participants became more and more willing to reveal and study their own thoughts and motives.

The common experience of participating in the simple (almost childish) ring toss game also helped to bring the group together. At this early stage this game, with its active, experiential flavor, increased each member's participation in the learning process. In addition, of course, concepts relevant to human motivation were introduced by the participants themselves. Whereas the earlier discussion often touched on concepts like "goals," "aspirations," etc., the discussion of the ring toss game was filled with words like "challenge," "incentive," "pressure," "risk."

The group was beginning to form; the participants were beginning to look at themselves; and issues about motivation were being raised.

A typical reaction of a participant, however, was a beginning uneasiness that a whole day had passed and "nothing had really happened."

DAY 2: TUESDAY

Tuesday began with a discussion of the activities of Monday. Typically, members reported both insights and frustrations. Often they requested that the staff play a more active part and tell them "how to motivate students." In response to emerging questions about human motivation, theory and research, and the purpose of the workshop, a staff member began a short presentation in an attempt to clarify some issues.

Input 4: Vignette on the Relationship between Thought and Action

A staff member presented as briefly and succinctly as possible the rationale that motivation may be seen as a mild obsession. When someone wants something, he is apt to think about it often even if he can do nothing about it. As a result motives can be discovered in thoughts. Ultimately, a motive, if strong, will transcend thought and be translated into action. But thoughts are freer than actions and should better reflect motives. The thought samples or stories that the participants wrote on Monday were given as an example of specimens of thought that can be examined by trained observers for indications of motives and related to behavior, just as blood samples can be examined for medical reasons to detect disease (see deCharms, 1968, Chapter 6, for the complete discussion on which this vignette is based). This introduction to motivation led the participants to discuss their motives and their thoughts and prepared the way for examining their stories later in the day.

Input 5: The Block-Stacking Game

Three chairs were placed around a table in the center of the room. On the table was a pile of 30 to 35 toy building blocks. A staff member recruited three volunteers to play the roles of child, parent and teacher. He told them that he wanted the "child" to stack as many blocks as he could in a five-minute period, adding that the "child" would have to stack the blocks with his non-preferred hand while blindfolded. Each player was asked to estimate independently how many blocks the "child" could stack and was told that eighteen blocks in a five-minute period was a national average. After the three members made their estimates, the staff member read them aloud and requested a final consensus, causing the three to enter into a decision-making interaction. Before the "child" was blindfolded, the group was told that the "parent" and "teacher" were allowed to speak to the "child," but could not touch him or the blocks.

After the first exercise, the entire sequence was repeated two or three times so that a variety of interpretations of the roles was demonstrated. This exercise was adapted from an experiment (Rosen & D'Andrade, 1959) which studied the relationship between goal setting and motivation. The discussion of the block-stacking game began with an analysis of the "parent's" behavior.

Some "parents" took control and dominated the "child" throughout the task. The task became the "parent's" and not the "child's." The "child" became anxious and fared quite badly as the "parent" badgered him with directions about which block to pick up, etc.[1] Other "parents" were less directive. They allowed the child considerable freedom in setting his goal, stressing realistic appraisal of ability. In the actual block-stacking, they gave help, usually responding to requests for help by the "child" rather than offering directions. The task remained the "child's," as did his success or failure.

Direction giving was often related to the amount of praise, support and warmth that "parents" gave in the game. Styles of reward tended to be related to styles of influence. Autocratic "parents" tended to be quite cold and critical, while others gave their "child" a great deal of support and affection. The relationship between the "child's" expectation and that of the "teacher" and/or "parent" was also important. If the expectancy of the helper was far below or above that of the "child," conflict often developed.

The behavior of the helpers generated questions, such as, "What is the role of the teacher as a helping agent?" "What kinds of help or influence facilitate or inhibit motivation?" The behavior and feelings of the "child" in the role play helped to answer the second question. "Children" who had been completely dominated by the "parent" or "teacher" felt unmotivated. They felt like Pawns. On the other hand, a "child" who was given relative freedom to tackle the task on his own, with warm support from his helper, felt in control of the task and felt motivated—he felt like an Origin.

One of the purposes of the input (and others like the Blindfold game, the Origin-Pawn game, and the Leadership game) was to generate positive and negative affect associated with freedom and constraint. Teachers who were treated as Pawns felt uneasy. At the same time they began to recognize that much of the time they treat others as Pawns in the classroom. This awareness led to discussion of what one can do in a classroom to avoid treating students as Pawns.

Input 6: Measuring Individual Motivation

The afternoon was devoted to further examination of personal motivation as the participants analyzed the stories they had written on Monday. A member of the staff began with an explanation of the technique of measuring motivation through thought samples (McClelland et al., 1953). He presented the use of content analysis by discussing the relationship between thought and action. The stories the group had written reflected the general types of thoughts and concerns they had.

He went on to explain in detail the method for identifying specific motives in the stories. Stories with achievement themes are concerned with competition and hard work, while stories with power themes are about people helping, advising or arguing with and influencing others. The participants learned how to identify the intensity of each concern by looking for the expression of needs, feelings associated with anticipation or occurrence of success or failure, obstacles, etc. The conceptual scheme of the scoring system is a goal-directed behavioral unit that a motivated person thinks through in the process of reaching his goal. The specific scoring categories are elements of the path between wanting something and reaching a goal.

Finally, the participants received a booklet (a similar manual for scoring achievement, affiliation and power motivation can be found in McClelland & Steele, 1972) that described in more detail the method for scoring their stories for the achievement motive. They broke into groups of three or four and spent most of the afternoon analyzing their stories for the kinds of concerns presented. The staff acted as consultants as the small groups read their stories to each other and measured their "achievement motivation."

After a couple of hours, the group returned to discuss the scoring and the role of the teacher as an influence agent, using friendship and power to benefit the children and to raise their motivation.

Finally, the group attempted to write a story that had a maximum score for the achievement motive. The goal was to help the participants to become aware of the way "highly motivated" people think and of specific changes they could make in themselves to raise their own motivation.

Input 7: Dramatic Presentation of the Problems of the School

After dinner, the group began to discuss the relationship between the workshop and their "real world," by identifying problems that the teachers had to deal with in the schools.

The participants broke into small groups and spent an hour preparing creative dramatic presentations which expressed their views of school. Each group was urged to be creative in selecting their medium—a one-act play, poem, song, etc. The task produced a subtle competition between groups and the presentations by each group were received with considerable enthusiasm.

Summary of Tuesday

The exercises and discussion on Tuesday built on Monday's experiences and introduced new variables. First, the group became more specific in their self-study as they struggled with the motive scoring. Members went beyond the actual scoring as they analyzed their own motives. Second, the Block-Stacking game introduced the concept of the helping relationship to the training. Issues related to freedom and control, spontaneity and inhibition, Origin and Pawn began to take a central role in the group discussions. Finally, some of the group's everyday concerns about school began to be more freely expressed.

DAY 3: WEDNESDAY

Input 8: The Blindfold Game

Prior to dismissal the previous evening, the participants had been asked to meet together before breakfast. At this early meeting the staff provided blindfolds for half the group. Volunteers were blindfolded and partners chosen to be their guides. The "sighted" person was responsible for helping his blindfolded partner to the dining area, eat breakfast and return to the lounge. The purposes of the game were to illustrate individual differences in giving and receiving help and to heighten individual awareness of and concern about issues of guidance and control.

When the group returned to the lounge, the initial discussion focused on a heightened sense of awareness in blindfolded partners and quickly moved to reactions to the feeling of dependence. For people in supervisory positions, such as teachers and administrators, this exercise constituted a "role-reversal." Some blindfolded participants were pleased when their partners allowed them to explore unguided. Others demanded a strong, protective leader and talked of their feelings of insecurity. The exercise generated discussion about children's needs for security in new tasks.

As the blindfolded members talked, it became evident that their sighted partners had displayed a variety of leadership styles. Some had been overprotective and had carefully directed the movements of their partners as they walked or ate. Few of the teachers were comfortable in letting their partner go completely by himself, lest he hurt himself. Many leaders played a role designed to develop independence in the blindfolded person. They provided help at the beginning of the exercise, when support was most needed, and gradually encouraged independent actions.

As the participants related their feelings and reactions to the game, they began to talk about motivation. People set free too soon had been too afraid to try anything. Others who were guided too closely felt bored by the task and were somewhat angry at their leaders. These reactions led to questions like "How *should* one help another to maximize his motivation?" and "What kind of leadership facilitates or is detrimental to motivation?"

Input 9: The Power Role Plays

After a break, a staff member asked for volunteers to have an arm wrestling match. Four matches were held, including one between two women. The observers became very absorbed in the matches.

Immediately following the last match a staff member announced that he was going to auction a nickel to the highest bidder. Assuming the role of an energetic auctioneer, he danced around the room, reporting bids, asking for more, lauding the virtues of the nickel. After the first nickel was sold, he auctioned off three more "brand new,

The Blindfold Game (see p. 51)

beautiful nickels." Each of the nickels sold for more than its face value.

After the auction, a staff member initiated discussion by asking the first purchaser to describe his feelings during the bidding. The winner responded by saying that he wanted to win—to beat the other bidders. This stimulated a discussion of competition. As the group expressed its reactions to the game, one of the members noted that if they had cooperated they could have made some money. As the strategy of cooperation was being discussed, the staff member introduced the concept of the "zero-sum game." He noted that it seemed that the participants had viewed the auction as a game in which one person had to win and others had to lose. This competitive feeling probably was partially induced by the arm wrestling matches, competition in which there had to be a winner and a loser.

After much interchange, the staff member summarized by suggesting that competitive situations arouse personal power needs, and that it is difficult to act cooperatively in those situations. He suggested that the group role play a situation in which the dimensions of power, control and competition dominate when cooperation is really needed.

Input 10: The Family Control Role Play

The staff member selected three participants to play the roles of mother, father and son. He gave them the following directions privately. *Mother:* her son is always getting into trouble because her drunken husband doesn't accept any responsibility for or show any concern for the boy. She detests her husband's drinking, and holds him responsible for the boy's wild ways. *Father:* his wife is a shrew. He often stays at the tavern to avoid her and her prodigal son. The mother pampers their son so much that the boy is going bad, and he holds her personally responsible for the boy's actions. *Son:* he is sixteen years old. His parents persecute, neglect and fight with him so much that he prefers to stay on the street corner with the gang as much of the time as possible.

The father and son were sent out of the room while the staff member supplied the mother and the rest of the group with the *setting:*

The mother has just received a phone call from her neighbor. A gang of boys has broken the window of the corner drugstore with a brick. Rumor has it that they stole watches and radios and the police are combing the neighborhood looking for the boys. It is early evening and the son is usually on the street corner with the gang.

The father was called in and the role play began. At what seemed an appropriate point the staff member called the boy in.

The discussion that followed the exercise began with an analysis of specific behavior and feelings exhibited and quickly evolved into a discussion of the parallels between the exercise and incidents in the lives of the participants. Throughout the discussion the participants talked about the difficulty of transforming conflict situations into cooperative problem-solving endeavors. The arm wrestling, auction and role play had generated many negative reactions to "power plays" and the group went to lunch talking about strategies that improve understanding and cooperation.

Input 11: The Goal-Setting Game[2]

After lunch, the group returned to a room equipped with large tables. The participants were given a box of tinker toys and were told that they were going to play a goal-setting game. Each was handed a mimeographed form containing detailed instructions.

The object of the game was to assemble specific models in order to make "money." Each individual first bought parts and contracted to assemble a given number of models in five minutes. The larger the number constructed, the greater the profit margin, but the larger the estimate, the greater the cost. Consequently, it was necessary that the participants realistically assess their manual abilities.

For each of three different models, the participants went through the same process: (a) they inspected a demonstration model and estimated how many they would make in five minutes; (b) they practiced assembling the model for one minute and then could modify their initial estimate; (c) they attempted to reach their goal; and (d) they computed their profit or loss after the staff checked their production for quality and quantity.

This procedure, which can occupy more than an hour, developed intense involvement in most participants. After the game each of the steps was discussed at length. Feelings of success and failure were expressed as were insights into the relationship between the goal-setting strategies of the ring toss game and the present game, and goal-setting in real life. A staff member summarized the experience and presented some research findings. He noted that "highly motivated" individuals approach goals in a consistent manner. They set realistic goals that challenge their skills, examine the outcome of their actions (feedback) carefully, take responsibility for their actions and, consequently, tend to be successful in reaching their goals. On the other hand, people who seem to be "unmotivated" tend to set very unrealistic goals when they do set them, and consequently don't experience success very often. They don't accept responsibility for their actions, so they feel relatively powerless.

The afternoon concluded with a discussion of the differences between long- and short-range goals and the importance of helping children to set goals and to be realistic about them.

Input 12: Evening of Relaxation

Tuesday, Wednesday and Thursday evenings were devoted to activities that relieved the tedium of being in one place and the emotional tension associated with the workshop. The creative dramatic session on Tuesday helped serve that function. On Wednesday, after the highly emotional power-play exercises and the exhausting goal-setting game, the participants went as a group to a restaurant for dinner followed by a party.

Summary of Wednesday

The power-control exercises of the morning produced in the participants an awareness of their own motivation and the effects of it in helping others. The goal-setting game helped the participants to identify personal goal-seeking behavior. As the group discussed the effects of time pressure and anxiety on productivity they moved to discussing the feelings of children in the classroom.

DAY 4: THURSDAY

Input 13: Motivation and the Need for Power

The morning began with a review of the relationship between motives and behavior. The staff member recalled that individuals who have high achievement motivation are concerned with excellence, that they take personal responsibility for their actions, set realistic goals and plan carefully. People who are very concerned with affiliation and are successful in finding friendship take risks in making friends, yet they actively seek friendship, take responsibility for their behavior and seek evidence concerning the success of their interpersonal relationships. No matter what the individual need or motive, be it achievement, affiliation or power, personal responsibility, realistic goal-setting, risk-taking and planning are important components of "motivated behavior."

Since the issue of power and influence seemed to be a central concern for teachers, the participants scored their stories for the need for power. Winter's (1968) definition of power motivation as "the need to establish or maintain impact, control, or influence over another group of persons" was explained. The participants then formed small groups to read, discuss and score their stories for power motivation.

When the large group reconvened, discussion turned to different kinds of power concerns and different styles of influence strategies. Some individuals need to be in complete control, to dominate, to make others submissive. Others are also concerned with influencing people, but their goal is to help others to learn. If teachers are to influence rather than dominate their students, they must develop strategies to help their students to grow, rather than to make them submissive.

Input 14: Role Play of a School Lunchroom

After a break, a staff member suggested that the group do some role-playing that would demonstrate different strategies of influence within a school context. Volunteers were selected to play a "principal" waiting in his office and a "teacher" acting as a proctor in the lunchroom. The staff member privately gave instructions to two "students." *Girl:* she was eating lunch and the boy next to her broke the rule by not returning his tray. She was to persuade him to return the food tray. *Boy:* refuse to do what the girl asks. Resist her strongly, swear at her, even push her away if she persists.

In several versions of the exercise different influence strategies appeared. The discussion that followed focused on influence strategies and conflict resolution.

Teachers playing the Goal-Setting Game (see p. 54)

Input 15: The Origin-Pawn Game

After lunch, the participants reassembled in the room equipped with large tables on which the tinker toys were again available. A staff member suggested that they could build anything they liked. For the next fifteen or twenty minutes they made a varied assortment of models in a free and open atmosphere. When most had completed their model, the staff member asked each participant to show his model to the others and to tell what the model represented.

Next, the staff member became much more serious and told the participants to disassemble their models and put the pieces back in their boxes. When the pieces were returned to their correct boxes, the instructor began to issue the following directions in an assertive manner:

"Arrange the boxes in the center of the table.
"Don't prop the boxes up . . . I want them flat.
"Remove everything else but the boxes from your table.
"Sit up straight . . . put your hands in your lap.
"You may not talk, smoke or chew gum.
"Listen carefully to me . . . don't leave the room . . . if you need something, raise your hand.
"Listen to these instructions . . . this is a yellow rod . . . this is a blue rod . . . this is a red rod . . . this is a cylinder.
"Follow these directions carefully.
"Get six spools with narrow holes and place them in a straight line in front of you.
"I said a *horizontal* straight line, not a *vertical* line . . . follow directions."

As these instructions continued the instructor gave contradictory directions and participants attempted to correct him. He refused to listen to criticism. After all of the parts were on the "assembly line," he proceeded to direct the participants in the construction of the model.

"Take a spool, connect it to a red rod on the round side of the spool.
"I did *not* say to put the assembly down.
"Put the assembly down now.
"Pick up the assembly.
"Connect another round spool to the other side of the red rod.

"Connect it to the *round* side . . . don't you know how to follow
directions?"

The Origin-Pawn game continued for approximately one-half
hour until the model was near completion. The insturctor maintained the strict, autocratic role, continued to blame others for his
mistakes and finally walked out of the room for a few minutes. When
he returned, he told the participants that the game was over and
asked them to put the pieces back into the boxes.

During the task, the participants at first followed instructions
carefully. Later, especially after the instructor made an obvious
mistake, the participants became frustrated and even rebellious.

After the group had discussed their reactions, one of the staff
introduced the Origin-Pawn concept in terms of the participants'
experiences and discussion. He suggested a dimension, the extremes
of which are feelings of complete freedom compared to complete
oppression or control. In the Origin-Pawn game the participants had
experienced freedom during the first part of the activity. During the
second part their behavior was strictly controlled. During the first part
each participant felt personally responsible for his behavior. He felt
free; he felt like an Origin, for he originated his behavior. In the
second part of the exercise the individual felt constrained; his behavior was determined not by him but by the leader. He felt powerless to
control his fate; he felt like a Pawn.

One of the important questions for teachers is, "How may I help
students to develop personal responsibility?" A teacher influences a
child to act as an Origin by *not* treating him as a *Pawn*. Arbitrary
rules with no explanations, busy work that requires no thinking and
the threat of physical punishment are all instances in which the locus
of choice and control lies with the teacher rather than with the child
and, as a result, the child is a Pawn. Two typical reactions to such
controlling acts are (*a*) passive acceptance and conformity behavior,
or (*b*) rebellion. In either case the child's freedom, creativity and
productive behavior are suppressed. Such autocratic methods
depress motivation and train people to be Pawns.

Teachers can adopt a helping or influence strategy that does not
depend on too much control, nor does it forego rules and structure.
They can help their children develop personal responsibility by *gradually* giving them more and more control over their own behavior. An
ideal strategy in the Block-Stacking task or the Blindfold game was to
provide security, structure and directions at first, followed by a
loosening of external control to allow responsible internal control.

Developing responsibility in the classroom follows the same principle. The teacher who creates an atmosphere of openness and trust, who sees the student as a unique human being rather than as just another puppet to be pushed around, who provides the right amount of structure and help, can develop in the student the feeling of being competent in controlling his life.

Input 16: The Leadership Game

Following dinner, the participants formed three groups of five and elected a leader for each group. Paper jigsaw puzzles were distributed in envelopes containing five pieces for each group member. The task was for the group to assemble five similar squares through sharing pieces. No talking was allowed during the task, forcing members to communicate through gestures.

The staff member privately gave the respective leaders different roles to play. The *Autocratic Leader* was to attempt to control all transactions in the group; the *Democratic Leader* was to help the group to cooperate, offering suggestions (non-verbally) only when they were needed; the *Laissez-faire Leader* was to allow his group complete freedom and not to intervene in any way with his group. The leaders were then briefly shown a diagram of the correct solution and told to play their roles in influencing the group.

The democratically led group finished the puzzle first, as is often the case. Frustration was generated by the autocratic leader's attempt to control the group and the laissez-faire leader's failure to give aid. Discussion of leadership styles and control naturally followed.

Input 17: Problems of Control in the School

The discussion of leadership developed concerns about the optimum amount of information or help that a teacher could give to children as well as the atmosphere in which it was imparted. As a next step, a staff member suggested that the participants explicitly focus on teachers' problems that were related to control, power and motivation. The discussion ranged from administrators treating the teachers as Pawns, to teachers and even other children treating children as Pawns. Staff members suggested that the participants might analyze why people acted in such a way and plan ways of treating others as Origins and of avoiding being treated as a Pawn oneself.

Summary of Thursday

Thursday served the purpose of focusing the participants' thinking on influence strategies, showing how closely related the strategies were to personal motives and beginning to relate these developing themes to concrete problems in the school.

DAY 5: FRIDAY

Input 18: Brainstorming Solutions to School Problems

While the teachers had been discussing school problems the evening before, one of the staff had written them on a chalkboard. After more problems were discussed and listed, the staff member suggested that the teachers try to produce ideas to help resolve some of these problems. He asked them simply to brainstorm solutions. The rules of the brainstorming were that each individual should blurt out ideas, no matter how wild, and that no ideas should be criticized. The participants began to suggest solutions and a staff member wrote them on the board.

The purpose of this exercise was to develop creativity in looking at different solutions to old problems. Most of the suggestions dealt with eliminating structural variables that seemed to be arbitrarily imposed by authority.

Input 19: The Teacher as Motivation Expert

After the "loosening up" of the brainstorming session, the staff member suggested that one of the things the group might do during the school year would be to develop classroom units that would become motivation training for the students. He suggested that the group break into small groups and attempt to design classroom units. After an hour, the large group reassembled to discuss the suggestions of each small group. The units initially designed at that time generated many of the ideas and units actually used in the classroom and presented in Chapter 5 below.

Input 20: The Future Planning Manual

After the ideas had been presented and discussed, a staff member passed out a mimeographed booklet called the *Future Planning Manual* (Behavioral Science Center, 1967). The manual was to help them identify more specifically their goals in all areas of their lives and incorporated many of the ideas they had been discussing during the week. The manual was designed to focus on goals, feelings, perception of risks, conflicts, etc., and was intended to help the participants to commit themselves to a course of action. The members spent about two hours in private or in pairs completing the *Planning Manual*.

Input 21: Sharing of Goals

After lunch, the members returned to talk about their goals and their reactions to the entire goal-setting process. After sharing goals, the group talked about their reaction to the workshop week, and the workshop terminated in the late afternoon.

Summary of Friday

While the description of Friday is the shortest of the individual days, the process of problem-solving, planning and commitment to change converged as each individual planned for his future in general and for the school year specifically. The group was very close by the week's end and seemed reluctant to disband. It was evident that the plans to continue working together during the year were very important. Follow-up after such a workshop was felt to be crucial.

Notes

1. Adults playing the role of "child" get quite involved in this game. In one instance, an extremely masculine man was badgered by an authoritarian "parent" and performed miserably in the task. After everyone had gone to lunch, he stayed at the table, blindfolded and tried to see how many blocks

he could stack. He said: "I simply had to see how well I could do on my own."

2. Adapted from the Business Game (Litwin & Ciarlo, 1959), which is available from the Behavioral Science Center of Sterling Institute, Suite 3750, Prudential Tower, Boston, Massachusetts, 02199.

Chapter 5

Motivation Development
with Children

(R. deCharms)

Motivation development in the classroom was attempted in two ways. First, the experimental children were taught by trained teachers who served as models, acting like Origins and treating the children as Origins. Second, the staff and the teachers developed classroom procedures to emphasize four fundamental concepts: (*a*) the Self-Concept, (*b*) Achievement Motivation, (*c*) Realistic Goal-Setting, and (*d*) the Origin-Pawn Concept. The exercises developed by the teachers and staff based on these concepts constituted the major concrete differences between the experimental and the control groups. Less concrete and less demonstrable but probably of equal importance, were the differences in classroom behavior of trained teachers as compared to the untrained teachers.

Units dealing with the Self-Concept were introduced into the experimental classrooms shortly after the fall term began. The sixth grade unit was called "The Real Me;" the seventh grade, "The Person Perception Training Unit." In the eighth grade the teachers were given some techniques designed by Blasi (1970) to increase personal development. Only a few of the teachers found time to use them in their classrooms. The Achievement Motivation concept was embodied in only one unit, called "My Stories of Achievement," introduced at mid-year in the sixth grade. Similarly, training in Realis-

Table 5.1 —Units Used in Motivation Development By Grade Level

UNITS

	Self-Concept	Achievement Orientation	Realistic Goal-Setting	Origin-Pawn Concept
Sixth Grade	I "The Real Me" pp. 66–67*	II "My Stories of Achievement" pp. 67–70	III "Spelling Game" pp. 71–73	IV "Origin Manual" (Shea, 1969) pp. 73–77
Seventh Grade	V "Person Perception Training" (Collins, 1973) pp. 77–82			VI "Origin Manual" (Plimpton, 1970) pp. 82–83
Eighth Grade	Ego Development (Blasi, 1970)			

*Page numbers refer to where the unit is duscussed in this chapter.

tic Goal-Setting was conveyed through a "Spelling Game" that was used only in the sixth grade year, following "My Stories of Achievement." The Origin-Pawn concept resulted in two different units, called "Origin Manuals," one each for the sixth and seventh grades. Table 5.1 presents the four concepts and the year each unit was introduced into the experimental classes. The remainder of this chapter describes the rationale for and development of each unit in chronological order.

HOW DO YOU HELP A PERSON TO CHANGE?

The fundamental step in helping a person to change is to get him to change himself for reasons that are important to him. If the change is to be genuine and to have lasting effects, the impetus for change must come from within the person, not be imposed from outside. To effect a real and lasting change the teacher must nurture the child's desire to improve himself. This process does not happen suddenly. The nurturing of a desire to change in an individual where the desire doesn't exist initially involves a change in the individual's conception of himself—a change in his self-image. What a person thinks of as an ideal image of himself develops over time as a result of interaction with people whom he likes and respects.

Charles H. Cooley (1902) referred to the self-image as the reflected or "looking-glass" self. Other people form the looking glass and we look to them to see what we are through their reactions to us. The development of the self-image or identity is especially crucial for children about to enter adolescence as Erik Erikson (1968) has pointed out in discussing the identity crises of adolescence. The self-image is most strongly affected by his primary identification with his parents and family. But increasingly as he moves through elementary school this image is challenged by the expectations of others. His mother wants him to get an education; his friends want him to play hooky. Is he to live up to the expectations of his mother and teacher by going to school, or is he to risk loss of favor with adults and live up to the expectations of his classmates? Clearly, what is expected of the child from various groups that are important to him affects what he does.

One method of minimizing his dilemma is to help the child see personal goal-directed change as desirable. The teacher must try to provide an atmosphere in which his friends approve of his development—an atmosphere of acceptance of personal goals within the group where all members of the group may gain support for their endeavors from each other.

Two principles can be deduced from the above. In order to help a person *to make up his own mind* to work on his own personal motivational development, one must help him to see personal development as an improvement in his self-image and one must provide group support and acceptance of personal development. McClelland (1965) has captured these ideas in two of his propositions for the development of motives.

"The more an individual can perceive and experience the newly conceptualized motive as an improvement in his self-image, the more the motive is likely to influence his future thoughts and actions" (McClelland, 1965, p. 327).

"Changes in motives are more likely to occur in an interpersonal

atmosphere in which the individual feels warmly but honestly sup-
ported and respected by others as a person capable of guiding and
directing his own future behavior" (p. 329).

These two propositions capture what we mean by treating a
person as an Origin. There is a basic conception of mankind implied
here: namely, a man will be good if he believes that people who are
important to him expect him to be good. To help a person attain his
highest potential, sincerely expect it of him.

SIXTH GRADE

Unit I: The Real Me

The aim of this unit was to engage the pupils in self-study to help
them gain a clearer picture of themselves and of their problems, and
to see how personal motivational development would help them.

The unit lasted for ten weeks starting in October. After introduc-
ing the idea of self-study to the class, the teacher asked each child to
write a paragraph in answer to the question, "Who am I?" This
procedure was repeated at the end of the ten-week period. These
paragraphs and other material written for the unit were kept in a
personal notebook. The children were encouraged to make these
books reflections of themselves and by the end of the ten weeks they
were usually elaborately decorated and contained self-portraits,
poems, photos and other personal artifacts.

Each week the teacher introduced and posted a thought for the
week. Each day, when the class had some free time, the children
shared their thoughts, and on Friday each child wrote a personal
statement for inclusion in his notebook.

The thoughts for each of the ten weeks were:

1. My favorite daydream.
2. If I had three wishes.
3. The perfect family.
4. I'm different.
5. What makes me angry.
6. My greatest success.
7. When I'm discouraged, I . . .

8. Why try?
9. Failure teaches lessons, too.
10. The kind of person I want to be.

These "thoughts" were chosen by the teachers from some twenty-five or thirty suggested in the planning sessions. Examples of what some of the children wrote may be found in Chapter 3.

One further technique was introduced in an attempt to help the children visualize their increasing self-knowledge. Each child made a picture poster of his name in any way that he wished. He then cut the poster into a jigsaw puzzle of ten pieces. Having chosen "his space" on a bulletin board, he added one piece of his name to "his space" each week, thus achieving a "total picture" of his name by the end of the ten weeks.

The effects of this unit on the children are difficult to evaluate. The measurement techniques used to evaluate changes in self-concept were not very successful (see Technical Note 5.1 for details).

The greatest value of the unit may have been its effects on the teachers. One teacher, who had taught the same children the year before in the fifth grade, said: "I didn't know them as well last year because I didn't find out as many crucial things about them last year as I did this year. . . . I learned more about them (from their) writing those ten stories than I had in a whole year that I knew those children, especially the ones who never say anything."

The enthusiasm, encouragement and inventiveness of the teachers in designing and implementing this unit and the trust relationships they enjoyed with their students were primarily responsible for the enthusiastic responses of the children. The childrens' response was evident in their reluctance to part with their notebooks even for the few days required for the research staff to copy the stories.

Unit II: My Stories of Success and Achievement

McClelland's concept of achievement motivation was an important antecedent to the present project, but it was felt that a broader concept of motivation development was needed. Achievement motivation is defined in terms of competition and, while the teachers were eager to increase achievement in general, they were extremely critical of any attempt to promote competition between students. As a result, in using the concept of achievement motivation in the project, competition had to be deemphasized. In training businessmen, McClelland

and Winter (1969) taught them to write stories that included achievement thoughts such as those that appear in stories written by people who score high on achievement motivation. Again the aim for students was broader and we specifically avoided teaching them directly the achievement motivation categories found in stories.

The goal was to elicit achievement thoughts from the children themselves rather than to tell them what specific thoughts to reproduce. The difference between (*a*) eliciting the children's own responses and (*b*) training them to respond in a certain way by recognizing achievement responses of others is related to the Origin conception of development. The achievement responses are sought *from the pupils,* not supplied *by the teachers.*[1]

In developing the unit the teachers and the staff reviewed the goal and developed a plan for the "Stories of Achievement Unit" which included ten weekly essays. The essays were to be creative stories— fiction, not directly related to the child himself. Skeleton plots were developed around which the children were to write their stories. The plots were derived from the basic criteria devised by McClelland et al. (1953) for measuring achievement motivation although the children were not told this.

The four major criteria for achievement motivation can be briefly summarized as follows:

1. Competition with others (doing something better than others).
2. Competition with a self-standard of excellence (doing something better than you yourself have done it before).
3. Unique accomplishment (doing something that no one else has ever done).
4. Long-term involvement (doing something that will take a long time but will result in personal success).

In addition to these major criteria there are subcategories in scoring for achievement motivation that help fill out a story sequence. All subcategories relate to striving for achievement and personal feelings about achievement. These subcategories are:

1. A statement of wanting to succeed (*Need,* in the McClelland et al. (1953) manual).
2. A statement of action or what the person is doing to help himself succeed (*Instrumental Activity*).
3. A statement of asking for help in attaining the achievement goal (*Nurturant Press*).

4. A statement of some personal defect that may interfere with success *(Personal Block)*.

5. A statement of some external obstacle between a person and his goal *(World Block)*.

6. A statement about looking forward to success *(Positive Goal Anticipation)*.

7. A statement about fearing failure *(Negative Goal Anticipation)*.

8. A statement of being pleased or happy with success *(Positive Affect over Goal Attainment)*.

9. A statement of being unhappy at failure *(Negative Affect over Lack of Goal Attainment)*.

For each week's story the skeleton plot was derived from one of the four major definitions combined with one of the nine subcategories. Thus, the children were told: "During this week you are going to think about a story that you will actually write on Friday. In the meantime we will think about it and share our ideas about it. The instructions for this week are to write a complete story in which the hero or heroine is trying to do something better than it has been done before and he actually says he wants to succeed in what he is doing."

This first plot is a combination of major criterion Unique Accomplishment (3) and subcategory Need (1). Each Monday such a plot was supplied to the children for them to think about. They were encouraged to select magazine pictures that suggested stories to them. Both the teachers and the project staff as well as the children supplied magazines for this purpose.

The story writing was used as a classroom essay contest. Each week the children selected a different panel of judges, who did not write stories themselves but who read all the stories and selected the best ones to be posted as "The Story(ies) of the Week." The criteria for selection was to be left entirely to the judgment of the panel.

In writing the stories, the children were encouraged to create as freely as possible without concern for grammar or spelling. This aspect often worried the teachers and many used the rough draft stories as the basis for grammar exercises.[2] The goal of the unit, of course, was freedom of expression, not technical skill.

At the teachers' suggestion a list of 15 achievement-related words, 10 selected by the teachers and 5 by the students, were studied each week. The children were asked to include these vocabulary words in their stories.

In summary, the Stories of Achievement Unit asked the children to write stories for a weekly essay contest based on a skeleton plot derived from achievement categories and including as many of the week's achievement-related words as possible. With these instructions it was probably inevitable that one child would write the following story:

"A boy is sitting at his desk trying to write a story about a hero or heroine who is trying to do something better than it has ever been done before. He is trying to use the following words: achieve, succeed, attempt. . . ."

More typical, however, was this sincere attempt.

"A boy is going to try to *achieve*[3] his way into high school. He had to decide whether you would finish school or not. He was a mean and unclear boy for a long time and now was the time for him to prove he was somebody so he told himself that he was *determined* that he would go on to school. The first year he *succeeded* in his work. He attempted to quit school but his mind just wouldn't let him quit everytime he would be *intenting* to quit his mind wouldn't let him quit, so he went to school another year and he *succeeded* again. The next year he made *standard* grades. He was so *determined* that school was the best place for him and soon he found that it was best for him to go on to school and that it was not *worth* him being knowbody. At the end of the year he was a young man. And in the year of 1808 he was a scientist and on the year of April 21, 1808 he did his first *experiment* with an egg. He was a very great scientist and he went on for years and years being a great scientist and in the late years he was *encouraged* to *explore* for more and mor science objects. And with *patience* and time he found everything he needed as a scientist An in the year of March 23, 1946. The young man died but he was remembered."

Although the unit was designed to last for ten weeks and the enthusiasm was high in the early weeks, the teachers reported that the children began to lose interest after seven weeks, so the unit was terminated in most classes after eight weeks.

Effects of the unit on a word-association test indicated that achievement words were more prevalent in responses of the children after the training than before (cf. Technical Note 5.2). Effects of this unit in combination with the other units on achievement motivation are discussed in Chapter 6.

Unit III: The Spelling Game

William James (1890) pointed out that the way to get yourself motivated to get out of a warm bed on a cold morning is not to concentrate on forcing yourself out and its immediate consequences, but to start thinking beyond to what needs to be done. As your plans develop you suddenly find yourself on the way to implementing them—without having to suffer the dreaded immediate consequences.

Similarly, with the unmotivated child direct pushing is probably the least effective motivator. Setting goals for the future tends to pull one out of present inaction and to get activity started. Unfortunately, however, some goals may be selected that actually subtly promote procrastination or insure failure. This may occur when a child does not want to participate in school activities but is forced to do so by the teacher. The child may choose a setting in which he cannot be successful in order to demonstrate to the teacher that it is hopeless. He will try something so hard that although he could not be expected to succeed, he would be considered brave for having tried. In many school-related activities the children in the motivation project exhibited this kind of behavior, which was essentially aimed at avoiding the task.

Carpenter (1967) found, for instance, that children, similar to the project children, chose tasks on which they knew they had a very low probability of succeeding. The children were asked to choose from lists of spelling words or arithmetic problems that were of varying difficulty levels. They typically chose items from lists on which they knew that their chances of succeeding were very low. This unrealistic goal setting was also found to be characteristic of the project children by Rothenberg (1968) and Shea (1969), (see Chapter 6). The child's goal apparently is to avoid revealing his real ability, probably because he inwardly is very pessimistic about success. Choosing an unrealistically high goal puts him in the hands of Fate; if he fails, no one can really blame him, nor can they evaluate his skill.

Since school-related goals are most often imposed by teachers and parents, the children rarely experience the full sequence of setting a goal themselves, realistically determining their skill, trying to improve and experiencing the joy of success or the pain but new self-knowledge that comes from failure.

Our aim in the spelling game was to give the children an academic task in which they would experience this sequence. The goal would be theirs. We hoped they would learn that a realistic goal is one which challenges them; neither so difficult that success is impossible nor so easy that failure is impossible. The most critical aspect of the game would be that each child must compete with his own level of skill.

In these sixth grade classrooms the teachers used a spelling book that presented twenty new words each week to the children. The Spelling Game was built around these books. On Monday the children took a pretest on the words for that week. Tuesday and Wednesday were devoted to practice in any way that the teacher or workbook suggested. Thursday was the day for the game. By Thursday the teacher had checked the Monday papers and had marked correct and incorrect words and kept the list herself. The children began by choosing two teams as in a traditional spelling bee. When they were ready, the teacher called on the first member of team A.

"John, what would you like to try, an easy word, a moderately hard word, or a hard word? If you spell the easy word correctly your team will receive 1 point. Correct spelling of the moderately hard word gives 2 points. Hard words result in 3 points. Incorrect spelling of any word results in no points and I will spell it for you."

John was faced with setting a goal and unbeknownst to him the difficulty of the words were scaled according to his own ability. The teacher had in front of her his spelling paper from Monday. An easy word was one he spelled correctly on Monday; a moderately hard word one he spelled incorrectly on Monday but had a chance to study; and, a hard word was from a future list tailored to his ability. John's teammates were allowed to consult with him on setting his goal, thus giving group support.

We decided not to tell the children the method of selection of words to see if they did, in fact, have more success with moderately difficult words and tend to choose them more often as time passed. The teachers were initially concerned that the children would think it unfair to change standards for each child, but their fears were quieted, as the children heartily approved. As the children said, even the worst speller could get two points for his team if he studied the words he missed. The teachers also wondered if the children would start looking at future spelling lists and apparently some did. In the context of the game this might be considered cheating, but hardly something to be discouraged.

With the children, the Spelling Game was clearly the most popular of the four units. The project staff collected data on it for five weeks, but all classrooms continued to use it for at least five more weeks and some used it until near the end of the year, from February to May.

Many of the teachers considered this the most successful unit: "It taught them how to set a moderate goal. They learned immediately the dangers of setting one that's too high and also they learned that there is no satisfaction in setting one that's too low. . . . Also this was something easy to transfer to areas other than just the spelling game.''

During the Spelling Game the teachers recorded the type of words each child chose. From these data we were able to demonstrate that the number of moderately hard words chosen increased progressively over a five-week period while the number of hard and easy words chosen decreased (cf. Technical Note 5.3 and Figure T 5.3.1). Apparently we had succeeded in encouraging the children to select their goals more carefully and realistically.

Unit IV: The Origin Manual

To complete the first-year design of the "motivation curriculum" the teachers and staff designed the "Origin Manual." In it were incorporated a review of the earlier units and an attempt to embody the Origin-Pawn rationale described in Chapter 1. The specific goal was to help the child to understand his goals and to help him to strive for them effectively.

The Manual was a forty-page booklet distributed to each child in the classroom. On the booklet was printed "CONFIDENTIAL." The booklet was the personal and private property of the child; he did not have to share the contents with anyone. The teachers set aside about twenty minutes per day and guided the children through the workbook.

The Manual contained twenty-five exercises, each designed for use on a particular day in the week over a five-week period. The following is a brief description of each of the twenty-five exercises.

Day I. My goals in life. The children simply listed and discussed the goals that they wanted. They were asked to focus on all aspects of their lives.

Day II. We must be aware of ourselves. The children were reminded of the "Real Me" unit and the importance of personal understanding. They then were given an example of one kind of goal: "to be kind to people today." They constructed a checklist and were asked to keep track of the number of times they were kind during the day. This checklist was used to help the children focus on the importance of using careful checks on progress in goal striving.

Day III. My goals for today. After looking at the performance relevant to the goal of yesterday, each child set a goal for himself for that day. After he stated the goal, he considered the activity necessary for reaching the goal, the help he could get and the issue of personal responsibility.

Day IV. Check on progress. This exercise was designed to help the child focus on the process of evaluating past performance, specifically referring to the goal set the day before. They focused on the activity actually done, the feelings associated with success or failure, personal responsibility, as well as the feelings associated with an easy, moderate and hard to attain goal.

Day V. My goals for the weekend. The children set goals for the weekend, paying attention to activity, help, and personal responsibility.

Day VI. Check on progress over the weekend. This exercise on checking their progress or feedback was quite similar to the exercise on Day IV.

Day VII. Training to be an Origin. In this exercise we tried to develop the concept of "being an Origin." In order to do this we developed a set of words that described Origin behavior and were, at the same time, a gimmick to hold the child's attention. The children were told that an Origin is someone who

a) takes *Personal Responsibility,*

b) *Prepares* his work carefully,

c) *Plans* his life to help him reach his goals,

d) *Practices* his skills,

e) *Persists* in his work,

f) has *Patience,* for he knows that some goals take time in reaching,

g) *Performs*—he knows he has to do things in order to reach his goals,

h) checks his *Progress*—i.e., uses feedback,

i) moves toward *Perfecting* his skills, paying special attention to improvement.

Following the introduction of those concepts, the children set another goal, "to help out around the house," and constructed a checklist.

Day VIII. Is it good to be an Origin? The children discussed the question of value, paying attention to how they saw people who acted like an Origin and how other significant people saw them. Following this, they set another goal for that day.

Day IX. Looking at an Origin. In this exercise, the children read a story by Jesse Owens in which the author discusses how he developed into a successful track star. His vocabulary contains many references to the concepts that were introduced during the earlier aspects of the training—personal responsibility, getting help, long-range planning, persistence. The children discussed the relationship between what they had been doing and the content of the story.

Day X. Being an Origin over the weekend. Again the children set weekend goals and planned how they would reach them. In this case the planning steps were constructed around the concepts introduced on Day VII.

Day XI. Checking our progress. Another feedback exercise.

Day XII. Treating others as Pawns. This exercise was not in the workbook. It was designed as an experiential learning technique similar to the Origin-Pawn game used in the teacher training (see Chapter 4). The teacher came into the classroom and passed out sheets of paper that had numbers and dots on them. The directions to the teacher read:

> The task is a connect the dots picture. The picture is very
> simple: a very simple house on the left, a tree on the right.
> It's up to you to give the children very explicit orders, to be
> very authoritarian, to treat them like Pawns. We have included
> some directions here. Follow them as closely as you can, and
> "lay it on" as much as possible (Shea, 1969, p. 152).

The teacher told the children to pick up their pencils, connect dot #1 to dot #2, put down their pencils, pick up their pencils, connect dot #2 to dot #3, etc. Near the end of the picture, the teacher collected the papers, ripped them up and threw them away, saying, "I've never seen worse art work." One teacher, usually a quiet, non-directive individual, performed his role so well that several of his students ran to the principal and said: "You'd better come quick. Mr. Jones has gone out of his tree!"

After the exercise, the teacher discussed the fact that she had treated the students as Pawns. Often this discussion went on for over an hour.

Day XIII. The experience of being a Pawn. Recalling the task of the day before, the children were asked to recall times when they were treated as Pawns or acted as Pawns, and to pay particular attention to the feeling associated with that experience.

Day XIV. Treating others as Origins. The task for this exercise was another "connect the dots" picture; however, the children were encouraged to be creative—connect the dots in any way, add color and/or details; they were free to ask for help, but were encouraged to do it on their own.

When the children had completed the task, they and the teacher discussed the Origin concept and the notion of personal responsibility once more.

Day XV. The experience of being treated as an Origin. Again recalling the previous day's activity, the children focused on the feelings associated with times when they were treated or acted as Origins. Following this, they set a goal for the weekend.

Day XVI. What I can't do. After checking their weekend progress, the children discussed the issue of a realistic appraisal of personal shortcomings.

Day XVII. What I can be and do. Again, to help the children be realistic, they analyzed their abilities.

Day XVIII. Goal sheet. This exercise forms the basis for much of the work that follows. The children were asked to clarify for themselves their goals for all phases of life. Some of the questions they answered were: What are my goals for today (this week) (this month) (this year)? What do I want while I'm in high school (after high school)? They also reviewed the goals that they used to have, but for some reason rejected.

Day XIXa. Examination of the importance of my goals to me. The children rated their goals along the importance dimension.

Day XIXb. Examination of my present ability to reach each goal. The children considered whether their goals were realistically set in relation to their abilities.

Day XX. My goals for the vacation. The children set goals for their spring vacation, again using the concepts introduced earlier.

Day XXI. Checking my progress over the vacation. Another feedback exercise.

Day XXIIa. Acknowledging the source of blocks. The children looked at their goal sheet and decided who was responsible (themselves or others) for their not reaching their goals.

Day XXIIb. Reducing personal and other blocks. The children discussed the ways they could do things to reduce blocks and to move themselves toward their goals.

Day XXIII. To get a goal—review and preparation. In this exercise the children reviewed the concepts they had been learning all year. They then wrote a story about "someone trying to do something better than he or someone else has done it before." In the story the children were asked to describe how the person acted as an Origin.

Day XXIV. To get a goal—achievement plan. In this exercise the children chose one specific and important goal and planned how to reach it. They then committed themselves to reaching it by signing an "Origin contract" with themselves.

Day XXV. Checking our progress. This exercise actually continued for the remainder of the year. At the end of the Origin Manual was a check sheet. On it the child wrote the date and the specific things that he had been doing to help him reach his goal.

The children liked this input. It gave them something of their own—a personal diary that continued the process begun with the "Real Me" stories. Teachers commented that the children regularly reminded them that they wanted to work on their Manuals and many took them home to work on at night. One boy, who was dismissed from the school during the Origin Manual unit, took the Manual with him. Several weeks later he visited his teacher and showed her his completed Manual.

Shea (1969 and Chapter 6) found indications that this unit did have effects on the behavior of the children. The experimental children became more realistic in their goal setting as compared to the controls.

SEVENTH GRADE

Unit V: Person Perception Training Unit

The third year of the Project began with a new group of trained teachers and, by this time, the children were in seventh grade. That fall (1968) the staff and teachers developed a new input designed to further the children's training in self-study and relationships with other people.

Recent theory and research in developmental psychology (Erikson, 1950; Kohlberg, 1964; Loevinger, 1966) have indicated that through a process of maturation and learning children develop into social beings who gradually become more and more skillful in dealing with other people. One characteristic that seems to be very important for healthy social development is increasing awareness of and sensitivity to other people. Thus, the very young child is almost oblivious to the people around him, while the mature adult is considerate and often very understanding of other people. During the time the young child is growing to adulthood, there seems to be a series of fairly well-defined stages of development of sensitivity to others.

An important element in the understanding of others is the degree to which one understands oneself, since we tend to attribute to others feelings we have experienced in ourselves. Another related factor that seems important in social development is the ability to see many aspects of another person rather than just a few. This so-called cognitive complexity (Harvey, Hunt & Schroder, 1961; Kelly, 1955) is the recognition of many aspects of another's personality. To be skillful in "reading" other people children must develop a very complex set of categories for judging another's personality based on self-knowledge and careful observation of others, plus a sensitivity to fine nuances in the behavior of others.

In the psychological parlance the three factors sketched above are self-knowledge, interpersonal sensitivity and cognitive complexity.[4]

The choice of these three concepts as an area of concentration for classroom exercises grew out of McClelland's (1965, also see Unit 1) postulate that motivation development must be built on a firm base of self-study and eventually self-initiated change. Idealistically, the most mature Origin is one who only feels that he is an Origin when he can be sensitive to others and *allow them to be Origins,* so that each can reach his highest potential.

Six techniques were designed to encourage the child to perceive other people from different points of view. Six incomplete sentences from a measure of ego development (Loevinger & Wessler, 1970) were selected as the focus for discussion, one for each of six weeks. The techniques used with these incomplete sentences (Items) were designed to develop a child's cognitive complexity. The incomplete sentences were:

Item 1. When a child won't join in group activities . . .
Item 2. Sometimes he/she wished that . . .
Item 3. My conscience bothers me if . . .
Item 4. The thing I like about myself . . .
Item 5. What gets me into trouble is . . .
Item 6. When people are helpless . . .

Each Item (above) was coupled with one of the following techniques:

Technique 1. Structured Role Play
Technique 2. Story Writing
Technique 3. Pairing Personalities
Technique 4. Two Points of View in a Story
Technique 5. Building a Person
Technique 6. Structured Brainstorming

For design purposes each Technique was paired with every Item by having, for instance, teacher 1 use Item 1 with Technique 1, but teacher 2 used Item 1 with Technique 2 the same week, and so forth. During any week all Techniques were used in different classrooms, but all were concentrating on the same Item. Technically, this design formed a Latin Square.

The children were asked on Monday to complete the sentence Item in as many ways as possible. This procedure was repeated on Friday, after the Item had been coupled with the training technique. It had been hoped to compare Monday and Friday performances to measure the effects of each technique. However, after three weeks, the children complained of repetition, so the Friday writing was discontinued. Tuesday, Wednesday and Thursday were devoted to the technique activity.

For *Technique 1* (Structured Role Play) the class was given the beginning of a short playlet based on an Item involving three or four characters. After studying and discussing the Item and the playlet for a couple of days, the children volunteered to play the roles and to finish the playlet in front of the class in an impromptu fashion.

Thus, for instance, the children were given the following playlet for Item 2 (Sometimes he/she wished that . . .):

Scene: THREE FRIENDS FOOLING AROUND AFTER SCHOOL.

1st Friend: You know, sometimes I wish I were dead or could run away or something. My mom's never home and I have to get the dinner for my brother and me and do all the dirty work at home.
2nd Friend: I know what you mean. My mom works until 9 o'clock every night. She makes me do a lot of work at home. But mom keeps telling me how much money she can make by working the late shift and this way we have lots more money to spend.

3rd Friend: My mom and dad don't talk much about money. They just keep telling us kids . . .

Usually two or three different groups played the scene in different ways. Each time, the play was followed by discussion emphasizing the feelings of the characters.

In *Technique 2* (Story Writing) the children were asked to think about, discuss and finally write a story suggested to them by the Item for the week. They were given a story cue and four or five possible plots to help them.

For Item 3 (My conscience bothers me if . . .), for instance, they were given the following:

Story cue: Bernice has been asked to babysit for her little brother while her mother shops for a new dress.

(1) Bernice wants to go with her mother because Bernice might get a new dress too.

(2) Bernice enjoys babysitting her little brother.

(3) Bernice refuses to babysit unless her mother buys her some special earrings.

(4) Bernice wants to help her mother because her mother does so many nice things for Bernice.

In *Technique 3* (Pairing Personalities) the children were asked to select in their minds two people whom they knew well. They were then asked to list as many ways as they could how these two people were alike or different. They did this twice for two different self-selected pairs.

Discussion centered around a list of attributes gleaned from all students, which the teacher put on the chalk board. The children were encouraged to discuss (*a*) which qualities were most important to them, and (*b*) what acts, statements, gestures, etc. led them to attribute certain qualities to their friends.

Technique 4 (Two Points of View in a Story) asked the children again to write a story (as in Technique 2), but this time from the points of view of two different characters in the setting. Thus, the students were given a story setting, and they chose one character and wrote a story from his point of view. Then they wrote the story from another character's point of view.

Using this Technique with Item 4 (The thing I like about myself . . .), they were given the following setting and characters:

Story setting: Sally asks her friend Marline why she spends so much money on cosmetics when Marline's mother has to go out to work to support the family.

Possible characters: Sally, Marline, Marline's mother, and Marline's brother.

Technique 5 (Building a Personality) involved incorporating new and often discrepant information about a person into a previously formed impression. The teacher gave the class four paragraphs all about the same imaginary person, but all contained different information. She read the first paragraph and then asked the children to write down their impressions. Then she read the second paragraph and they wrote about any new impressions. She continued reading the paragraphs, to which the children gave their written responses. There followed, after all four paragraphs had been read, a discussion of their changing impressions.

Thus, the children built an imaginary Mr. Stoddard from the following paragraphs:

Paragraph 1: Mr. Stoddard is a tall, slender man about 50 years old. He is a high school science and mathematics teacher.

Paragraph 2: Mr. Stoddard has a reputation for being a very strict teacher. When Bill Jones, the basketball team captain, turned in an incomplete homework assignment because the team played a big game that week, Mr. Stoddard gave him a zero on it.

Paragraph 3: Mr. Stoddard is devoted to his four-year-old son, Steven. They love to sit together at bedtime while Mr. Stoddard tells Steven an exciting imaginary story.

Paragraph 4: Mr. Stoddard insists that Mary Jane, his oldest child, practice her piano lesson immediately after school. Mr. Stoddard has taken an evening job so that he can pay for Mary Jane's lessons.

Technique 6 (Structured Brainstorming) asked the students to complete the Item in as many ways as they could within a given setting. Four settings were supplied, one by one.

Thus, the child would respond to Item 5 (What gets me into trouble is . . .) in each of these settings:

1. While fooling around after school.
2. In the principal's office.
3. Saturday morning at home.
4. Monday morning in history class.

In the discussion that followed the teacher led the children to list on the board various responses and to note their variety and the feelings expressed.

Of critical importance in all of these Techniques was the discussion and sharing of ideas and feelings. The teachers tried to allot thirty minutes every day throughout the six weeks to the various Techniques. As additional aids to learning throughout the six-week period the children kept a personal notebook into which they put all their written materials and any other work they wished to add. These were to be strictly private and not collected by the teacher or the project members.

Unit VI: Origin Manual

The *Origin Training Manual* developed by Plimpton (1969) had the same goals as the first Origin Manual, i.e., to help the child to determine his own goals and to plan activity to attain them.

As a result of observing classroom behavior in an experimental classroom during the spring of the sixth grade year (described in Chapter 7) Franziska Plimpton concentrated on six major factors that seemed to be characteristic of Origin behavior.

1. Internal Control
2. Internal Goal-Setting
3. Internal Determination of Instrumental Activity *publicly tell someone I sang*
4. Reality Perception
5. Personal Responsibility *record keeping*
6. Self-Confidence *% men believes I sang*

Only the first five factors were used in the classroom exercises. The training lasted for seven weeks. Each week the children wrote a composition or story that followed discussion of the particular Origin factor considered that week. The writing of the composition was itself followed by discussion of what the children had written. The topics for discussion and the compositions were:

Week 1. "I look at myself. Who am I and what do I want out of life?" The teacher discussed with the children Internal Goal Setting and Internal Control over what happens to the person.

Week 2. "How am I going to get what I want?" The teacher discussed what the children could do (Instrumental Activity) in order to attain their goals.

Week 3. "There are Origins and there are Pawns." The teacher discussed with the children what Origins and Pawns are and the children wrote a description of them.

Week 4. "Personal Responsibility." No composition was written this week. After extended discussion, the children looked for examples of heroes taking personal responsibility in stories.

Weeks 5 and *6.* "Reality Perception." Again no composition was written, but the teacher developed the concept with the children under these subheadings:

Insight—the ability to analyze a cause and effect relationship where one's behavior is the cause; and how to plan and act accordingly.

Adjustment—the ability to adjust to insurmountable obstacles.

Help—the willingness to seek help and advice from those who know.

Obedience—a form of adjustment by internalizing social rules.

Seeing Blocks—the ability to foresee obstacles to be overcome in pursuing a goal.

Week 7. Review. During this week all the major factors were reviewed and the children attempted to write a story in which the hero demonstrated all of them.

This unit directly trained the students in categories that were to be scored in their thought samples that were written several weeks after the class completed the unit. As such, it is different from the first Origin Manual (Shea) used in the sixth grade. Its effects on the Origin score derived from the thought samples should be more direct than the former unit.

We developed no direct measure of the unique effects of this unit on the children's behavior. However, this unit and the Person Perception unit together showed dramatic effects on Origin scores. (For details see Chapter 7.)

EIGHTH GRADE

The last year was essentially a follow-up year, as was mentioned in Chapter 2. Only one unit was given to the teachers and it was only used by some of them. Its effects were apparently minimal; consequently, we will not describe it here. It was an outgrowth of work reported by Blasi (1971) and it was intended to increase social maturity in a way similar to the Person Perception unit.

SUMMARY

By way of summary the reader may wish to look back at Figure 5.1. This chapter described each unit listed on the chart and presented available evidence of the specific effects of each unit. Evidence of such effects was reported for Achievement Stories, the Spelling Game, the first Origin Manual in the sixth grade year and the Person Perception unit in the seventh grade. The majority of our data, to be presented in subsequent chapters, deals with overall effects of the units on measures taken at the end of each year. In Chapters 6 and 7 effects on motive measures (Achievement Motivation and the Origin-Pawn Variable) are discussed and in Chapter 8 the effects on academic achievement measures are considered.

Technical Note 5.1

Before and after "The Real Me Unit," a semantic differential measure (Osgood, Suci & Tannenbaum, 1957) of self-esteem was administered to each student in the experimental group. This self-report measure was composed of twelve pairs of qualities. The child rated himself on a six-point scale on each of these twelve pairs. The twelve pairs of qualities used were:

Friendly-Unfriendly	Good-Bad
Smart-Dumb	Good Athlete-Bad Athlete
Success-Failure	Brave-Cowardly
Happy-Sad	Sharp-Dull
Clean-Dirty	Good Grades-Flunking
Honest-Dishonest	Strong-Weak

On this measure of self-esteem the children, on the average, rated themselves considerably higher than their academic performance or teacher obser-

Table T 5.1.1 — Semantic Differential Self-Esteem Measure: Mean Scores on a Six-point Scale Before and After The "Real Me" Unit

	Before Training	After Training
Males (N = 114)	4.74	4.74
Females (N = 92)	4.81	4.72
Total (N = 206)	4.78	4.73

vations could substantiate. Table T 5.1.1 presents mean scores on the Semantic Differential Scale before and after training. Very little change in self-concept is reflected in these scores for the experimental group as a result of the ten-week training unit.

After the unit was complete, a revised self-concept measure was developed. In the revised measure the child rated himself on each quality in comparison with his own selection of the highest, lowest and average children on these qualities. He also was asked to show how he thought his mother, his teacher, and his best friend would rate him on these twelve qualities. This measure was given as a post measure to all experimental and control children at the end of the sixth grade training year (after all four units). Our hypothesis was that the experimental students would reflect a more realistic attitude toward themselves than would the controls, as evidenced by lower mean scores and greater

Table T 5.1.2 — Self-Concept Measure: Mean Scores on a Five-point Scale

Sex	Control Group	Experimental Group
Males	3.51 (N = 36)	3.58 (N = 67)
Females	3.63 (N = 49)	3.60 (N = 75)

variation within individual protocols. Table T 5.1.2 presents mean scores on a five-point scale. The hypothesis of a significant difference between experimental and controls was not supported.

Technical Note 5.2

A word-association test to assess the use of achievement words was administered to experimental classes before the Achievement Stories unit and again after the fifth week, and to experimental and control classes after the tenth week. Carefully selected and pretested words were read to the class as a group. After each word was read, each child wrote down the first word that occurred to him. Words thus elicited were scored if they fell into one of three categories. The two fifty-word lists used in training periods constituted the first two categories. Fifty easier achievement words not used in training constituted the third category.

The mean number of words in each category produced in the first-, fifth- and tenth-week word-association measures were computed for experimental subjects. The same means were available for controls for the tenth week only. Figure T 5.2.1 indicates that experimentals started somewhat higher on the measure than controls for all three word categories. The effects of the training are most obvious for the first word group as Part A of the Figure indicates. The fifth week test scores for the fifty words used in the first five weeks of training were substantially higher than scores for the same words in the first week. Scores for these words remained high five weeks later. Part B of the Figure indicates a smaller training effect for the second word group during the second five-week period. Part C of the Figure indicates that the easy words not used in training continued to be used with relatively high frequency through all three tests.

The actual number of words produced is very small, averaging about one word. To analyze the data we resorted to comparisons of subjects who have more or fewer words after training than before. When the percentages of subjects who increased and decreased in achievement word use as a function of training are compared, the effects show a highly significant difference in favor of increases as a function of training in both training periods. As might be expected the training on the first fifty words that continued for the full five weeks was more effective than the training on the second fifty that was stopped after three weeks. In other words experimental children increased their achievement vocabularies.

The effects of the whole year's training on need for achievement was assessed at the end of the year and will be discussed in Chapter 6.

Technical Note 5.3

Figure T 5.3.1 illustrates the choices that the children made in each of the five weeks we collected data.[5] The Figure shows that the moderate risk choice was preferred by the classes from the first week and that as the unit progressed the children increased their percentage of choice at the moderate risk level.

The statistical analysis of the data was accomplished by first transforming the percentage scores by the arcsin transformation. The fit of orthogonal polynomials and the analysis of variance of the data indicate a linear trend (in the moderate level choice) at the .05 level.

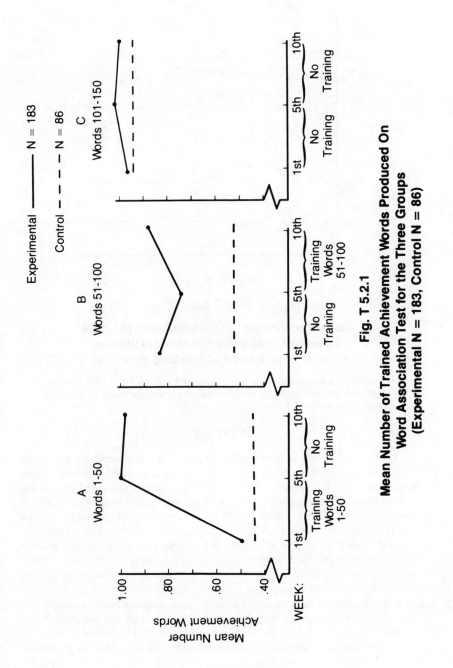

Fig. T 5.2.1

Mean Number of Trained Achievement Words Produced On Word Association Test for the Three Groups (Experimental N = 183, Control N = 86)

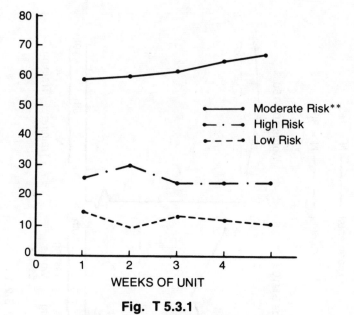

Fig. T 5.3.1

**Mean Percentage of Choices Made at Three
Levels of Risk in Experimental Classes
(N = 9) Over Period of Spelling Risk Unit.**

** ANOVA of moderate risk taking curve indicates a significant (p < .05) linear trend.
Data was analyzed by arcsin transformation of percentages and fit of orthogonal
polynomials to (k = 5) weeks.

Notes

1. This difference is also similar to the difference between a specific response more or less forced out of an organism in classical conditioning and a response that spontaneously occurs and then is rewarded in operant conditioning. Compare the amount of freedom of a dog in a harness whose response is to withdraw his foot when it is given an electrical shock (called a "respondent" by Skinner, 1938) and a child who is rewarded with candy when he more or less freely emits the response of pressing the correct button on an electronic teaching machine (an "operant" in Skinner's terminology). Compare a measure of motivation in which the child more or less freely emits responses in a story and the researcher must search for the underlying motive (an operant measure) with a questionnaire where the child can only choose between responses prescribed by the psychologist (a respondent measure). This distinction is discussed by McClelland (1966).

2. One teacher reported that when a rough draft was posted as the story

of the week the principal remarked, "How can this be a story of the week? There is no punctuation!"

3. The underlined words are the achievement-related words for the week.

4. They are major factors in Kelly's (1955) theory of personal constructs, Harvey's (1963) theory of cognitive styles, Loevinger's (1966) theory of ego development and even Kohlberg's (1964) conception of the development of morality.

5. We would like to thank Mr. Jay Noell for his help in collecting the data used in this analysis.

Part 2

Effects of Motivational Development

Chapter 6

Achievement Motivation, Control of Reinforcements and Goal-Setting Behavior

(D. J. Shea & R. deCharms)

How can you measure the effects of motivational development? This
is the basic problem of this section of the book and it is a formidable
task. No single measure can be counted on, for the basic reason that
effects of increasing motivation should have broad effects on behavior. Our conception of motivation led us to look for effects of the
training in the thoughts produced by the children, in the eagerness to
come to school as shown by promptness and attendance records, in
their goal-setting behavior and even in their school grades and academic achievement records. Academic achievement is, of course, the
most practical potential outcome and there are standardized measures
to assess it. However, to predict that the kind of training received by
these children should affect their academic achievement involves a
rather long chain of inferences that assume that increase in such
things as realistic goal-setting, planning, etc., will convince the children that success in academic achievement is an important goal and
that they will, therefore, devote more energy to it than untrained
children. The chain of reasoning connecting the effects of motivation
training to the thoughts of the children is not so long, but the measures
are less well standardized than those of academic achievement.

The measures of motivation available when the Motivation Development Project started had been designed to measure concepts related to the Origin-Pawn concept, but none of these was originally designed to measure it directly. It is paradoxical that in the areas most directly affected, the measures were the least well developed and standardized. Thus, during the first two years of the project we used related measures to assess the effects of the training while, at the same time, we devoted considerable energy to developing a measure of the Origin-Pawn concept. Altogether during the four years of the project we used several motivation measures that showed effects on related concepts, one new measure designed specifically to show effects on the Origin-Pawn variable, evidence of school behavior and standardized measures of academic achievement.

In this chapter we will discuss the mixed bag of measures of motivation that were available when the project began, i.e., measures of achievement motivation, control of reinforcements and goal-setting. All show some indications that the motivation development had effects. In Chapter 7 we shall discuss the development of the new Origin-Pawn measure and review the very clear evidence for effects on it. In Chapter 8 we move to academic achievement measures and here again we will find positive effects of motivation development. Finally, we will look at classrooms as a unit, rather than children, and ask, in Chapter 9, whether the Origin Classroom is different.

ACHIEVEMENT MOTIVATION

For theoretical reasons (see deCharms, 1968, and Chapter 7 below) we chose for our primary tool for measuring motivation a technique called "thought sampling" developed by McClelland and his associates at Wesleyan University. We hoped to use thought samples to measure both achievement motivation and the Origin-Pawn variable.

The rationale for the use of thought samples derives from the work of McClelland et al. (1953). McClelland noticed that the thoughts of successful people as expressed in words seemed saturated with ideas about competition, about liking to win and hating to lose and about plans that could lead to success. Following this lead, he asked college students to write very short stories and found that people who wrote about competitive situations, planning, working and winning were indeed different from those who didn't. He described this difference by the term "achievement motivation." McClelland's technique of having people write very brief stories or thought samples and then analyzing the content for references to achievement has subsequently been standardized into a measure of the motive.

A motive is like a mild obsession; a person with a motive for a specific goal thinks about that goal and ways that he may obtain it. When a motivated person writes an imaginative story, more often than not he will write about a character who has thoughts about goals similar to his own. In trying to discover a person's motives, thought samples have several advantages. Thoughts are free; that is, a person may be constrained from *doing* what he wants to do, but he can still think about it. If we wish to know what he *wants* to do, his freer thoughts may give a better indication than his actions. Further, what a man wants to do when free of constraints is more in keeping with our notion of an Origin. If we wish to know in what way he will act when not constrained, we must let him produce a sample under more or less free circumstances rather than measure what he can do when we push him.

For these reasons at the end of each year of the Motivation Project we asked the students to compose six short imaginative stories. To help them with the stories we gave them a booklet with a sentence that briefly described a scene at the top of each page. The scene described was commonplace, such as "Two men are working at a machine." The sentence was read to them, they all closed their eyes to think of a story and when they had an idea, they began writing. Since they had to complete each story in four to five minutes (a frustratingly short time which, however, was found in McClelland's research to be an optimum amount), they were given four questions to guide them through a complete story. On each page equally spaced down the page were the questions: (*a*) What is happening? (*b*) What happened before? (*c*) What is being thought or wanted? and (*d*) What will happen?

The whole procedure takes about thirty minutes in a classroom. The results, though rarely literary gems, do often contain stories of achieving characters. The presence of this kind of story in a person's writing can be used to predict some of his other behavior. Even a story composed of a one-sentence answer to each of the four questions may be a clear indication of motivated thoughts.

Achievement Content in Stories

The word "achievement" has very broad meaning. If ten people are asked what they consider an achievement, they will probably produce ten different answers. Thus, in confronting the task of specifying achievement thoughts or fantasies, the McClelland group had to be quite explicit. They defined the "need to achieve" as the desire to compete with some standard of excellence. In identifying the kinds of thoughts that reflected the need they found four major concerns about achievement in the thought samples people wrote.[1]

1. Competing with an external standard of excellence, either an impersonal standard (an athletic record) or another person.
2. Doing better than one's self or improving one's skill.
3. Attaining a unique task (an invention).
4. Working for a long-term goal (a career).

These categories appeared in Chapter 5, where they were used to develop story plots for the classroom exercise "My Stories of Achievement" designed to increase achievement motivation in the children.

In scoring a story, if the goal of a story is identified as an achievement goal, the story is searched for indications of the intensity of concern for reaching the goal. The following categories, also mentioned in Chapter 5 above, are taken as indicators of intensity.

1. Concern with excellence expressed as a need.
2. Concern with activity designed to move the individual closer to his goal.
3. Concern with the outcome of his endeavor expressed as hope of success.
4. Concern with the outcome of his endeavor expressed as fear of failure.
5. Concern with feelings about the task expressed as present success feelings.
6. Concern expressed in present feelings of failure.
7. Concern with getting help in attaining the goal.
8. Concern with personal inadequacies that might hinder his progress.
9. Concern with impersonal obstacles that might hinder his progress.

10. Concern with only an achievement theme uninterrupted with other concerns.

These are the categories, as carefully defined and elaborated by McClelland et al. (1953) that are looked for and counted in the thought sample stories of the children. A child's achievement motivation score is simply the total number of such categories found in his stories that have a stated achievement goal. A high score indicates high achievement motivation.

The classroom exercise ("My Stories of Achievement") designed to increase achievement motivation was only used in the first year of the training, when the children were in sixth grade. We would expect, then, that if achievement motivation increased as a function of training, the largest effect would occur during the sixth grade year in the trained classrooms. Effects of other exercises used in the seventh grade might affect this achievement motive score but should not be as strong.

In fact, the effects of the training on achievement motivation scores were not very strong at all. Effects did appear, however, in the one place where the strongest effect would be expected. During the sixth grade training the achievement motivation scores of the *boys* increased significantly as compared to scores of similar boys who did not receive training. These results may be seen most clearly in Figure 6.1, where the mean scores for trained and untrained boys are shown for the end of the fifth grade before any training and for the end of the sixth grade after the trained students had received all four classroom exercises described in Chapter 5 (see Table 5.1), including "My Stories of Achievement." The *boys* who experienced the "My Stories of Achievement" exercise were more likely than the girls to show an effect, because the measure of achievement motivation was originally developed and validated for boys and the measure has produced inconsistent results of achievement motivation in girls (Veroff, 1969; McClelland et al., 1953; French & Lesser, 1964; cf. Technical Note 6.2).

A comparison between boys' and girls' sixth grade achievement motivation scores may be seen in Table 6.1. and Figure 6.2. The table also shows the effects of Origin training (that did not include an achievement motivation unit) in the seventh grade. (See Technical Note 6.1 for details of sampling and analysis. Since we first encounter longitudinal data here, Technical Note 6.1 gives an account of procedures used to handle loss of subjects over time.) For the girls the

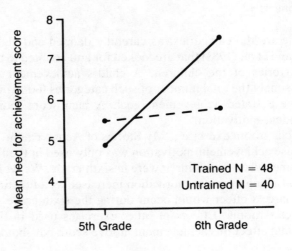

Fig. 6.1

**Mean Achievement Motivation Scores
for Trained and Untrained Boys
Before and After One Year of Training**

*Table 6.1 — Mean Achievement Motivation Scores By Sex
Comparing Sixth Grade Experimental and Controls*

| | | | Sixth Grade | | | | | | |
| | | | Experimental Grade Level | | | | Control Grade Level | | |
		N	5th	6th	7th	N	5th	6th	7th
BOYS	$\overline{X}$	48	4.98	7.65	5.96	40	5.55	5.75	5.60
	s.d.		4.17	5.24	4.39		5.42	4.59	3.83
GIRLS	$\overline{X}$	60	6.77	7.68	6.45	60	4.30	6.07	5.42
	s.d.		5.22	4.87	4.53		3.86	4.34	4.51
TOTAL	$\overline{X}$	108	5.97	7.67	6.23	100	4.80	5.94	5.49

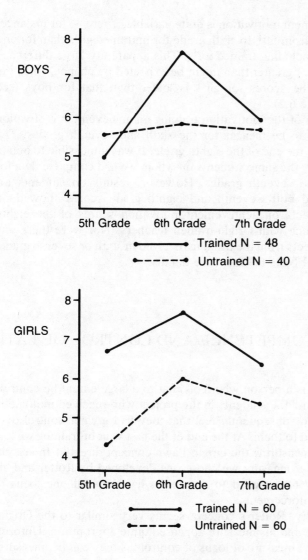

Fig. 6.2

**Mean Achievement Motivation Scores
for Fifth, Sixth and Seventh
Grades* by Sex and Treatment**

*No achievement motivation training was given in seventh grade

mean achievement motivation is quite variable. There is, for instance, a greater gain from fifth to sixth grade for untrained girls than for any other group, including trained girls. This apparently large difference is, however, not greater than might be expected by chance, since the reliability of the scores for girls is lower than that for boys (see Technical Note 6.2).

The results of the motivation training on achievement motivation scores appear to be meager for the sixth and seventh grades. The same is true at the end of the eighth grade. It was impossible to obtain data on exactly the same students on whom we had complete data for fifth, sixth and seventh grades. However, results on students for whom we had both seventh and eighth grade scores showed no significant effects on achievement-motivation scores of the eighth grade experience with Origin-trained teachers. Nor were there any carry-over effects from the training received in sixth or seventh grade. (See Technical Note 6.3 for more details.)

COMPETENCE AND CONTROL OF FATE

An Origin is a person who feels that to a large extent he controls his own fate and the students in the project who received motivation training should subsequently feel that they had greater control over what happened to them. At the end of the first year of training we had no means of measuring the Origin-Pawn concept directly. In searching for a similar measure we chose one developed by Rotter and his associates (1966) designed to measure what they call the locus of control of reinforcements.

Superficially, Rotter's concept seems very similar to the Origin-Pawn concept and his measure appeared quite appropriate. Unfortunately, the best measure of locus of control (as they call the measure) is a questionnaire the wording of which we found to be too advanced for our population of fifth grade students. We did, however, find that a less well developed measure constructed by Esther Battle (Battle & Rotter, 1963) could be used. This measure had the advantage of allowing the student to produce his own responses, as in thought samples, rather than asking him to respond to predetermined items, as in a questionnaire.

The measure presents the student with six cartoons in which one child appears to be talking with another. The first child asks the second a question by way of a "balloon" over his head as in newspaper comic-strips. Typical questions are: "How come you didn't get what you wanted for Christmas?" or "Do you think you can be anything you want when you grow up?" The student responds to the question by writing in his answer in the balloon above the second child's head in the cartoon. Responses are coded in a way that determines whether the response indicates a feeling of internal or external control.

Unfortunately, the results from this measure were not very reliable, despite the fact that Rothenberg (1968) had found some interesting relationships between it and socio-economic status and with goal-setting behavior. Although we had hoped to show a change from "External" responses to "Internal" as a result of the Origin training, there was no such evidence in the data. The obvious similarity between the locus of control concept and the Origin-Pawn concept makes this a puzzling result. It is probably attributable both to theoretical differences and to the low reliability of the measure, so we shall not pursue the finding here but consign a more detailed analysis to Technical Note 6.4.

It should be noted here that Rotter's concept of locus of control emphasizes reinforcements, that is, concrete rewards or satisfaction. The emphasis is on feeling that one can obtain rewards. The Origin-Pawn concept stresses the feeling that one has determined his own action and goal and is realistic about his actions. These theoretical differences may account for the negative results presented so far. The concept of locus of control was not a complete failure, however. In the next section we shall see that it helped us to predict which students would learn to be more realistic in their goal setting as a function of the Origin training.

REALISTIC GOAL SETTING

Psychologists have been developing measures of goal-setting, risk-taking and levels of aspiration at least since the early work by Kurt Lewin and his students (Lewin, Dembo, Festinger & Sears, 1944). An outgrowth of this research has been the finding that motivation, especially achievement motivation, is related to realistic risk-taking (Atkinson & Litwin, 1960). As we saw in Chapter 4 the ring-toss game was used in teacher training to develop the idea of realistic goal-setting. In Chapter 5 we discussed the rationale for developing the Spelling Game to teach the students realistic goal-setting. Although we already had evidence (see Chapter 5) that the Spelling Game had the desired effect on choices of spelling words in the game, we wanted another measure to assess more general effects on school behavior.

Fortunately, Carpenter (deCharms & Carpenter, 1968) had developed such a measure for arithmetic. The measure of arithmetic skill was composed of sixty items divided equally into six levels of difficulty. Arithmetic problems were taken from a series of arithmetic textbooks used in the schools from early elementary grades to junior high school. Extensive pretesting was conducted to assess empirically the validity of the various levels and to assure a very high degree of success for all children at the easiest level, and increasing difficulty up to a level at which little success could be expected from any child. For example, the first several arithmetic problems, along with their difficulty level were:

Difficulty Levels	Problem
I.	1) $1 + 2 =$ _____
II.	2) $9 + 7 = 10 +$ _____
III.	3) ¼ of $8 =$ _____
IV.	4) What is a six-sided figure called?
V.	5) A child when 1 year old usually weighs 3 times its weight at birth. What is the percentage increase in its weight? _____
VI.	6) 12 pounds = _____ kilograms?

A week or so after the children had taken the skill test in their classroom as a group the investigator met with each child individually. He explained to the child the six levels of difficulty and showed the child that he had correctly solved almost all of the easiest problems and fewer of the problems as they became more difficult. Very few of the children solved any of the ten problems at the most difficult level (Level VI).

Then the child was told that he would now take a test similar to the first. On this test, however, he would have ten problems and he himself would choose the difficulty level of each problem. The investigator made it clear that the test items were divided into levels comparable to those on the pretest.

The object was to obtain "points," and the number of points that could be won by correctly solving the problem increased with the difficulty of the item chosen. These points were determined individually for each child according to the empirically established level of difficulty *for him*. This procedure enabled us to equate each child's choice on the basis of his skill. For example, a skillful child who had solved many problems at Level III would receive fewer points for a correctly solved problem at that level than would a less-skillful child who had solved fewer problems at the same level.

After the child made a decision as to the level of problem he wished to solve, and recorded how many points he would receive by solving a problem at that level, the investigator gave him the problem. After he completed his work, the investigator told him if he had completed it correctly or not, and the child recorded the number of points won. This process—choosing a level, recording the decision, attempting the problem and recording success or failure—was repeated a total of ten times.

For each child we could derive a goal-setting score that indicated whether he was choosing problems in which his chances of success were (*a*) high (easy problems), (*b*) moderate or (*c*) low (very difficult problems for him).

On this measure of goal-setting behavior the students at the end of their sixth grade most often chose problems for which their chances of success were very low (approximately 40% of the choices were of problems on which they could expect to be successful less than two times out of ten or 20% probability of success). Many of these children, then, seem to be characterized by extreme risk-taking and unrealistic goal-setting.

The reader will recall that in Chapter 5 this type of behavior was hypothesized to be the result of attempts to avoid the task altogether, to choose problems where success could hardly be expected. It was one of the goals of the Origin training to attempt to change this behavior and to encourage the children to choose more realistic problems on which their chance of success was higher. If we were successful in the training, the Origin-trained children, subsequent to training at the end of the sixth grade, should choose more moderately difficult problems and fewer extremely difficult ones. The results of the statistical analysis showed a trend in this direction, i.e., the trained children chose fewer high-difficulty arithmetic problems and more moderately difficult ones than the untrained children.

The results, however, were very striking when the trained and untrained groups were further divided into students classified as high on Battle's measure of *Internal* locus of control or high *External* locus of control. In general, students who felt that fate and external sources controlled their rewards were the most extreme risk-takers, i.e., the least realistic in setting goals. And it was this very group that was most affected by Origin training. Figure 6.3 shows that "Externals" who received Origin training chose the fewest extremely difficult problems (32%) and the most moderately difficult ones (40%), while "Externals" who did not receive the training chose the most extremely difficult problems (49%) and the least moderately difficult ones (29%). The "Internals," who even without training did not choose so many extreme problems, were not strongly affected by the training. (Statistical analyses were performed on the mean probability of success scores that are presented in Technical Note 6.5).

In short the evidence shows that the "Externals" were strongly affected by Origin training and became more realistic in their goal setting; became in fact more like the "Internals," who, even without training, chose fewer extremely difficult problems.

SUMMARY

The results reported in this chapter give us some evidence that motivation training does in fact affect measures of motivated behavior. The evidence cannot be considered very strong, however. Achievement motivation scores did increase for boys who received achievement motivation training in the sixth grade. It did not increase for girls who received the training, nor did it increase as a function of the Origin training given in the seventh grade. The training did not significantly affect the locus of control scores for either boys or girls, a fact probably attributable both to the low reliability of the measure and to theoretical differences between Rotter's concept of locus of control and the Origin-Pawn concept.

Realistic Goal-Setting behavior, a variable that is thought to be an integral part of the Origin-Pawn concept, was enhanced by the training, especially in the external locus of control students who without training showed the greatest propensity to be unrealistic.

These results do demonstrate that the training produced some

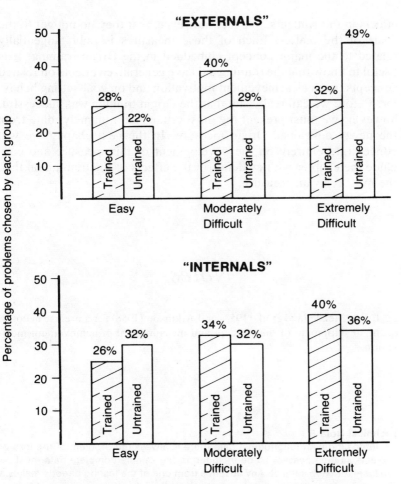

Level of Difficulty of Arithmetic Problems Chosen*

Fig. 6.3

**Effects of Origin Training on Choice of Problems
in Arithmetic Goal Setting Task, showing differences
between Internal and External Locus of Control Subjects.**

* Easy problems = 100 to 60% probability of success,
  Moderate = 50 to 30%
  Extremely difficult = 20 to 00%.

Approximately ⅓ of the choices were made in each of these portions of the distribution.

effects in the students. We feel, however, that they do not get to the heart of the matter. Each of these measures is only tangentially related to the major concept embedded in the Origin training. It is useful to know that the training did have generalized effects on related concepts, such as achievement motivation and on goal-setting behavior. Before we can really say that the Origin training was successful, however, we must present the most crucial data; namely, data from the newly developed Origin measure. In the next chapter we will concentrate entirely on the development of this measure and conclude the chapter with evidence of the effects of the training on this, the most relevant measure.

Notes

1. See McClelland et al. (1953) and Atkinson (1958) for a precise account of the development of the concept and measurement of achievement motivation.

Technical Note 6.1

In dealing with longitudinal data there is always the problem of the loss of subjects as time passes. To be included in the sample complete data must be available for each subject. Any absence from one of the testing periods makes a subject unusable. Since attendance at school (and therefore presence at testing periods) may be a function of motivational variables, it was necessary that we try to assess the effects of attrition on our data. We could not afford to return to each school to test children who were absent, nor could the schools arrange it.

Measures were taken to assess the effects of attrition, since it could not be completely controlled. As the Project progressed data were analyzed for samples each time data were collected. This meant that, for instance, we would have a large batch of achievement motivation scores for children in the fifth grade and another batch for children in the sixth grade. Some of the scores would be for the same children for both years and some for children only in the fifth grade or only in the sixth grade. The most useful data, of course, were those where we had both years. Before we were satisfied that those data were not contaminated by attrition, the means for subjects on whom we had complete data were compared with those on whom we had only partial data. For achievement motivation (and for academic achievement data discussed in Chapter 8 below) the data were handled in this way for pairs of years (fifth and sixth grade, sixth and seventh grade). Finally, subjects on whom we had data for all three years (fifth, sixth and seventh) were analyzed and compared with individual year and paired years. It turned out that attrition apparently tended to mask the effects of training. The mean differences between fifth and sixth grade achievement motivation scores were larger, for instance, for the subjects on whom we had both of those scores, than the differences between fifth and sixth grade scores on the smaller sample of subjects on whom we had scores for all three years (fifth, sixth and seventh). To be conservative we here report differences only if they appear significant in *all* of the analyses. Since attrition appeared to decrease rather than increase differences attributable to motivation training, we run the risk of underestimating the effects of the training. This conservative approach seems preferable, however, to running the risk of reporting differences that were not, in fact, attributable to the training.

A specific example of a difference that did not meet our criterion was the achievement motivation data for girls. Our first analyses of differences between trained and untrained girls for change in achievement motivation from fifth to sixth grades produced a small but significant difference. Subsequent analyses did not support this, however, and convinced us that the variability of achievement motivation means for different samples of girls was such that we could not consider the findings reliable.

The only finding that held up under the strict criterion was that of the effect of motivational training on the achievement motivation scores of boys in the sixth grade. There was no apparent effect of the seventh grade training (which did not stress achievement motivation) on the achievement motivation scores of either boys or girls.

Table T 6.2.1 — One-Year Achievement Motivation Repeat Reliability Coefficients for Boys and Girls Who Received No Training (Controls) between Testings*

		5th Grade Compared to 6th Grade	6th Grade Compared to 7th Grade
Boys	N	36	27
	r	+.46	+.17
Girls	N	61	47
	r	+.14	+.40

*Average correlation over all conditions equals +.29. The reader may wish to compare this with the overall reliability of the OP measure to be reported in Chapter 7.

Effects of Motivational Development

Technical Note 6.2
Repeat reliability coefficients were computed separately for boys and girls, for fifth compared to sixth grade scores and for sixth compared to seventh grade scores for students who had no training (controls) between two tests. Table T 6.2.1 presents the results. The significant increase attributable to training found for boys (fifth and sixth grade) occurred where the highest reliability coefficient occurred. The comparable coefficient for the girls (fifth compared to sixth grade) was very low.

Technical Note 6.3
Table T 6.3.1 presents the mean achievement motivation scores for the students at the end of their eighth grade year. Analysis of variance shows no significant differences in any of the effects.

Table T 6.3.1 — Mean Achievement Motivation Scores in Eighth Grade

		Teachers				
		Trained		Untrained		
		Male	Female	Male	Female	Total
Previously Trained Students	N	21	24	36	41	122
	$\overline{X}$	4.81	5.09	5.83	7.25	5.98
Previously Untrained Students	N	30	29	38	26	123
	$\overline{X}$	7.00	5.27	5.60	6.46	5.97
Total	N	104		141		
	$\overline{X}$	5.55		6.29		

Technical Note 6.4
The inter-item correlations between the six pictures in the Battle measure of locus of control (called the Children's Picture Test) were all very low, ranging from $-.10$ to $+.13$. The correlations of each item with total score averaged about $+.42$ (range $+.23$ to $+.52$). Shea (1969) reported means for students given motivation training in the sixth grade compared to control students. Pre-training (fifth grade) and post-training (sixth grade) means did not differ. It is apparent that the Origin training did not produce more internal scores in the trained students.

In scoring the Battle measure we felt uneasy about some of the responses that were scored Internal. They did not seem to coincide with our concept of

Origin responses. For example, according to Battle any answer to the question "Do you think you can be anything you want when you grow up" that implies a positive response is scored Internal. On the other hand, any response that implies "no" is scored External. But we found that many answers were qualified by very realistic statements. We felt that a realistic Origin might well say no he couldn't be anything he wanted to be because, for instance, he didn't have enough money to go to college.

Based on such notions about realistic qualifiers, Ina Coor, in an unpublished study, developed in a preliminary way rules for scoring the Battle measure for the Origin-Pawn variable. Even with this set of rules the measure did not prove very reliable. However, in validating the measure of the Origin-Pawn concept to be presented in Chapter 7 we compared it with both Battle's measure and Coor's Origin-Pawn adaptation of the Battle measure (see Table 7.5 for the correlations). The apparent resemblance between the Origin-Pawn concept and Rotter's control of reinforcements is not borne out by the empirical data, a result that is probably attributable both to real theoretical differences between the concepts and to the fact that the locus of control measure that we used because of the age of our students was not the best measure available, i.e., the questionnaire measure designed for adults.

Technical Note 6.5

Figure 6.3 presents percentages of choices at three levels of difficulty for students divided into groups comprising trained and untrained and internal and external on Battle's measure for locus of control of reinforcements. This is a convenient way to summarize the data descriptively, but the statistical analysis was performed on mean probability scores for each student. On each trial in the goal-setting task the student chose a difficulty level and was informed of his own empirical probability of success at that level. From the previously administered skill task his score (out of ten problems) had been determined. When the students chose their ten problems, they did so with a knowledge of their empirical probability of success at each level of difficulty. A mean probability score for each subject was computed. The higher the mean probability of success score, the easier the problems were for the subject. Students scoring an average of about .50 were tending to choose problems at a truly "moderate level" of difficulty. Students choosing problems of low probability were tending to choose very risky problems. Because all students tended to choose problems at a probability level less than .50 (mean probability level for all students was .35), those students who have higher relative mean probability levels are, in fact, closer to the .50 probability level and are taking "more moderate" risks (and are being "more realistic").

The student's score then is the average of his own empirically determined level of probability for each of the ten problems he chose in the goal-setting task. Whether he solved the problem chosen correctly is irrelevant in computing his mean probability score.

Table T 6.5.1 presents the mean probability scores for students divided by sex, training and locus of control. The analysis of covariance shows significant sex differences, a marginally significant interaction between locus of control and training and a significant regression of mean goal-setting scores on IQ, i.e., higher IQ students set more realistic goals.

Table T 6.5.1 — Probability of Success Scores and Analysis of the Data

	Pretraining Locus of Control Score	Trained Subjects	Untrained Subjects	Total
Males	Internal	$\bar{X} = 0.35$ s.d. $= 0.15$ $N = 27$	$\bar{X} = 0.39$ s.d. $= 0.19$ $N = 25$	$\bar{X} = .37$
	External	$\bar{X} = 0.35$ s.d. $= 0.14$ $N = 23$	$\bar{X} = 0.28$ s.d. $= 0.14$ $N = 25$	$\bar{X} = .31$
				All Males: $\bar{X} = .34$
Females	Internal	$\bar{X} = 0.43$ s.d. $= 0.15$ $N = 24$	$\bar{X} = 0.39$ s.d. $= 0.16$ $N = 17$	$\bar{X} = 0.41$
	External	$\bar{X} = 0.43$ s.d. $= 0.15$ $N = 26$	$\bar{X} = 0.37$ s.d. $= 0.18$ $N = 33$	$\bar{X} = 0.40$
				All Females: $\bar{X} = 0.405$
Both Sexes	Internal	$\bar{X} = 0.39$	$\bar{X} = 0.39$	$\bar{X} = 0.39$ *All Internals*
	External	$\bar{X} = 0.39$	$\bar{X} = 0.33$	$\bar{X} = 0.36$ *All Externals*
	Total	$\bar{X} = 0.39$	$\bar{X} = 0.36$	$\bar{X} = .375$

Analysis of Covariance Summary Table*

Source of Variance	df	MS	F
(A) Treatment	1	0.037	1.662
(B) Sex	1	0.121	5.378**
(C) Locus of Control	1	0.077	3.427
A × B	1	0.001	0.033
A × C	1	0.084	3.725***
B × C	1	0.005	0.202
A × B × C	1	0.009	0.390
Regression	1	0.576	25.663**
Residual	191	0.022	

*I.Q. = covariate
**$p < .05$
***$p < .06$

Chapter 7

Origins and Pawns in the Classroom

(F. Plimpton & R. deCharms)

The development of a measure of the Origin-Pawn concept was undertaken by Franziska Plimpton (1970). Starting with extensive discussions in seminars based on the concept of personal causation (deCharms, 1968), she planned to observe in one classroom, attempting to identify children who showed primarily Origin or primarily Pawn behavior. From these observations the characteristics of each type of behavior were to be listed. This step was to be followed by an attempt to develop a coding manual to identify Origin and Pawn behaviors in the characters of stories written by the students in the project. This procedure embodies what Bridgman (1959) has called the "operational analysis" of a concept, such as the Origin-Pawn concept, that is not completely objectifiable. The difficult step from observations to a measure will be discussed in more detail after the presentation of the classroom observations.

THE OBSERVATIONS

One sixth grade experimental classroom was observed on three days during the week (Tuesday, Wednesday and Friday) over a period of eight weeks. Unless the class was involved in unscheduled activities involving the whole school or several classes, the observer spent the time from 10:00 A.M. to noon and 1:00 to 3:00 P.M. in the classroom. Intending to impose her presence as little as possible on the students or the teacher, the observer was seated at a table in the back of the room. No interaction with the students was sought. The observer did not indulge in any activities or conversations with the students unless asked by them to do so.

According to an agreement with the teacher, no notes were taken initially by the observer while in the classroom. After two weeks, the observer asked the teacher for her permission to take notes while observing. This permission was willingly granted. In addition to the notes taken in class, the observer wrote down her personal impressions and inferences immediately after each observation session.

The observations were interrupted partly by the Easter break of the university and by the one-week Easter vacation of the school.

The fact that this class was part of the Motivation Project made the initial contact easy. The observer arranged the date of the first observation with the teacher by telephone. On the first day she introduced herself to the school principal, outlined the purposes of the study and was granted permission to come and go freely, without checking with the main office each time she entered the building. She described the purpose of her observations to the classroom teacher and offered to present her report in its final form to her. It was understood that the observer would not discuss either the students or the class or her observations with the teacher during the course of the study, but that once the observations were terminated the teacher would provide an interview and technical information.

The large and well-illuminated classroom was situated in a fairly new school building furnished with movable desks for the students. The twenty-seven children of the class had arranged their seats so that they all faced the center of the room, with the teacher's desk unobtrusively placed in one corner of the room.

In this setting Mrs. Strong[1] had created a relaxed mood at the time the observations began in March of the sixth grade year of the project. This class had experienced the first three classroom units (described in Chapter 5) and was working daily on the Origin Manual. The resulting atmosphere of the classroom will be the topic of Chapter 9. Here we will report observations of individual children.

GRANT. March 29, 10:15 A.M.: Mrs. Strong is standing in the center of the room. She and the children have started work on the Origin Manual. Mrs. Strong says:

"We have just talked about what an Origin is and what a Pawn is.

The Manual asks you to write how it feels to be a Pawn and an Origin. Please write what you think in the space provided.''

Most of the class starts writing immediately. Violet, Marianne and Matt seem to be thinking. Marianne sits motionless for quite a while thinking. Finally, she starts to write. Grant has been writing rapidly all the while and when Mrs. Strong starts to move to the next topic, he and Marianne are still writing.

"The Manual next wants to know which is better, to be an Origin or to be a Pawn," Mrs. Strong continues. "Let's discuss that."

After several students say that it is better to be an Origin, Grant looks puzzled and asks,

"Mrs. Strong, can you be an Origin and a Pawn at the same time?"

Mrs. Strong hesitates, letting the children think. After some reflection, Grant continues, "But you can't be an Origin all the time— sometimes you just gotta be a Pawn. . . ."

April 17, 11:00 A.M., after recess, Arithmetic:

Mrs. Strong reviews yesterday's lesson on fractions. Marianne is still writing in her Origin Manual when Mrs. Strong explains converting fractions and common denominators. Grant says to the teacher, "I don't do it that way. The way I do it is . . ." and he explains his way.

"That's a correct way, too," says Mrs. Strong, "you get the right answer that way. That's all right."

Marianne is still writing but looks up from time to time and gives an answer. Mrs. Strong moves to Matt's desk, since he doesn't understand. "Matt, can you show me how to do this problem?" Grant interrupts, giving the right answer.

"I want Matt to understand it, too," the teacher says, trying not to dampen Grant's enthusiasm. She assigns several problems to those who have caught on and Grant proceeds, apparently, to teach Marianne his method. When Mrs. Strong glances their way, he laughs, embarrassed, and ducks.

During the remainder of the class Grant makes several proud but embarrassed gestures. When he and Marianne start toward the teacher simultaneously, he bows stiffly and gestures for her to go ahead. They laugh, but the class does not respond.

As Mrs. Strong begins to sum up the lesson, Grant complains that he has had no chance to apply his knowledge (his way of solving the problem).

In yet another incident (April 16, 1:35 P.M.) in an English lesson Mrs. Strong asked the class to use the word "shine" in several ways

Mrs. Strong (pseudonymn) and class (see chapters 7 & 9)

in an exercise. Grant, not satisfied with "her" word, wanted to substitute the word "polish" in his exercise.

Grant was not a model of decorum and could be a nuisance to a teacher. From the field notes we can see that he was more restless than the average student of the class, that he walked around more and talked more often than the rest of the group. But we also can see that this behavior was largely work-oriented and that he rarely indulged in play and deviant behavior. His work behavior followed a fairly distinct pattern of concentration on the task and asking for information, mainly from Marianne and the teacher. His interaction was restricted almost exclusively to Marianne and Leonard, both of whom sat next to him. He usually initiated the conversations with Marianne.

He frequently volunteered to do tasks, to help others and to have a turn at the board. He also found his own way to solve problems, as in the arithmetic lesson. But he was not totally independent of attention from the teacher and class, as he showed in his "complaint" to the teacher about his method and also in his clownish behavior in the class. He often appeared to perceive the deeper meaning of problems, concepts, interrelationships and consequences, as shown by his question: Can you be an Origin and a Pawn at the same time?

Overall, Grant's behavior realistically concentrated on finding meaning for himself in the classroom and on making what he did make a difference. Grant seemed to us to be more often an Origin than a Pawn.

VIOLET. From the field notes we can reconstruct certain patterns of behavior characteristic of Violet. She was the first girl on whom we focused our attention.

Violet's working behavior appeared to be highly independent of the class' influence. She was observed to work with great concentration on a task despite any external disturbances. She would ask for help, mainly from Grant and Marianne, and occasionally from the teacher, but would then return immediately to her work. Once her work was finished, she found other related work or constructive activities. More often than the rest of the class she offered to help other students. She approached reluctantly tasks that apparently did not interest her, but as her involvement grew her concentration increased. She was not a model student and could be distracted, although she rarely was a Pawn. In one incident, however, she could not cope with a constraining situation; and, unable to find a solution to her problem, indulged in deviant behavior and rudely resisted any further communication with the teacher.

MARIANNE. On checking the field notes we found that more notes were taken on Marianne's behavior than on any child that was closely observed. She attracted our special attention, however, only late in the observations when the teacher asked her to arrange each student's report on the board for an open house. Her determined and independent behavior was striking. She worked continuously from 1:30 P.M. until the end of school amidst considerable confusion arranging and rearranging the reports until the display satisfied her. Often she engaged in discussions with Grant, Susan and others about the display. Once she tactfully returned the display to her original arrangement, after Grant had tried a different one.

Marianne was a quiet student, rarely indulging in play or distracting behavior, but rather going quietly her own way. Occasionally, she asked for information from Grant, but apparently not from the teacher. When she worked, she appeared to be committed, working with concentration and persistence, ignoring anything that could interrupt her work. She even seemed to approach tasks that had little interest for her with considerable investment. When finished with a task, she took a break and then turned to some uncompleted work. She very rarely moved around the room. Her steady, stable behavior appeared to be guided by the pursuit of a long-term goal rather than just the completion of assignments step by step or day by day.

In the interview with the teacher following the termination of observations, it was revealed that Marianne, while absent from school for months with rheumatism, had sent for books and homework on her own account. When she returned to class, she had no difficulties.

SHIRLEY. The above portraits are all of children whom we later found to be of average or slightly above average intelligence. Shirley, on the other hand, appeared to be below average, an impression that was confirmed subsequent to the observations. Her tested IQ was 77, a score that placed her considerably below most of her classmates.

Although at first Shirley's main activity appeared to be "doing nothing," a closer look revealed that when she understood a task, she became committed to its solution. Her apparent passivity occurred most often when the task was beyond her ability. Her written reports showed an independent effort, such as original and creative drawings. Although she often asked for information, too often it was of little use to her. She seemed to accept this situation and never appeared anxious or ingenuously pretended zeal or understanding. Her passivity did not appear to be resignation, but rather acceptance of her own limitations. She showed no dependence on the teacher or class for encouragement, although the teacher must have tactfully nurtured her best qualities for her to show such security.

LEROY: *A Pawn?* Grant, Violet, Marianne and Shirley all helped clarify the concept of Origin behavior. But what about Pawn behavior? At first it seemed that such behavior would be so prevalent that it would be easy to spot. However, as observations continued, it developed that because Pawn behavior was so characteristic of the students, it was actually harder to identify. In a sense it formed a background against which Origin behavior stood out more clearly. We later found a similar situation while classifying the behavior of the characters in stories written by the children. Pawn behavior was more prevalent than Origin behavior in their stories also. The scoring categories which are developed and presented later in this chapter concentrated on Origin behavior.

Perhaps one of the difficulties of identifying Pawn behavior stems from the very concept of Origin and Pawn. By definition Origin behavior is related directly to the child and it demands little analysis of other forces. Pawn behavior, on the other hand, always involves some outside agent, and therefore its identification demands some knowledge of those forces. When the outside forces are present, as they always are in the schools, any behavior occurring independently of them, namely Origin behavior, is more outstanding.

But it cannot simply be said that Pawn behavior is everything that Origin behavior is not or that a Pawn is the opposite of an Origin. To illustrate Pawn behavior we tried to pick an extreme case of a child who apparently did nothing unless he was told.

If Leroy worked at all, it was reluctantly and with much interruption. He was easily distracted into aimless "fooling around" and was also quickly, though only temporarily, brought back to work by the influence of the teacher or his peers. He seemed helpless when confronted with a problem or with interpersonal conflict, as shown in this incident recorded in the field notes.

April 26, 1:35 P.M. Mrs. Strong leaves the room and soon Leroy and Sarah start grabbing at a set of keys held by Joyce. Several children pass the keys around and finally Leroy gets up to get them from Sarah and pulls her desk toward his. The rest of the class begins to get restless as the commotion increases. Several others move to the area and Sidney gets involved in a quarrel with Diana. Violet looks briefly from the other side of the room, but returns to her work. Grant passes the quarreling students, shows some interest, and then goes back to his work. Sarah now succeeds in dumping Leroy and his desk on the floor with a loud crash. While Sarah loudly makes jokes about Leroy, James and Joyce fight over the keys. Finally, Joyce comes to the observer and gives her the keys. Leroy stretches out his hand for the keys, but Sarah urges the observer to keep them. The observer asks whose keys they are and Sarah finally admits that they belong to Leroy.

This and other incidents made it clear that Leroy was usually ineffective in asserting himself. He was especially submissive and obedient to the teacher. These characteristics, possibly central to Pawn behavior, are more often seen in the children than are some of the examples of independent behavior presented above.

Observable Characteristics of Origin Behavior. On the basis of the observations and the analyses of Grant, Violet, Marianne and Shirley we tried to derive some behavioral traits that were common to the four and might be used to identify Origins. These students, when compared to the others, often show:

- more commitment to the task,
- more work-oriented behavior,
- more concentration and attentiveness,
- more assumption of personal responsibility as expressed in volunteering for extra tasks, support of others and aid to weaker students,
- more creativity in artistic arrangements and illustrations,
- less overt anxiety and pretentious behavior,
- more interaction with better students and the teacher,
- more capability to master problems and to cope with situations.

Observable Characteristics of Pawn Behavior. Although our observations here were less convincing, our tentative conclusions about extreme Pawn behavior in comparison with the "norm," indicate:

- more submissive behavior,
- more strict obedience to authority,
- greater dependence on external reinforcement,
- more pretentious behavior,
- greater anxiety and helplessness.

DEVELOPMENT OF THE ORIGIN
MEASURE

The Internal Focus and Objective Observations

In Chapter 1 we started with internal concepts, such as meaning, purpose, commitment and responsibility. These are first-person words that describe what I experience subjectively when I am motivated. The states described by the words are private and not objectively observable. They are, however, related in my mind to my behavior; they give meaning to it for me. Behavior, on the other hand, can be observed objectively. Behavior can have a third-person, public, verifiable referent. Yet purely objective descriptions of behavior have no meaning until such meaning is inferred by a person. To understand behavior we must do two things at once. On the one hand, we must observe it objectively so that we know the facts. The facts can be checked from one person to another. On the other hand, we must attribute intention or purpose to the actor in order to place the behavior in a meaningful context. Here again we may check with another person, but the primary source of knowledge is not objective but personal and often private.

As suggested in Chapter 1 behaviorism has replaced the study of human consciousness, because it is possible to verify publicly the objective facts of behavior. The basis of behaviorism is the philosophical doctrine of *physicalism*. Carnap (1959) presents the fundamental thesis as stating that "every sentence of psychology may be formulated in physical language . . . all sentences of psychology describe physical occurrences, namely, the physical behavior of humans and animals" (p. 165). The definition of a psychological concept must be in terms of physical concepts.

The reason for and importance of this doctrine is that it allows psychology to use the verification principle, viz., the meaning of a statement is no more than what is testable about it through its objective method of verification. To translate this doctrine into psychological sentences about motivation is to say, for instance, that the statement "he is motivated to achieve" says no more than that he is behaving in such and such a way. Assuming that everyone could observe the behavior, they could probably agree that "he" is "running" and that objectively his speed is fast and that "he" is looking at a stop watch after each run, etc. That much, the behavior, is verifiable. But from what objective verifiable element(s) comes the meaning "he is motivated to achieve"? It comes from an inference that this instance of behavior is of a class of behaviors that fall under the rubric of competition with a standard and that the goal of the runner is to be successful. If the only meaning comes from the verifiable facts, then the concept "motivated" is meaningless. But the objective description leads to the inference and the meaning is derived from the inference. The facts come from observation, but are made meaningful only when interpreted by a human being drawing on past observations of others *and* personal experience.

Since we accept the value of verifiability and at the same time insist that meaning comes from first-person concepts partially grounded in private personal experience, we are confronted with two very fundamental problems. First, we must make some assumptions about the relationship between experience and behavior, private and public, first-person and third-person, subjective and objective. Second, to produce reliable evidence concerning the relationship, we must find a way to communicate about and verify the first-person subjective experience.

There are many pseudo-problems in dealing with subjective knowledge without falling into the traps encountered by solipsism, introspectionism or phenomenology. The fundamental error of introspectionism was to assume that we could observe objectively our own experience and avoid the "stimulus error" of attributing "meaning" to experience (see Malcolm, 1964, and deCharms, 1968, for a more complete critique). Phenomenology, on the other hand, accepted experience as "raw truth" in a way that hampered analysis and verification.

In order to proceed in a systematic study of motivation we must accept the following:

1. Inferences about observed behavior give *meaning* to the behavioral sequence.
2. Inferred motivational concepts such as intention, purpose, commitment come from personal knowledge (Polanyi, 1958).
3. Personal knowledge is a combination of observed behavior that is objectively verifiable and subjective experience that is not.
4. Personal experience is more than observation of my own behavior (Malcolm, 1964).
5. Reports of subjective experience are notoriously fraught with error and bias and hence some means of assuring their verifiability

similar to the test for objective sentences by reducing them to physical terms must be found.

A very useful technique of verification in the physical sciences is operationism. The meaning of a concept is wholly contained in the physical operations (cf. Margenau, 1950) through which the phenomenon named by the concept is produced.

The meaning of a psychological concept such as the Origin-Pawn concept, however, is not totally contained in physical operations. If we conceive of the process of inference as an operation performed by the brain of a man, we can maintain an operational point of view and seek verification of the personal knowledge used in inference. The operation of inference is quite different from physical operations used to define physical concepts. Attempting to use operational analysis to verify more subjective concepts is not new. In fact, it dates from the classic statement of operationism by Bridgman (1927).

> In general, we mean by any concept nothing more than a set of operations; *the concept is synonymous with the corresponding set of operations.* If the concept is physical, as of length, the operations are actual physical operations, namely, those by which length is measured; or if the concept is mental, as of mathematical continuity, the operations are mental operations, namely those by which we determine whether a given aggregate of magnitudes is continuous. It is not intended to imply that there is a hard and fast division between physical and mental concepts, or that one kind of concept does not always contain an element of the other; this classification of concept is not important for our future considerations (pp. 5–6, italics in original).

This distinction between physical and mental operations first noted by Bridgman in 1927 was at first dismissed and soon forgotten by physicists and apparently not noted by psychologists, such as Stevens (1939), who began to apply operationism to psychological concepts. Bridgman himself, however, reintroduced the concept of mental operations (Bridgman, 1959) and stressed the uniqueness of one kind of operational analysis. His example of that kind is the operation involved when *I* verify that I have a toothache. The operation that I perform is quite different from the operations that *you* might perform to verify that I have a toothache. *You* would use objective observation, but *I* would use immediate experience. You could ask a friend to make similar observations independently to check the reliability of your observations, but I could not. *I* am the only person who could experience my toothache. The basic distinction, then, is between the number of people who can perform the operation. Operational analysis of physical concepts can be stated in third-person objective terms and be performed by anyone. Operational analysis of personal states can be stated in first-person–present subjective terms and can be performed only by the subject.

Operational analysis of motivational concepts, such as the Origin–Pawn concept, involve observations of behavior like that presented above, inferences from behavior to concepts and analysis of the first-person states of experiencing personal motivation. In order to derive a measure of the Origin–Pawn concept a technique had to be found to communicate about the subjective states and to check the reliability of inferences drawn.

Plimpton, in concert with several others, became thoroughly familiar with the Origin concept as she experienced it and others reported it. She then observed the behaviors of children in Mrs. Strong's classroom and made inferences from her personal knowledge about the subjective motivational states of the child. These observations and inferences helped to clarify the concept and to apply the concept to the concrete world of children in the classroom. The next step was to find some check on the reliability of her observations and inferences.

Behavior observed on the fly, so to speak, has the disadvantage of being gone in an instant. With only one observer present there is no check even on the objective observation. While this problem can be overcome by many observers or video-taping, another problem cannot. Samples of any behavior are subject to external constraints and variability attributable to situational variables. What is needed is a sample of behavior where situational variables are controlled as much as possible and at the same time the person feels as free from external constraints as possible so that he can express his motivational states in his behavior.

A technique for obtaining maximum freedom and minimum situational variability is the technique of thought sampling. Thoughts are free, but they are not directly accessible. However, a sample of behavior closely related to free thought can be obtained under standard conditions by asking a person to write a story. Assuming that motivational states affect thoughts and behavior (a motive is a mild obsession) allows us to analyze the thought samples for indications of motive states; that is, we may draw inferences about internal states from the behaviors described in the story.

Written personal documents, such as thought sample stories, become a permanent record of behavior and the content may be reviewed as often as necessary and by as many people as is necessary to assure reliable analysis. The problem, now, is not to verify that the behavior occurred, but to make reliable inferences from the stories to concepts such as the Origin concept. From the objective record, the stories, concrete instances leading to the Origin inference, can be catalogued into a scoring manual so that anyone understanding the concept can learn to count reliably the number of instances that led him to the Origin inference. If two people can read the same stories independently and make the same number of inferences from exactly the same materials, a check on reliability of inferences is obtained. In short the operational analysis of subjective states is combined with objective observation and verified. The number of inferences thus reliably found may be turned into a scale for stories from several people. Using the scale, the assumption that the more instances of Origin behavior produced the more Origin behavior will occur under other circumstances in that individual can be objectively checked i.e., the construct validity of the measure can be determined.

Origin Behavior in Children's Stories

Thought samples were available from the students in the project in the form of stories written to six verbal cues. For details of the technique of collecting the stories see below (section entitled "Data and Instrumentation," p. 127).

Here is Plimpton's description of how she developed the Origin–Pawn measure from the students' stories.

"After intensive discussion of the Origin-Pawn concept in a semi-nar and after the classroom observations described above, I sat down with 240 stories written by forty different children. I read each story carefully and tried to determine whether I thought it indicated behavior of a Pawn or an Origin.

"At this stage I was not trying to be 'objective' or even to clarify my criteria of judgment. That would come later. I was trying to use all my personal experience and knowledge to make me sensitive to the implications of the story. I tried to allow my mind to register, as a sensitive instrument, what thoughts had passed through the mind of another human being as he wrote the story.

"First, I divided the stories into two piles: those that had struck me as Origin and those that had struck me as Pawn stories. Then I went back to find the similarities in stories within each pile that related to the Origin-Pawn theory.

"The Origin-Pawn concept is not a *motive*. A motive, such as the achievement motive, entails a fairly specific class of goals which the motivated person desires. The Origin-Pawn concept is not restricted to specific goals, but rather is an orientation toward the pursuit of goals of any and all kinds. Thus the most prominent characteristic is the elaboration of goal-seeking behavior. The goal can be anything. Stories were classified not as to what type of goal was mentioned but who determined the goal and how the person went about reaching his goal.

"Of prime importance in distinguishing Origin from Pawn behavior is whether the goal of the person in the story was his or whether it was imposed on him by someone else. Any sign of this aspect should be indicative of whether the writer felt like an Origin or a Pawn. Thus one difference between Origin and Pawn stories is the theme of *Internal Goal Setting* in the stories.

"The Origin chooses his own activities as well as his own goals. Accordingly, we classified as *Internal Instrumental Activity* any indications in the stories that one of the characters was engaged in doing something that he himself decided upon.

"Being realistic about goals and instrumental activity is important to the Origin. But to decide whether a long term goal is realistic for a child is complicated: one can say that it is not realistic for most children to strive to be President of the United States, but what about becoming a pilot or a physician? Can I pass judgment on realistic goal setting without knowing a host of factors about the child's ability, skills, and situation? For me to decide what is realistic for him, I need to consider many factors. The same is true for *him;* he must consider many factors. Judging another's goals, with insufficient evidence, would not produce a reliable index. Rather, we looked for indications that the writer himself was considering the relevant factors; his ability, skills, and situation. If he is realistic, he will be considering such factors. On the other hand, if he is unrealistic, he will simply dream an impossible dream and even plan and engage in unrealistic activities. We found, then, that the realism that characterized Origins, was not identified by trying to assess the child's goals alone, but by looking for indications that the child himself was considering things about himself and his life situation that may help or hinder him in reaching his goals. We called these *Reality Perception* about self and the world.

"An Origin who sets his own goals will probably desire recognition when he reaches them. He also has no one to blame but himself if he doesn't reach his goals. An Origin should, therefore, take responsibility for his behavior. He should acknowledge mistakes; worry about the consequences of what he does; show determination to do things; and show concern for the effects of his acts on others. Such indications of concern we called *Personal Responsibility*.

"When a person is effective in reaching his goals, he has more confidence in himself. Confidence was apparent in the stories in several ways. Most often, Origin stories seemed to end successfully. Obstacles intervening between the hero and his goal were usually overcome (by his own actions) and the stories were written as if success were expected. Such indications in the stories were classified as *Self Confidence*.

"Throughout all of this analysis, the distinction has been made between internal determination by the character himself and external determination by someone else. Some examples of this might be found in internal determination of goals, internal determination of acts, internal decisions about reality and responsibility, even an inner sense of confidence. One story may have one or two of these and show traces of Origin behavior; others may be saturated—nearly everything in the story is internally determined. Despite this saturation, however, the story may be short or not elaborate on all of the other categories. A story in which no external determination of goals, acts, etc. was indicated and in which all behavior appeared internally directed we classified as an indication of *Internal Control of Behavior*.

"In theoretical discussions of the Origin-Pawn variable we talked of the Origin as being 'intrinsically' motivated and derived the conception of such a person becoming totally absorbed in and committed to his activity. Theoretically, we had hoped to find indications of such *Self-Investment* in the stories. In fact, because it appeared very rarely and seemed too elusive to capture, we gave it up in our analysis of these stories."

In looking at the first batch of Origin and Pawn stories Plimpton tried to elaborate the Pawn side of the picture as has just been done for the Origin stories. Although considerable effort went into this, the Pawn characteristics, more often than not, turned out to be the opposite of Origin aspects discussed above and seemed to add little to the clarity of the concept. The same phenomenon that occurred in the classroom behavior was apparent in the stories: the Pawn characteristics were so prevalent that they were hard to pick out, whereas the Origin characteristics stood out against a background of Pawn behaviors. Since a statistical analysis also indicated that Pawn categories failed to distinguish between children (they occurred almost as often in the Origin stories as in the Pawn stories), we decided to discard them and concentrate on Origin categories described above.

In summary, the six Origin aspects that seemed to make a difference and to be fairly clear were: (*a*) Internal Goal Setting, (*b*) Internal Instrumental Activity, (*c*) Reality Perception, (*d*) Personal Responsibility, (*e*) Self-Confidence, and (*f*) Internal Control.

Considerable refinement of these six aspects resulted from looking at more and more stories, ultimately more than 3500. The final results were careful definitions of each aspect, which may now be called scoring categories, and a manual written with instructions and examples to enable others to learn to score children's stories for the Origin-Pawn variable (see Plimpton, 1970, and Appendix A).

The manual for scoring the Origin-Pawn variable translated the Origin-Pawn *concept* into an Origin-Pawn *measure*. The development of the measure was completed at the end of the seventh grade year of the project. Fortunately, however, the categories were designed to be used with an instrument (the Test of Imagination) that had been administered to the children each year of the Project. Our plan was to use the measure to assess the effects of the training on the children.

Reliability and Validity of the Origin-Pawn Measure

Before one can accept a new measure, especially one originally derived from subjective impressions of stories, it is necessary to assess its value. As with any instrument, the question is: Can different people, with training, see the same things every time they look; and are the things that they see telling them anything valuable? Such checks are crucial with a new measure of motivation.

The following steps were taken to determine the reliability and validity of the new Origin-Pawn measure.

1. Establishment of coder reliability.
2. Assessment of test homogeneity.

3. Assessment of test stability.

4. Determination of the discriminant validity of the test.

5. Determination of predictive validity.

6. Establishment of the experimental validity of the test by direct experimental manipulation of an Origin-trained group to be compared with a non-trained group.

Step 5, predictive validity, involved relationships between the Origin-Pawn measure and academic achievement. These relationships are the subject of Chapter 8 and will not be presented here.

Step 6, experimental validity, was determined by comparing means for trained and untrained children. Since these are the major data of this chapter, they are discussed in detail in a separate section below.

Steps 1 through 4 were designed to establish reliability and validity of the measure. Reliability was assessed by computing *(a)* split-half reliabilities of four samples of data, *(b)* intercorrelations between scores on each individual story and all other stories, *(c)* intercorrelations between each category score for each protocol and all other category scores, *(d)* a homogeneity ratio and *(e)* test-retest reliability coefficients.

Discriminant validity was assessed by comparing the Origin-Pawn measure with other measures, some derived from the same method of content analysis, some derived from different methods.

Data and Instrumentation. The data submitted to operational analysis to derive the Origin-Pawn score resulted from the Test of Imagination. The Test of Imagination (sometimes referred to as the Thematic Apperception Test) was administered under conditions described by McClelland (McClelland et al., 1953) using verbal cues from Winterbottom (1958). The children wrote six stories to the following cues: (1) A father and son talking about something important, (2) Two men working at a machine, (3) A boy with his head resting on his hands, (4) A mother and her child look worried, (5) A young person sitting at a desk, and (6) Brothers and sisters are playing—one is a little ahead.

In the classroom an experimenter passed out protocols with one of these cues printed at the top of each page plus the following four questions equally spaced down the page: (1) What is happening? (2) What happened before? (3) What is being thought or wanted? (4) What will happen? Subjects were instructed to write imaginative stories to each cue and were allowed four minutes for each story. The subjects in this study produced a mean of approximately forty words per story and the protocols had previously resulted in valid need for achievement scores.

Coder Reliability. After the preliminary manual was developed, a second scorer learned the scoring system to a criterion of 90% agreement with the expert scorer.[2] Training for approximately two hours daily, the new scorer reached the reliability criterion after about one and one-half weeks and about 250 practice stories. The two scorers worked independently while scoring and then discussed intensively their discrepancies. These discussions are crucial and should result in written agreements between scorers complete with examples from stories for the scorers to consult in future scoring. Thus, while learning to score, the scorer develops a supplementary manual for himself. This is in the spirit of the concept of operational analysis of introspective material in the subjective mode (Bridgman, 1959). Our impression is that in general learning to score may take longer than the example given above, since the novice discussed above had the advantage of lengthy discussions with the person who developed the manual.

After reaching 90% agreement, the second scorer coded a one-third random sample of 525 protocols (N = 175 × 3 protocols for each subject). The percentage of agreement on all categories for these (the actual data) was 90.2%. In scoring each protocol of six stories the scorer made a binary decision for each of the six categories for each story. That is, for each story the scorer decided whether it contained evidence (as specified in the manual) for each of the following categories: (*a*) Internal Goal Setting, (*b*) Internal Determination of Instrumental Activity, (*c*) Reality Perception, (*d*) Personal Responsibility, (*e*) Self-Confidence, and (*f*) Internal Control. Thus, for each protocol the scorer made thirty-six such binary decisions. Chance agreement between two scorers working independently would be 50%.

Each category is scored only once per story so that the maximum score that one story can receive is six, the minimum zero. Since the protocols contained six stories, the possible range of scores per subject is from zero to thirty-six (actual range = 0–31).

Test Homogeneity. The homogeneity of the test was assessed in four ways: (*a*) split-half correlations were computed on the scores of the odd vs. the even numbered stories written by each subject; (*b*) intercorrelations were computed between each story score and all other story scores; (*c*) intercorrelations were computed between each category score for each protocol and all other category scores; (*d*) Scott's (1960) homogeneity ratio was computed.

Table 7.1 presents the split-half reliabilities for the four samples

Table 7.1 — Split-half Reliabilities of Six Verbal Cues of the Origin Measure (Cues 1, 3, 5 vs. 2, 4, 6)

	N	r	Spearman-Brown Prophecy
1st Sample	40	+.43	+.60
2nd Sample	40	+.84	+.91
3rd Sample			
Cell 1	57	+.50	+.67
Cell 2	41	+.55	+.71
Cell 3	27	+.51	+.68
Cell 4 (Controls)	50	+.21	+.35
Combined	175	+.66	+.80
4th Sample (Controls)	58	+.65	+.79

used. Sample 3 (N = 175) is here divided into the various groups of the experimental design used for experimental validation. Reliabilities range from .35 to .91. The Spearman-Brown (Brown, 1910; Spearman, 1910) prophecy formula was computed for a test twice as long as either half, i.e., the actual length of the test.

Table 7.2 presents the intercorrelations between each story cue

Table 7.2 — Intercorrelations of the Six Story Cues on the Origin Measure (Untreated Controls Only)

	Story Cue Number				
	1	2	3	4	5
1					
2	.17				
3	−.08	.04			
4	−.16	.27	.27		
5	.05	.09	.23	.30	
6	−.08	.16	.15	.11	.07

Table 7.3 — Intercorrelations of Subcategories of the Origin Measure (Untreated Control Subjects Only)

	Internal Control		Goal-Setting		Instrumental Activity		Reality Perception		Personal Responsibility		Self Confidence		Total Origin Pawn Score	
	6th*	7th	6th	7th	6th	7th	6th	7th	6th	7th	6th	7th	6th	7th
Internal Control														
Goal Setting	.35	.17												
Instrumental Activity	.58	.09	.33	.37										
Reality Perception	.26	.16	.20	.17	.36	.16								
Personal Responsibility	.41	.13	-.04	.03	.31	.19	.21	.36						
Self Confidence	.33	.07	.46	.08	.34	.26	.30	.37	.26	.55				
Total	.72	.27	.67	.53	.75	.56	.59	.68	.46	.67	.71	.69		
Mean Score	0.51	0.07	1.68	1.60	1.00	0.82	0.89	1.36	0.57	1.10	1.01	0.86	5.64	5.77

Homogeneity Ratio (Scott, 1960)
  Sixth Grade = +.22
  Seventh Grade = +.31
*Six Grade N = 53, Seventh Grade N = 108

(Items 1 through 6) and each other story cue for each group of the experimental design.

Table 7.3 presents intercorrelations between the scoring categories for control subjects only (Group D) for both sixth grade (N = 53) and seventh grade (N = 108). Presented here also are the homogeneity ratios for the two samples.

Test Stability. The stability of the test was assessed by computing test-retest correlations. Table 7.4 presents test-retest data for tests administered a year apart, either at the end of the fifth grade and again at the end of the sixth, or at the end of the sixth and again at the end of the seventh grade.

Table 7.4 — Test-Retest Reliability
Fifth, Sixth and Seventh Grades

	N	r
Fifth and Sixth Grades	91	+.414
Sixth and Seventh Grades	49	+.384

Discriminant Validity. As a test of discriminant validity (Campbell & Fiske, 1959) the Origin-Pawn scores were compared with (*a*) achievement motivation scores derived from the same story protocols and the Origin-Pawn scores (same measure, different trait), (*b*) an Origin-Pawn score derived from content analysis of Battle's Children's Picture Test (Battle, 1962) (different measure, same trait), (*c*) an Internal-External Control of Reinforcements score (Rotter, 1966) derived from the Children's Picture Test (different measure, related trait), and (*d*) a Goal Realism score (Shea, 1969) (different measure, related trait). Table 7.5 presents the intercorrelations between these variables.

Discussion

In general, the stability and homogeneity of the Origin-Pawn measure are all of the order that might be expected from this type of measure. It is a mistake to expect data comparable to those based on objective tests, such as standardized achievement tests or questionnaires. This is a measure of more freely emitted responses. These procedures for assessing reliability were originally developed to be

Table 7.5 — Intercorrelations between Two Methods and Three Measures (N = 35)

Method	Measure	Method I (Imaginative Stories)		Method II (Children's Picture Test)	
		Measure A Origin-Pawn	Measure B Need for Achievement	Measure A Origin-Pawn	Measure C Internal External
I	A Origin-Pawn	(.41)*			
	B Need for Achievement	.22	(.29)*		
II	A Origin-Pawn	-.12	-.02		
	C Internal External	-.13	-.02	.22	(.53)*
	Goal Realism	.32	.19	.12	.02

*One year repeat reliability

applied to what McClelland (1965) called a *respondent* measure rather than to a freer *operant* measure like the Origin-Pawn measure. In the operant measure the subject is allowed freedom to produce his own responses (stories) and the psychologist must find ways (content analysis) to assess his responses. In the respondent measure (questionnaires) the psychologist defines the number of answers which the subject can use. The subject is responding to what the psychologist has presented in a predetermined form. The Origin-Pawn measure is an attempt to find out about the subject at his level—what he *will do* on his own, not what he *can do* when specifically instructed.

In this light the measures of reliability of the Origin-Pawn measure are quite satisfactory when compared, for instance, to the similar and well-established measure of achievement motivation. McClelland (McClelland et al., 1953) reports interscorer reliabilities (measured by percentage of agreement) of 78%, 85% and 91% for achievement motivation (p. 186). In the years since the achievement motivation measure was developed it has been customary to strive for 90% agreement. A split-half reliability similar to that reported here was reported for achievement motivation (p. 188) to be +.65. The two Origin-Pawn reliabilities from our data reported in Table 7.1 that can be compared to that for achievement motivation are those for the third sample (Controls) and the fourth sample (Controls). The first (+.35) is inferior, but the second (+.79) is higher than the achievement motivation figure.

Repeat reliabilities for a measure of motivation are also problematic. Much can happen to a person's motives between measures, especially when the intervening interval is one year. For the Origin-Pawn measure administered a year apart the test-retest reliability is +.41 for one sample and +.38 for another. By comparison McClelland et al. (1953, p. 192) reported a correlation of +.22 for equivalent forms of the achievement motivation measure administered a year apart. Atkinson (1958) reports a correlation of +.54 on two forms administered three weeks apart. In our own data the test-retest reliability (a year apart) for achievement motivation was +.29 for a sample of 185 subjects.

The data presented in Table 7.5 concerning discriminant validity are not very revealing. The correlation between the Origin-Pawn measure derived from the stories and alternately from the Children's Picture Test is −.12. This result, where a positive relationship would be expected, may be attributed to the differences between the two methods of collecting data (imaginative stories vs. the cartoons of the Children's Picture Test). Unfortunately, however, it can also be attributed to the possible unreliability of the scoring of the Children's Picture Test. It had been hoped that this scoring could be developed to a point where a valid comparison could be made, but when this negative correlation was found, it was decided to terminate perfecting the content analysis of the Children's Picture Test for the Origin-Pawn measure and to concentrate entirely on the Manual for the imaginative stories, which produced a much larger sample of thoughts that had already been demonstrated to yield a reliable and valid measure of achievement motivation. In Table 7.5 it can be seen that the Origin-Pawn measure from the imaginative stories does correlate with goal realism ($+.32$, $p < .05$). This is a first step toward assessing predictive validity.

Origin-Pawn Scores of Plimpton's Five Subjects of Observation

Before turning to the data from the total project we can report scores on the Origin-Pawn measure for the five students that Plimpton observed in detail as reported above. Were Grant, Marianne, Violet and Shirley, in fact, Origins as indicated by their scores; and was Leroy a Pawn? If so, Leroy's score should be lower than the others'. Subsequent to the observations, Origin-Pawn scores were obtained for these students who were observed in Mrs. Strong's class. Table 7.6 shows that the children selected as Origins did have higher scores (above the average score even before training). Leroy (the Pawn) had a low score even after training. It is important to emphasize that these scores were not known to the observer when she selected these children for observation.

The Effects of the Training on the Origin-Pawn Measure

Now we can turn to the important question: Did the training given to the experimental children affect their motivation and if so, is the effect reliably indicated by our new measure?

The design of the project (discussed in detail in Chapter 2) divided the students into experimental and control classes during their sixth grade year. During their seventh grade year the students were divided into four groups: (*a*) students who had training in both sixth and seventh grades, (*b*) students who were trained only in sixth grade, (*c*)

Table 7.6 — Origin Scores for Students Observed in Mrs. Strong's Class[1]

	Origin Scores	
	Fifth Grade	Sixth Grade[2]
Grant	6	15
Marianne	not available	11
Violet	8	11
Shirley	not available	8
Leroy	not available	1

[1]The Origin scores were derived several months *after* the observations.
[2]After one year of training.

students trained only in seventh grade and (*d*) students who had no training (see Table 2.1, Chapter 2). The data analysis concentrated on these four groups and comprised a longitudinal study of their scores at three points in time: at the end of fifth grade (before any training) and again at the end of sixth and seventh grades.

Such longitudinal data are subject to special problems of sampling and attrition of subjects. The technique used in Chapter 6 with achievement motivation scores taken from the same thought sample protocols gave an indication that attrition tended, if anything, to reduce differences between experimental and control groups, thus making any differences reported conservative. The technique involved analyzing samples of scores from each year, pairs of years, and finally all three years and reporting only data found significant in all analyses. This technique could not be used for the Origin-Pawn measure without entailing extensive additional scoring. If analysis had shown initial differences between the four groups, then the additional scoring would have been deemed necessary. Since it did not, the effects of attrition of subjects from the data pool over the three years was assumed to make the longitudinal data a conservative estimate of the effects of the training.

The rationale for the above is as follows: if subject loss by attrition had somehow affected the means of trained subjects in a different way from the untrained, then the means before any training occurred (fifth grade) should be different. But the pretraining mean Origin-Pawn scores are all remarkably consistent and similar to the control means.

Taking all seven means (from all three years for subjects before training and for those who had no training) the range is only 1.57 on the Origin-Pawn scale (see Table 7.7, Both Sexes Combined). Differences between pre- and post-training means are of the order of seven points on the same scale.

Apparently, whatever the effects of loss of subjects, the differences between means attributable to training vs. none are large enough to overshadow any artifacts of sampling.

Table 7.7 presents the mean Origin-Pawn scores for students in the four groups for fifth, sixth and seventh grades. Here the differences between sexes may be seen. Overall the girls have slightly

Table 7.7 — Mean Origin Scores By Sex, Group and Grade

Origin	Scores	5th Grade	6th Grade	7th Grade
Males	Group A N = 29	$\bar{X}$ = 5.03	$\bar{X}$ = 11.24	$\bar{X}$ = 15.24
	Group B N = 8	$\bar{X}$ = 3.25	$\bar{X}$ = 7.75	$\bar{X}$ = 7.50
	Group C N = 16	$\bar{X}$ = 4.37	$\bar{X}$ = 4.06	$\bar{X}$ = 11.06
	Group D N = 25	$\bar{X}$ = 5.28	$\bar{X}$ = 5.80	$\bar{X}$ = 4.60
	Total	$\bar{X}$ = 4.79	$\bar{X}$ = 7.67	$\bar{X}$ = 10.18
Females	Group A N = 28	$\bar{X}$ = 6.71	$\bar{X}$ = 14.60	$\bar{X}$ = 17.46
	Group B N = 19	$\bar{X}$ = 4.74	$\bar{X}$ = 13.63	$\bar{X}$ = 13.16
	Group C N = 25	$\bar{X}$ = 4.40	$\bar{X}$ = 5.40	$\bar{X}$ = 11.96
	Group D N = 25	$\bar{X}$ = 6.08	$\bar{X}$ = 6.72	$\bar{X}$ = 6.20
	Total	$\bar{X}$ = 5.57	$\bar{X}$ = 10.01	$\bar{X}$ = 12.30
Both Sexes	Group A N = 57	$\bar{X}$ = 5.86	$\bar{X}$ = 12.89	$\bar{X}$ = 16.33
	Group B N = 27	$\bar{X}$ = 4.29	$\bar{X}$ = 11.89	$\bar{X}$ = 11.48
	Group C N = 41	$\bar{X}$ = 4.39	$\bar{X}$ = 4.88	$\bar{X}$ = 11.60
	Group D N = 50	$\bar{X}$ = 5.68	$\bar{X}$ = 6.26	$\bar{X}$ = 5.40

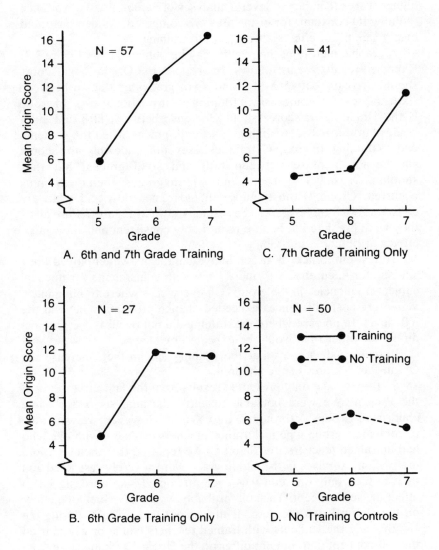

A. 6th and 7th Grade Training

C. 7th Grade Training Only

B. 6th Grade Training Only

D. No Training Controls

Fig. 7.1

**Mean Origin Score
Before and After Motivational Training
(Longitudinal Data, Plimpton, 1970)**

higher scores than boys. Several analyses of variance and covariance (holding IQ constant, for instance) were computed. All demonstrated highly significant effects attributable to training.

A graphic picture of the results may be obtained from Figure 7.1. Expected results are as follows. In group A the Origin-Pawn scores should increase between fifth and sixth grades and again between sixth and seventh grades, since training occurred both years. In group B the Origin-Pawn scores should increase between fifth and sixth grades but not between sixth and seventh grades when the students had no training. In group C (training in seventh grade only) the scores should not increase between fifth and sixth grades, but they should increase between sixth and seventh grades when the training occurred. Group D (no training) should remain low and relatively constant for all three years. The results shown in Figure 7.1 are all as they were predicted to be, are remarkably consistent and show large effects attributable to training.

To test differences between individual means we employed the *t* statistic for fixed effects (Winer, 1962) with adjustments for unequal subject frequencies in the groups. In every case where training intervened pre-post differences exceeded chance probability beyond the .001 level. In no case where the training did not occur is the pre-post difference other than would be expected by chance.

It seems safe to say that the training did, in fact, increase the Origin-Pawn scores of the children.

So far we have only presented results from the first three years of the Project. We were not able to carry the analysis of the same children in Groups A through D into Year 4. However, we were able to compare a group who had trained teachers in Year 4 with one who had untrained teachers. In Chapter 5 we reported that the classroom motivation exercises in the eighth grade were severely restricted and that, in fact, only one unit was even attempted—a unit designed to affect the self-concept. This unit probably would have had little effect on the Origin-Pawn measure. It turned out that, in fact, during the eighth grade the students with trained teachers (some of whom used the self-concept unit) did not differ on the Origin-Pawn measure from children with control teachers.

Table 7.8 presents the mean Origin-Pawn scores for students in the eighth grade. They are divided into students who had previous training (in sixth or seventh grades or both) or no previous training, and again into those who had trained teachers in the eighth grade and those who did not. Analysis of variance indicates that training of the

Table 7.8 — Mean Origin Score after Eighth Grade
(Departmentalized and Self-Contained Classrooms Combined)

| | | Eighth Grade Teacher | | |
		Trained	Untrained	Total
Student Previously Trained*	N	45	77	122
	X̄	8.5	10.1	9.5
Student Previously Untrained	N	59	60	119
	X̄	5.8	6.6	6.2
Total	N	104	137	241
	X̄	7.0	8.6	7.9

*These students received training either in sixth or seventh grades or both.

eighth grade teachers had no significant effect on the Origin-Pawn score of their pupils. Note that the pupils themselves had no training in eighth grade. The effect of training in previous grades, however, carried over, since the difference between previously trained students and untrained students is significant. (The analysis was done for departmentalized and self-contained classrooms separately and the resulting probabilities were $p < .02$ and $p < .0001$ respectively.)

Apparently the training during sixth and seventh grades did affect the Origin-Pawn scores and the effects persisted with no further training for at least a year. The Origin-Pawn scores were not affected either by the small amount of self-concept training in eighth grade or by the fact that the experimental children had trained teachers.[3]

SUMMARY

In this chapter we have presented the Origin-Pawn concept in its most concrete form: what may be technically called the attempt to "operationalize" the concept. Out of direct observations of children in a classroom and by drawing on the theory of personal causation (deCharms, 1968), we selected certain characteristics that seemed to differentiate the behavior of highly motivated children from those less strongly motivated. We called these characteristics Origin behavior.

An investigation of the imaginative stories written by the children showed that six characteristics differentiated the stories emphasizing Origin behavior from stories about Pawn behavior. These six characteristics were refined and more carefully specified to form scoring categories from which an Origin score could be determined for each child. Extensive investigation of the reliability and consistency of these scores was reported.

The major result reported in this chapter was the finding that the Origin scores reliably reflected the effects of motivation training on the experimental children.

Notes

1. These are, of course, code names.

2. Karen Cohen served as the second scorer and also assisted in data analysis of the reliability and validity study.

3. Preliminary results (just available as this goes to press) indicate that there is still a difference between trained and untrained students after four years. Mr. Horace Jackson (unfinished doctoral dissertation) interviewed a sample of 79 students concerning their career aspirations and scored the transcripts for the Origin-Pawn categories. The trained students (compared to untrained) showed almost twice as many categories, a difference that was highly significant statistically.

Chapter 8

Motivation Training and Academic Achievement

(R. deCharms)

We turn now to the effects of motivation training on the school behavior and academic achievement of the students. Did the training help them in their school work? First, we must look to see if there was an overall effect on measures of academic achievement. If such effects appear, we must try to find out to what these effects are attributable. For instance, it could be that the major effect of the training was simply the result of greater enthusiasm (or morale) in the trained classrooms, a feeling of being "special," an effect similar to the so-called "Hawthorne effect" (Roethlisberger & Dickson, 1939). Such an effect is not to be discounted simply because of its generality (Sommer, 1968). After all, feeling special may increase motivation and that is just what we set out to do. If this increased enthusiasm was the major effect, then we could expect to find very general enhancement on many measures of motivation and behavior, an overall doing more and better on everything.

If we succeeded in having more specific effects, however, they should show themselves in recognizable patterns of effects that are related to factors in the training. Such effects would be more interesting and more useful in planning future motivation development projects. In a sense, they would tell us something about what we did that was most useful and what we did that seemed to have little effect.

Specific effects of the training could be of at least two types: (*a*) truly motivational effects, and (*b*) effects attributable to incidental aspects of the training. The best evidence for motivational effects are, of course, effects on motivation measures such as reported in Chapters 6 and 7. Motivational effects may be seen in academic achievement measures also and may be discriminated from incidental effects if they can be directly related to changes in motivation measures. Incidental effects may occur and even be quite valuable, but may not be directly attributable to enhanced motivation. For instance, during the first year of training the students engaged in the spelling game. As we have already seen, this game achieved its motivation goal in that it taught the children to set more realistic goals. In addition, increased attention to spelling may have increased the children's general spelling ability. If so, was it because of more careful goal-setting, and becoming Origin-like (a motivation phenomenon), or was it because they spent more time on spelling (a more incidental, fortuitous outcome)?

Our tools for probing these questions are not very precise, since it was impossible to isolate specific factors experimentally. Once we have established differences between trained and untrained groups, our investigation becomes exploratory, an after-the-fact look to see if we can find meaningful tendencies in the data to support assumptions about specific relationships. The result will not be conclusive evidence but suggestive leads to guide future research and to help the teacher in considering the merits of motivation development in the classroom.

ACADEMIC ACHIEVEMENT

Did Academic Achievement Scores Increase?

Academic achievement is measured every year in late spring by the school district. The Iowa Test of Basic Skills (Lindquist & Hieronymous, 1955) is administered in every classroom and the teachers and administrators use the grade equivalent scores of the children as one way to gauge success and failure of both the children and the teachers. The test is a multiple response instrument covering five major areas: vocabulary, reading comprehension, language skills (with four subsections), work study skills (three subsections), and arithmetic skills (two subsections). The Work Study skills part is not used in the district, so we will be concerned here only with the other four areas. A battery comprising these four areas allots approximately one hour to each area, with the exception of the vocabulary test, which is only seventeen minutes long.

For each subsection a grade equivalent score can be derived.

> The grade equivalent of a given raw score on any test indicates the grade level at which the typical pupil makes this raw score. . . . For example, if a pupil makes a grade equivalent of 6.3, this means that his raw score on the test is the same as that made by the typical or median pupil in the sixth grade at the end of the third month in that grade (Lindquist & Hieronymous, 1964, p. 21).

A normal year's growth is ten points, i.e., ten months. For a battery taken at the end of a year the composite grade equivalent can be subtracted from the grade that the child is about to enter (his grade placement), giving a discrepancy from grade placement and allowing comparison from grade to grade in terms of relative gain or loss.

By fifth grade the children in the district are typically more than one-half year behind national norms in grade equivalent scores. As the years pass and the children go on to higher grades they fall farther behind. This trend of gaining less than a full year in grade equivalent score over a year of school was somewhat alleviated by the personal causation training. Figure 8.1 shows the mean decrement in grade equivalent score from grade placement for a group of motivation trained and a group of untrained children at the end of fifth, sixth and seventh grades. The experimental group received personal causation training in both sixth and seventh grades, the controls received no training.

This most global analysis of academic achievement scores shows significant effects of the training during both years. The trained children are beginning to gain on the average a little more than the normal year's growth for the "typical child," while the untrained children continue to lose ground at a rate of between one and two months per year.

These longitudinal data for three years could not be extended to the eighth grade, but a comparison of eighth grade scores was available for 83 pupils who received training in sixth and seventh grade but not in eighth, and a group of 119 who received no training, thus giving

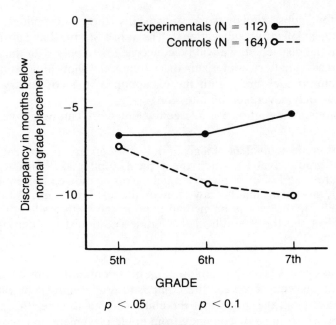

Fig. 8.1

**Mean Discrepancy in Months from
Normal Grade Placement on the
Composite Iowa Test of Basic Skills**

a follow-up after a year. After a year of no training for either group, there is still a large difference between the formerly trained and untrained children. The trained group is only one-half month behind normal grade placement, while the untrained group is more than six months behind. (Trained group mean discrepancy $= -0.5$, $N = 83$, Untrained group $= -6.3$, $N = 119$, $p < .01$.)

It is dangerous to compare these means directly with the means in Figure 8.1, for such a comparison gives the erroneous impression that the trained group gained even more in eighth grade than in sixth and seventh. Since this is a different group, they must be compared with their own mean at the end of seventh grade. Such a comparison shows that formerly trained and control groups gained equivalently in eighth grade, but that the formerly trained group did not slide back, nor did they increase their advantage in the follow-up year.

Some of the children in both of these groups had trained teachers in the eighth grade. The teachers were trained in anticipation of continuing the training in the classrooms. No significant classroom training in motivation occurred, however, because all of the teachers (trained and untrained) were involved in another district-sponsored project. Comparisons were made between the children's academic achievement scores for eighth grade trained and untrained teachers and no differences were found. This result would suggest that merely training the teachers in the fall and not working with them to develop classroom exercises is insufficient to produce changes in academic achievement. This conclusion can only be tentatively drawn, however, since the district-sponsored project was very time consuming. Hence, trained teachers may not have had time to use the motivation training in ways that they would have time permitting.

In general we can say that personal causation training of teachers and children had very significant positive and lasting effects on the academic achievement of the children. These effects raise these questions: Why should training in self-concept, achievement motivation, realistic goal-setting and Origin feelings affect the way children respond to multiple-response questions about the meaning of words (Vocabulary subtest), the content of short stories (Reading), spelling, capitalization, punctuation and usage (Language), and arithmetic concepts and problems (Arithmetic)? Did the training teach these things directly or could increased motivation of a more general nature produce such effects? Did increases in Origin feeling help academic achievement? To answer questions such as these more detailed analyses of the data are necessary.

Special Academic Achievement Results

Detailed analyses of the results of the Iowa test reveal that the effects of training are not equally observable on all subscales. This suggests that the training resulted in something more specific than a general "enthusiasm effect" and that we may look at the specific effects to see if they produce a meaningful pattern.

Briefly, the specific results can be summarized as follows:

1. Training effects were stronger in the sixth than in the seventh grade.
2. Language achievement was most strongly affected by training, and reading achievement was unaffected.
3. Boys apparently make gains in more areas than girls as a result of the training.

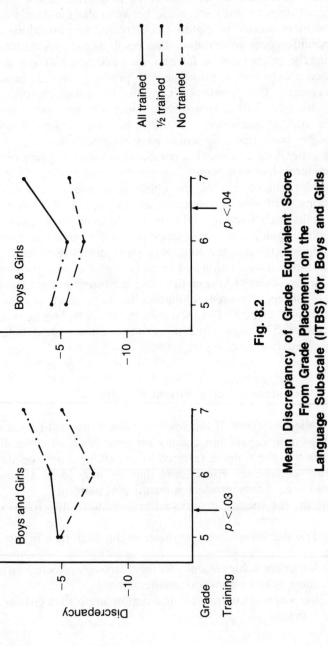

Fig. 8.2

Mean Discrepancy of Grade Equivalent Score From Grade Placement on the Language Subscale (ITBS) for Boys and Girls

These effects can be seen by comparing Figures 8.2, 8.3 and 8.4. The data in these figures combine students from the middle school and all other schools for reasons discussed in Technical Note 8.1.

Figure 8.2 shows mean discrepancy of grade equivalent score from grade placement on the language subscale of the Iowa test for both boys and girls. On the left the group that received training in sixth grade is shown compared with the group that received no training. Between the end of fifth and sixth grades the trained group moved from 4.7 to 4.1 months below grade placement, gaining a full year plus .6 of a month. (In Figure 8.2 a horizontal line would indicate a gain of exactly ten months per year or no change in grade equivalence relative to grade placement.) The untrained group dropped from 4.8 months below grade placement to 7.3 months below, gaining only 5.5 months when they should have gained ten.

When these two groups (shown in the left portion of Figure 8.2) entered seventh grade, each was divided and part of each given training. Thus, the results shown between sixth and seventh grade (in the left portion of the figure) do not show a difference between trained and untrained groups in seventh grade, but simply show what happened to the groups as divided according to training in the sixth grade. (See Technical Note 8.2 for explanation.) The results indicate that the sixth grade trained group maintains its superiority after a year during which the two groups were comparably treated, i.e., part of each were trained.

The right portion of Figure 8.2 divides the students into those who received seventh grade training and those who did not. The gain of the trained group from sixth to seventh grade is relatively and significantly greater than the untrained group. These data show that language achievement scores were significantly affected by the training in both years for both sexes. The effects appear to be stronger during the first year. Further, the effects of the training are not lost during the second year (Technical Note 8.2:).

Figure 8.3 shows vocabulary achievement for boys only. The results are reported in the same format as the previous figure and show significant effects both years for boys and again no loss of the effect of sixth grade training by the end of seventh grade. The trained and untrained girls did not differ in vocabulary achievement.

Figure 8.4 shows results on arithmetic achievement for boys only. Here the trained boys gained significantly in sixth grade only.

We have then one significant finding in language for both sexes, one in vocabulary for both years for boys only, and one in arithmetic for sixth grade boys only. Note that no significant results were found

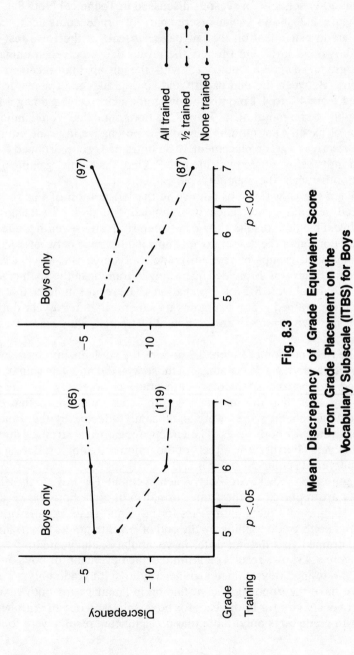

Fig. 8.3

**Mean Discrepancy of Grade Equivalent Score
From Grade Placement on the
Vocabulary Subscale (ITBS) for Boys**

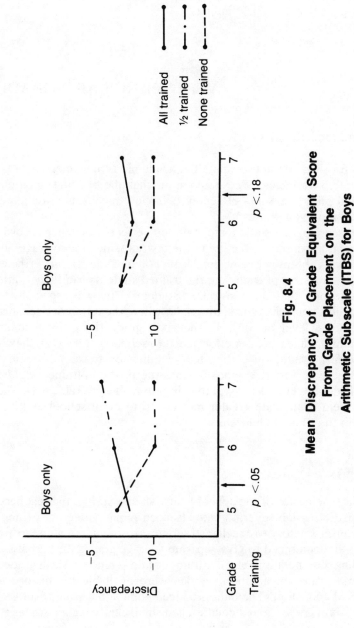

Fig. 8.4

**Mean Discrepancy of Grade Equivalent Score
From Grade Placement on the
Arithmetic Subscale (ITBS) for Boys**

in any of the groups on reading. We have no real explanation for the arithmetic findings. In a later section, after we have looked at attendance and grades, we will propose a tentative explanation for the language and vocabulary findings.

ATTENDANCE AND GRADES

Attendance Results

Before we attempt to relate the academic achievement results to motivation variables, we should note that the training apparently affected other measures of school behavior, specifically attendance, tardies and even grades.

Pressure on the students to maintain perfect attendance records is great and apparently effective in the district, since the average number of days absent per semester is small (about 5 days). Nevertheless, in both semesters of each year the trained students had higher attendance records than the non-trained students. This was especially true in the fall semester of the sixth grade, where the difference reached a significance level of .003. In the sixth grade the trained children apparently made a greater effort to get to school on time than they had in the fifth grade, since they had significantly fewer tardies in the training year. Just the opposite was true of the untrained children, who had more tardies in sixth than in fifth grade (cf. Table 8.1). These data seem to indicate greater motivation to be in school and be on time in the trained children.

Grades

Each semester of the school year, fall and spring, the teachers in the district assign several grades to each pupil. The grades (ranging from unsatisfactory to excellent) were transformed into numbers from 1 to 5 and combined to give separate average grades for verbal skills (reading, composition, etc.), arithmetic and science in sixth grade. In seventh grade, in addition, grades were available for history and physical education. The data produced some interesting results.

In sixth grade trained children had significantly higher grades than

Table 8.1 — Percentage of Subjects with More (% More) and Fewer (% Fewer) Tardies in Training Year than in Year Prior to Training

	Experimental Subjects (N = 206)	Control Subjects (N = 155)
% More	19	39
% Fewer	31	25

Experimental—Control Comparison
$\chi^2_{(1)} = 9.95, p < .005$
Experimental Against 50–50 Probability
$\chi^2_{(1)} = 5.52, p < .02$

untrained children in verbal and arithmetic skills in both fall and spring semesters. There was no difference between the two groups in science grades. In seventh grade differences were found in verbal skills and science in the spring semester and in history (a grade not available the year before) in both semesters. There was no differences in arithmetic or physical education.

In order to interpret these findings we must recall that the teachers assigning the grades to trained children (with the exception of physical education) were trained themselves. We cannot, therefore, completely discount the possibility that trained teachers simply gave higher grades in general. The evidence against this is persuasive, though probably not conclusive. Consider the comparison of the differences in grades with those found with the standardized (non-teacher-administered) tests. In both teacher-assigned grades and the Iowa test differences were found in the verbal area in both sixth and seventh grades. In arithmetic the pattern again is similar, i.e., differences between trained and untrained groups only in sixth grade. The evidence that sixth grade science did not show differences indicates discrimination on the part of the trained teachers rather than overall assignment of higher grades. The results with grades when seen in conjunction with the academic achievement test results strengthen the case for specific effects both years on verbal skills and on arithmetic skill in sixth grade only (Technical Note 8.3).

How Can We Interpret These Specific Findings?

The major effect of language achievement seems reasonable for the first year in view of the fact that three of the four personal causation training units involved either writing an essay each week ("My Real Self" and "My Stories of Achievement") or special attention to spelling ("The Spelling Game"). We might conclude from this that gains in language achievement were merely the result of emphasis on language skills in the units. The training in the seventh grade, however, did not contain such language emphasis, yet the gain in language achievement appeared there as well as in sixth grade.

On the one hand, our data seem to show specific effects rather than a general overall enhancement in all test scores. On the other hand, the evidence is not convincing that emphasis on specific skills produced all of the effects. If we can tie some of the changes in academic achievement to changes in motivational variables produced by the training, we will have the most direct evidence for our hypothesis that personal causation training increases motivation and thereby enhances academic achievement rather than merely enhancing skills directly.

MOTIVATION AS A MEDIATING CONCEPT

If we could establish that a measure of motivation was related to academic achievement, that the training enhanced that motivation measure and that changes in it due to training were themselves related to differences in academic achievement, then we would have evidence to tie increases in academic achievement directly to motivation induced by training. This more theoretically interesting analysis would place the motivation measures in an intermediate position, mediating between the training and the changes in academic achievement. We need to use the data, then to demonstrate three steps:

1. In the natural state (without any special training) the motivation variable is correlated with academic achievement—high motivation produces high achievement.
2. Personal causation training enhanced the motivation variable.

3. The training-produced changes in the motivation variable are themselves correlated with changes in academic achievement.

This three-step procedure was first used to investigate the specific effects of two of the four classroom units used in the sixth grade. It was further applied to change scores on four motivation relevant measures, i.e., goal realism, ego development, need for achievement and the Origin-Pawn measure.

As we said in Chapter 5 the measures used to assess the specific effects of the classroom units were not very powerful. No significant change was found in self-concept as a result of the "Real Me Unit" (see Table T 5.1). Small but significant changes were found in the number of achievement words produced as a result of the "Stories of Achievement" (see Figure T 5.1), and significant changes were demonstrated toward more moderate risk-taking as a result of the Spelling Game (see Figure T 5.2).

Applying our three questions to the self-concept measure and the spelling risk-taking measure results in interesting comparisons, although the findings are inconclusive with regard to demonstrating a mediating relationship between the training and academic achievement. The self-concept measure (administered at the end of sixth grade) was significantly related to academic achievement. (Vocabulary scale $r = +.31$, reading $= +.46$, language $= +.35$, arithmetic $= +.44$ for N $\doteq$ 77. In each case $p < .01$.) But change was not significant (Questions 2), nor was change related to academic achievement (Questions 3). Moderate risk-taking in the Spelling Game during the first week (before much change had occurred) was not related to academic achievement (with the possible exception of the small $r = +.24$ with reading), but the children did change toward more moderate risks as the weeks passed (see Figure T 5.2).

We might conclude from this that had we succeeded in changing self-concept it would have enhanced academic achievement, but even our success in increasing moderate risk-taking did not. Before we can accept the latter part of this statement, however, we must note that Shea (1969) found significant changes in a goal-realism measure (involving risk-taking) using arithmetic items (see Chapter 6). Using Shea's data we found a very provocative relationship between goal-realism and arithmetic achievement for boys ($r = +.48$, N $= 48$, $p < .01$). What was remarkable about this finding was that the above correlation was higher than between IQ and arithmetic achievement ($r = +.22$, $p < .20$). By the use of partial correlation it was determined that when the goal-realism was partialed out of the relationship between IQ and arithmetic achievement it was no longer significant. These data make it appear that the motivation relevant measure goal-realism may be more important in determining arithmetic achievement than is IQ. This result occurred in only one sample and only held for boys. It does indicate that some measure of risk-taking or goal-realism might be very useful in predicting academic achievement, but before this can be stated definitely further evidence would be needed.

Shea's goal-realism measure was the first to pass the test of our first two questions. Unfortunately, the third and crucial question could not be asked of the data. Since Shea had no pretraining goal-realism measure, change on that measure as a function of training could not be related to change in academic achievement. We may conclude, with regard to risk-taking and goal-realism, that our data are insufficient to be conclusive, but it stands as a good candidate for further investigation as a mediating variable.

Chapter 10 discusses in detail Loevinger's (1966) concept of ego development that figured heavily in our thinking during the year the students were in seventh grade, guided the development of the person perception unit (Collins, 1972, see also Chapter 5) and led to the measurement of ego development at the beginning of and again later that year. We can, as a result, apply analyses to the data to answer our three questions and determine whether ego development qualifies as a mediating variable between the training in seventh grade and academic achievement. Briefly, the answer is no. Ego development is significantly related to academic achievement (Question 1), but was not significantly changed by the training (see Chapter 10). Nor were changes in ego development related to changes in academic achievement.

Coming closer to the original goal of the training, especially in the sixth grade, we may use our three questions to investigate achievement motivation. Surely here we will find positive results. But, as in the case of goal-realism, the need-for-achievement measure passed the first two tests for boys only but failed the last. Need for achievement in boys is moderately related to both reading ($r = +.28$, $N = 76$, $p < .02$) and language achievement ($r = +.24$, $p < .05$). In Chapter 5 we saw that the boys changed significantly on need for achievement as a function of training. The change, however, was not related to change in academic achievement.

We come at last to the measure of the most central concept in the training, i.e., the Origin-Pawn concept. Here our perseverance is rewarded and we find a positive answer to all three questions. Figure 8.5 presents data relevant to the three questions. Here the results are presented in terms of mean discrepancy of grade equivalent score from grade placement. Since all of these means are below national norms for grade placement, all of the bars of the graph extend downward from zero, which represents normal grade placement. The ordinate is discrepancy from normal grade placement in months. The graph presents results for sixth grade students on the left and seventh on the right. Each grade is divided into motivation trained and untrained groups. The trained group was further divided into "Natural High Origins," subjects above the median Origin score before training (fifth grade); "Changers," subjects below the median before training who showed high change as a function of training; and "Resistors," subjects below the median who showed low change as a function of training. The untrained group was divided into "Natural Highs" or "Natural Lows" on the Origin scale that was administered before training.

If we look only at the control subjects for the moment, we can see that without training naturally high Origin subjects score significantly higher (closer to normal grade placement) than do naturally low Origin subjects in both sixth and seventh grades. A further confirmation of this finding occurred in the fifth grade, where the composite academic achievement scores were also significantly related to the Origin score ($p < .02$). The answer to our first question is positive— the Origin scale is related to academic achievement in the absence of training even with IQ covaried.

The answer to question two is also positive, as reported in Chapter 7 (see Figure 7.1). The training clearly had large and significant effects on the Origin scale.

To answer question three we divided the experimental subjects into three groups: (a) Natural Highs, (b) Changers, and (c) Resistors.

Figure 8.5 displays the mean discrepancy from grade placement for these three groups for both sixth and seventh grades under "experimentals." Here it can be seen that in both cases the Natural Highs score highest, the Resistors lowest and the Changers in between. This finding is in the predicted direction for both sixth and seventh, but significant only for the sixth grade training. In the sixth grade change on the Origin scale was related to increased academic achievement (Technical Note 8.4).

A comparison of Changers in the experimentals to Natural Highs in the controls reveals that Changers compare favorably with the Natural Highs (sixth grade, Changers = −8.2, Natural Highs = −8.2; seventh grade, Changers = −7.7, Natural Highs = −7.1). Both the Changers and the Natural Highs are significantly above the Natural

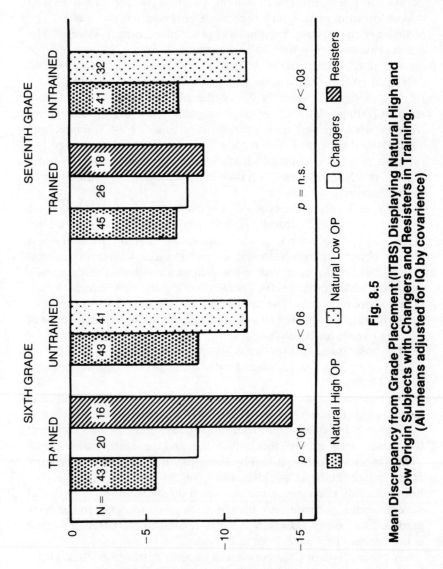

Fig. 8.5

Mean Discrepancy from Grade Placement (ITBS) Displaying Natural High and Low Origin Subjects with Changers and Resisters in Training. (All means adjusted for IQ by covarience)

Lows. Apparently, the training brings academic achievement of Changers up to a level comparable with that of subjects originally high on the Origin scale.

These data seem to establish the Origin concept as a mediator between the personal causation training and increased academic achievement.

SUMMARY

We started this chapter with a question: Did personal causation training help the students with their school work? If it did, we further asked, was the effect simply a matter of greater enthusiasm in the trained classrooms or was the effect attributable to the more specific increase in motivation related directly to the Origin concept? We have seen that the trend for these students to fall increasingly farther behind national norms on standardized tests was significantly reversed in the Origin-trained students as compared to non-trained controls. Moreover, this difference between the trained and untrained students persisted after the eighth grade year, when neither group had training. The difference remained a significant six-month advantage in grade placement for the formerly trained students.

In view of the negative results of most follow-up data from more conventional "compensatory education" programs, this result was very encouraging. Note, for example, that in 1967, when the present research was starting, the United States Commission on Civil Rights (1967) concluded:

> The commission's analysis does not suggest that compensatory education is incapable of remedying the effects of poverty on the academic achievement of individual children. . . . The fact remains, however, that none of the programs appear to have raised significantly the achievement of participating pupils, as a group, within the period evaluated by the commission (p. 138).

Since that report, of course, the whole concept of compensatory education and especially "cultural deprivation" has been severely criticized (Ginsburg, 1972), and efforts are turning to more sophisticated attempts to understand the culture, language and values of the child from a low-income home (cf. Labov, Cohen, Robins and Lewis, 1968).

The present research was never conceived as "compensatory," but rather as an attempt to enhance the potential for personal causation inherent in all human beings. Evidence in this chapter suggests that we were successful and that the techniques used had specific effects on academic achievement that were related to changes in motivation over and above a more generalized initial enthusiasm for the new program among the teachers and students.

Technical Note 8.1

In Chapter 2 it was noted that between sixth and seventh grade about one-half of the children moved to a middle school. The data for both sixth and seventh grade were analyzed separately for the children and it was found that children who remained in self-contained classrooms and did not change schools made greater gains than did children who changed. This caused a technical problem to be discussed here.

In the sixth grade all children in the study were in self-contained classrooms, with one teacher in one room for all major topics of study. About one-half of the children moved to a large middle school for seventh grade. In this school the classes were scheduled in a semi-departmentalized arrangement such that each group of children had a homeroom teacher who taught them one block of subjects (e.g., language and reading skills) and another teacher who taught them another block (e.g., science and math). The motivation training was conducted by only one of these teachers and she, having two blocks to teach every day, did each motivation exercise twice, with two different groups of children. The fact that stronger effects of the training were produced in the self-contained classrooms in seventh grade, then, makes sense. In the self-contained classrooms the children had contact with a trained teacher all day; in the middle school the contact was only for one-half day. Further, the self-contained classroom teachers only conducted the training exercises once, whereas the middle school teachers had to do it twice, with two different groups, and were responsible for twice as many students.

The trouble is that the difference existed between the two groups in *sixth grade* before one-half of them transferred schools! That is, even in sixth grade those who were going to transfer gained less from the training than those who were not going to transfer schools. Extensive search of all the available data produced no concrete evidence to explain this difference in sixth grade where there should have been none. There were, for instance, no significant differences between the two groups on any of the subscales of the Iowa test in fifth grade prior to the motivation training. There seemed to be no evidence to suggest that the sixth grade teachers of the two groups differed in any meaning-ful way either.

We are left with speculation about possible differences. It has been sug-gested, for instance, that teachers who pass their classes on to someone they know in the same school (as in the Kindergarten through eighth grade self-contained classroom school) are more determined for their children to do well than are teachers whose children move on to another school (as in the Kinder-garten through sixth grade schools that feed the middle school). We have no evidence for or against this idea.

Since we could find no empirical reason to justify separating the groups in the sixth grade, and since such a separation produced spectacular results in the self-contained classrooms and significant but more modest changes in the middle school group, it was decided that a conservative analysis would combine groups. The results to be reported, then, occurred in both the self-contained and middle school in seventh grade (when analyses were separated) and the figures and statistics reported are for analyses combining the two groups.

The group trained only one year (either first or second) were composed entirely of students who changed schools. The two year training and no training groups were equally represented from all schools. This makes comparison of all four groups misleading. Consequently, the data have been arranged to be sure that relevant comparisons are always made, i.e., either to confound differences between middle school and self-contained classroom schools (as in Figures 8.2, 8.3 and 8.4) or to leave out one year training groups (as in Figure 8.1).

Technical Note 8.2

The data in Figures 8.2, 8.3 and 8.4 result from the 2 × 2 design where some of the students trained the first year were not trained the second, etc. (see Chapter 2 and Technical Note 8.1). Means for all four groups were as shown in Table T 8.2.1.

It will be noted that the group trained in sixth but not in seventh grade is very small and that in fact they did not gain from sixth grade training. This is the group discussed in Technical Note 8.1 above that went to the middle school for seventh grade. There was no reason to separate them in sixth grade and therefore the combined data were presented in Table 8.1.

Technical Note 8.3

Having found that trained students' verbal grades were higher than untrained students' during training, we looked to see if students trained the first year and then mixed with untrained students for seventh grade were still recog-nized by untrained teachers as superior. We have very few such cases (N = 26) and although their average grade was higher than that for previously untrained students, the difference was not large enough to inspire much confidence. But the verbal grades in seventh grade of these students (trained only in sixth grade) were significantly correlated with their Origin scores, a result unique to this group. Although grades are not related to Origin score generally, the finding that they are in this group suggested that in the year after training the higher motivation of trained children is reflected in verbal grades assigned by untrained teachers.

Effects of Motivational Development

Table T 8.2.1 — Mean Discrepancy of Grade Equivalent Score from Grade Placement (Language Achievement, ITBS)

	Sixth Grade								
	Trained			Untrained			Total		
	5th	6th	7th	5th	6th	7th	5th	6th	7th
Seventh Grade Trained	(N = 112)·			(N = 113)			(N = 225)		
$\overline{X}$ =	4.4	3.0	0.0	4.0	8.0	4.4	4.2	5.5	2.2
Untrained	(N = 38)			(N = 164)			(N = 202)		
$\overline{X}$ =	5.8	7.5	7.6	5.3	6.8	5.4	5.3	6.9	5.8
Total	(N = 150)			(N = 277)			(N = 427)		
$\overline{X}$ =	4.7	4.1	2.0	4.8	7.3	5.0			

Technical Note 8.4

The actual analysis of all the data in Figure 8.6 comprised four separate analyses of covariance. One each for experimentals and controls in sixth and seventh grades. The design in each case was a 2^3 factorial. The variables were high-low Origin score (Median = 4.5), high-low Origin change (Experimentals median = 7.5, Control median = 0.5) and sex. After these analyses the individual comparisons displayed in Figure 8.6 were tested (Scheffé, 1959).

Chapter 9

The Origin Classroom Is Different

(R. deCharms, F. Plimpton & S. Koenigs)

The children in the experimental classrooms differ from other children on the results of measures of motivation and academic achievement. One might expect that these differences were mediated by a different atmosphere or mood in the experimental classrooms. Can these subtle differences be observed in the classroom? Can they be measured? Can we say, in fact, thar the Origin classroom is different?

We have two sources of information on which to base answers to the above questions. First, we have a careful non-participant observation study of one experimental classroom at the end of the sixth grade year. Second, we have a questionnaire measure devised specifically to measure the children's perceptions of the Origin nature of their teacher and classroom. This questionnaire was administered to many classrooms at the end of the eighth grade year. Let us look at the observation study first.

OBSERVATIONS IN AN ORIGIN
CLASSROOM

Although we can use the observation study as a general view of what an Origin classroom looks and "feels" like, the initial purposes of the study were more specific. The first purpose was to attempt to select children who seemed to act like Origins. This, of course, was the topic of Chapter 7 and was discussed in detail there. The second purpose of the study was to observe the role of the teacher in the Origin classroom and the resulting classroom atmosphere.

What is the teacher's role and function in an Origin classroom? Can she do nothing? As one student teacher said, "Do we need to have teachers go through all that training anymore? Can't anyone teach? As a form of group leadership 'laissez-faire' is the label attached here." The student teacher implied that laissez-faire groups are characterized by lack of norms and rules, lack of structure, leadership and discipline, and result, probably, in chaotic conditions. When we talk to teachers about treating children as Origins, they often assume that it means giving the children complete freedom to do anything. They may even renounce some or all of their responsibilities for leadership under the guise of treating the children as Origins. But true leadership places great responsibility on the teacher and is, we think, completely compatible with treating the children as Origins.

The term laissez-faire simply means, "let them do whatever they want." White and Lippitt (1960), in their study of three forms of leadership, describe "laissez-faire" as complete freedom of group or individual decision with a minimum of leader participation. Unfortunately, White and Lippitt do not specify details of this form of "leader participation." Instead, they concentrate on the comparison of "democratic" vs. "autocratic" leadership. They analyze the three types of groups in terms of "patterns of relationship" and "efficiency." In what follows, our Origin classroom will be analyzed in terms of social interaction, activity patterns, productivity and performance.

The School and The Class. Mrs. Strong's classroom was located in a fairly new school building on a quiet street lined with large trees and small one-family houses. (Since the time of these observations, many of the houses have been boarded up or torn down.) The attractive modern concrete school building was surrounded by a large paved recreation area and a small lawn. The classrooms were large and well illuminated, the furniture and equipment, in general, were well kept and in good condition.

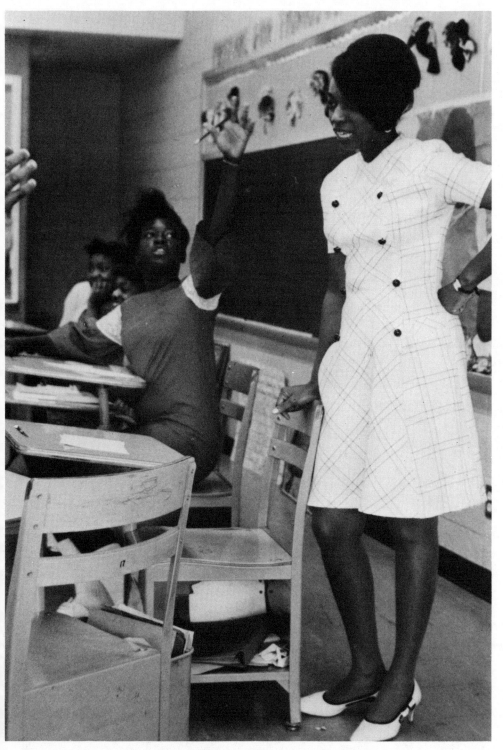

Mrs. Worthington (pseudonymn) and student

The principal and her staff were almost exclusively black; only two white teachers were employed. The students, kindergarden through sixth grade, were children from the neighborhood and, with very few exceptions, they were all living within walking distance of the school. The building and the staff radiated a friendly and accepting atmosphere that made the observer feel welcome. In the particular classroom being observed, the ages of the twenty-eight children ranged from eleven to eighteen years, most being twelve years old. Their mean IQ was about 95.

The Schedule. The schedule of the class repeated itself with little variation each day. From 8:30 till 9:50 A.M. the students joined their reading group, assigned by ability, not grade level. The various teachers of these grades thus taught a group composed of children from all the classes between fourth and sixth grade. At 9:50 A.M. the students returned to their home room and the lesson, lasting until 10:20 A.M., was normally arithmetic. Following recess at 10:50 A.M., seat work in arithmetic was continued, which then was followed by spelling and grammar. Lunch period lasted from 12 noon till 1 P.M. The class typically started the afternoon with English (grammar, spelling or composition) followed by geography from 2:20 P.M. til the end of the school day at 3:15 P.M. There was no recess in the afternoon.

Pattern of a Typical Lesson. As the class resumed after the morning reading lesson, the students quickly settled down. For about ten minutes the teacher recapitulated with the students the material of the day before and then related it to the new material to be introduced. Recapitulation took place on a verbal basis, the teacher posing questions that were answered either by individual students or by the whole class. Occasionally, the teacher used the blackboard for an explanation and then called on the class for answers or asked them to work a similar problem through with her. For introduction of new material the teacher primarily used the blackboard.

Following this short lesson period, the teacher assigned seat work on which the students worked for about fifteen minutes. The teacher then called the class to attention again and assigned each student a problem which he had to solve at the board. Once the problems were solved at the board, the students went back to their seats and each student read his solution from the board. The class discussed whether the problem was solved correctly or not. If the solution was wrong, the student went to the board and solved the problem again with the help of the teacher and class.

One typical aspect of all lessons was the short teacher presentation period as compared to the long period of seat work.

The general course of the day was determined by the monotonously repetitive schedule, imposing a structure and a basic framework upon the day's events.

Patterns of Interaction. The teacher maintained a free setting in the classroom and allowed interaction patterns to evolve as a natural process. These patterns were partially determined by the geography of the room. The desks were arranged in three "wings," so that the children faced each other. The flow of interaction was most often concentrated within the wing. Even student-teacher interaction seemed to be influenced by the seating arrangement; the students sitting closest to the teacher's desk were most likely to ask the teacher questions or to indulge in conversation with her.

Weak and average students tended to go for help to students of the same standing, while good students typically sought help from the best students. The top students in the class received their information directly from the teacher. Although the one top student was never observed to ask questions of the teacher and rarely from anyone else, on one occasion she obtained information by sending another good student to ask the teacher the question.

Communication in the class about information seemed to go through well-established channels. Similarly, social interaction followed the same hierarchical pattern. Although the best student of the class did not assume a leadership position, she ranked highest in status with the group.

Friendship was also a factor in the interaction structure, although only one friendship group consisting of more than two students could be observed. Incidentally, this group consisted of what Smith & Geoffrey (1968) call the "court jester," who here was the group leader, and his two followers. The jester was one of the better students in the class, while the other two were average to weak students. In this subgroup the leader provided help and information to the followers, while in exchange they provided ample applause whenever it was called for, although in this case it appeared that non-work oriented interaction was more frequent than the work oriented interaction. No other subgroups or cliques were observed in the classroom interaction. There were some students who seldom interacted with anybody, who did their work quietly and rarely spoke unless called upon.

Discipline, Freedom and Security. Aside from the general behavioral rules established early in the year and aside from some occasional "calling to order" by the teacher, no discipline appeared to be imposed upon the students. The class seemed to be governed by self-imposed discipline. The communication was mainly devoted to exchange of information. Moving around in the room consisted of either walking to some other student's desk for information or material or visiting the class library. Except for some very weak students, the class completed the work as assigned and kept pace with the year's curriculum. The teacher was not observed to have disciplinary difficulties, although she did have some students in the class who had been assigned to her after they had become intolerable disciplinary problems in their former classes. Such rather common deviant behavior as throwing chalk or erasers was not observed.

In the great freedom granted to them, the students had worked out a self-regulatory disciplinary system. The individuals seemed to feel secure and at ease within the group and the system. It may be this last factor that accounted for the fact that they completely ignored distracting factors external to their group. Although the class was not used to being observed, they paid very little attention to the observer's presence in the classroom. The students generally ignored the many messengers coming into the room. The door was always open and yet noises from the hall had no influence on the class.

An incident involving James, a sixteen-year-old student who rarely appeared in school, gives a specific example of how stability and security enabled this group to deal with distraction and disruption. One day James did appear after weeks of absence. He obviously intended to shock both the teacher and the class, as he put a cigarette behind each ear and then played with matches on his desk. The teacher and the class showed neither reaction to, nor interest in, his behavior. After fifteen minutes, James quietly took up working on a drawing and worked until the end of the session.

Cooperation and Competition. Another notable feature displayed by the class was their high degree of cooperation and helpfulness. A student was never refused help by another student. Just as the teacher always was present for the students whenever they needed her and always had time for them, so the students helped each other. The students seemed to be eager to offer assistance and advice to their peers. This phenomenon was of special interest when we consider that these children came from an environment where, reputedly, fighting and competition were learned early. During all the hours of observation there was but one incident when students were rude or hostile to each other. No fights and no rude language were noticed, not even in the absence of the teacher. Except for James, there were no usual signs of competition within the class, either for achievement or for attention from the other students or the teacher.

Individual and Social Maturity. Neill (1960) calls sincerity the most important trait to be developed in a child. Sincerity, as opposed to false submissiveness, means the freedom of a child to express how he feels and what he thinks. Sincerity in this sense would also include a class's freedom to express their feelings toward the teacher and about her actions.

Early in the observations Mrs. Strong directed a rather pedantic geography lesson and shortly thereafter the students frankly told her that they did not enjoy geography in the form that she taught it. It was agreed that the class would think of new forms of structuring these lessons and so would the teacher. Next day one of the students proposed that the students should give individual reports. The class and Mrs. Strong accepted the suggestion and the students prepared their reports during the week in the class, giving one report per week. The reports were individually structured and, on the whole, each student worked to his best ability.

A similar "experiment" was tried in arithmetic. Each student was allowed ten minutes to teach the class, and even the weakest students had their turn. Here it was interesting to observe how the class tried to help a weak student.

In one arithmetic session, we see how an eleven-year-old boy subtly handled a diplomatic problem involving one of his classmates. Morris was teaching the class and asked Carl to solve a problem at the board. Carl seemed reluctant to go to the board, so Morris promised that he would give him an "assistant" if he needed one. Morris then began assigning assistants to others working at the board. Carl smiled and went to the board, where, after trying to solve the problem, he received step-by-step instruction from one of the most able girls in the class.

Carl, eighteen years old, was a student who was planning simply to sit in class until he could drop out of school. When pushed too hard, he often resisted and became aggressive. On this particular day, as usual, Carl was showing no interest in class. Morris' suggestion to send him an "assistant" once he had tried the problem not only saved Morris the embarrassment of Carl's resistance, but also gave Carl a chance to save face, an opportunity to perform well in front of the class. Thus he fostered Carl's self-confidence and self-respect. The incident also resulted in other students' volunteering to help their peers. This in turn distracted the attention from Carl and made "help" a most natural thing, not something aimed only at the worst student.

An Origin Classroom

We have now established a basis to face the question whether this was a "laissez-faire" classroom as defined above. Apparently, our classroom did not fit any of the three types of leadership described by White and Lippitt (1960). In fact, democratic decision-making and discussions, autocratic disciplinary intervening on the part of the teacher and a rather well-delineated social and emotional structure of the class all seemed to exist side by side.

This was not a haphazard situation, with a classroom that ran the way the wind blew it, with a passive teacher who just let the students do whatever they wanted. Once the rules were established in the beginning of the year and the students were grooved (Smith & Geoffrey, 1968) by the teacher, she intentionally gave the students all the freedom possible within the limits of a classroom setting. But with the freedom the students also had to assume *personal* and *collective responsibility*. The teacher was neither a threatening authoritarian figure nor powerlessly at the mercy of the class. She was, rather, an authority by what French and Raven (1960) call "referent" power. The teacher-student relationship was one of mutual respect and confidence, and she drew on their respect to maintain control, sometimes in directive ways, sometimes in ways that drew out and developed the controls from within (Redl & Wineman, 1952) the children.

The teacher who succeeds in creating an Origin orientation in her classroom develops a warm, accepting atmosphere, where the children know the boundaries beyond which they may not step. Because they know the boundaries, they feel secure—the teacher's behavior is predictable and hence produces security. Because they helped to establish the boundaries and know that these boundaries, whenever possible, are not arbitrary, the students begin to make them their own rules. At this point, the students will defend the rules and begin to internalize them. For this to happen it is important that the students feel that the rules are for their benefit and not just for the convenience or whim of the teacher. In such an atmosphere the children can learn to take more and more responsibility and will enforce *their own* rules.

Once this system of working together has developed, the teacher does very little to control the children. Indeed, the children are controlling themselves. *But* a classroom society built on controls from within, warmth, acceptance and mutual respect is not created overnight. Nor is it developed by a laissez-faire teacher. She must be firm and consistent in her behavior, consistently seeking the good of the children in ways that they can understand. She must use *socialized power* for *their* good, not *personalized power* (McClelland, Davis, Kalin & Wanner, 1972) to enhance her own image.

Since the teacher is a member of the society, she has rights. She has the right to demand some things for her own convenience, but she should clearly label them as such.

The Origin-enhancing teacher is not afraid to be firm and directive—an authority but not an authoritarian—when she is pursuing the improvement of the children. She should always question herself as to her motives and reflect on her actions, but when she is sincerely seeking the good of the children, she should have no fear of being directive in enforcing the structure and boundaries agreed upon. Such direction is not treating children as Pawns; rather, it is instrumental in helping them reach their own goals. External control is often necessary, but the goal is to convert it to internal control.

Although Mrs. Strong's classroom was not perfect, it did differ from many others in her school and it did manifest many of the characteristics of an Origin classroom.

THE CHILDREN VIEW THE ORIGIN TEACHER

At the same time that we were measuring the effects of the motivation project on the classroom we were also attempting to measure the effects of the project on the Origin teachers. Except for follow-up data on the teacher's advancement within the school system (cf. Chapter 4), we have very little evidence about the effects of the Project training on the teachers. This is unfortunate, since our major effects were probably on the teachers and only indirectly on the children. But to threaten the teachers with critical evaluation of their effectiveness would certainly not have been treating them as Origins and would have seriously interfered with our cooperative working relationship. If we had employed measures of the teachers' classroom behavior, the entire Project might have been jeopardized.

As a result, we now have very little systematic comparative evidence on what actually happened in the teachers' classrooms. For the first three years of the project we had to rely entirely on rather unsystematic observations of individual classrooms, such as those described in the first section of this chapter. At the end of the eighth grade year we had remedied this situation to an extent by measuring the children's perceptions of their teacher and their classroom.

What trained teachers actually do that differentiates them from untrained teachers is important. But possibly more important is the students' *perception* of what the teachers do. After all, the teacher can do everything in her power to develop motivation, but if the students perceive no difference, their behavior probably will not be different.

To shed some light on the students' point of view, we developed a questionnaire to measure the pupils' perception of the Origin orientation of the teacher and of her classroom. The questionnaire served to give us one more type of answer to the question, "Is the Origin classroom different?"

Since the teacher training (Chapter 4) and the classroom exercises (Chapter 5) were designed to help the teacher produce an Origin orientation, there should be differences between the classrooms of the trained and the untrained teachers. Specifically, the trained teachers should encourage more internal goal-setting and instrumental behavior, expect more personal responsibility and realistic aspirations, and foster self-confidence and student-centered control of behavior. These are the aspects that should encourage motivation development and ultimately help the pupils to learn more. These are also the six Origin categories scored in the children's stories (cf. Chapter 7).

Development of the Origin Climate Questionnaire

As part of a graduate research methodology course Sharon Koenigs and Robert J. Hess set out to develop the questionnaire. After familiarizing themselves with the Plimpton Origin Content Analysis Manual (Chapter 7), they developed an equal number of positively and negatively worded items intended to measure each of the Origin subcategories, namely: (*a*) Internal Goal-Setting, (*b*) Instrumental Activity, (*c*) Reality Perception, (*d*) Personal Responsibility, (*e*) Self-confidence and (*f*) Internal Control.

The following items are examples:

In this class I can decide how to use the extra time (Internal Goal-Setting).

The teacher lets us try new ways of doing things (Internal Instrumental Activity).

The rules we have in this class are made to help the students (Reality Perception).

We must try to do a problem ourselves before the teacher will help us (Personal Responsibility).

I can do even the hardest work in this class if I try (Self-confidence).

We get to decide what we do in this class (Internal Control).

Armed with a battery of from four to six items for each subcategory, they administered the questionnaire to a sixth grade classroom in an integrated suburban school (N = 24). Testing time totaled approximately twenty minutes.

A complete item-by-item analysis (point biserial r's and phi coefficients) was computed, as well as an odd-even, split-half reliability coefficient. Inter-item phi coefficients ranged from +.17 to +.66. Point biserials of each item with total score ranged from −.30 to +.77. Three point biserials out of twenty-eight were negative, while ten were greater than +.40. The odd-even reliability coefficient (with Spearman-Brown correction) was +.87.

As a result of these computations four items were dropped and a few were reworded, resulting in the final scale of twenty-four items, twelve positively and twelve negatively worded. The definition of each subcategory and the items intended to measure it are presented in Appendix B.

More evidence of the internal consistency of the measure was obtained from the data collected from the project children. Table 9.1, for instance, presents the Pearson product-moment intercorrelations by subcategory for the measure based on data (N = 132) obtained from the eighth grade classrooms of both trained and untrained teachers.

The final form of the scale is a Likert-type (Likert, 1932) instrument. Items are always phrased in terms of teacher's behavior or things that happen in the classroom. The child circles the choices "always," "often," "seldom," "never." Instructions to the child read:

This questionnaire will help us to understand how you feel about your class. It is not a test and will not count as part of your school work.

Table 9.1 — Origin Climate Questionnaire Intercorrelations by Category for Eighth Grade, Trained and Untrained Teachers (N = 132)

	Internal Control	Goal-Setting	Instrumental Activity	Reality Perception	Personal Responsibility	Self-Confidence	Total
Internal Control	—						
Goal-Setting	.44	—					
Instrumental Activity	.40	.23	—				
Reality Perception	.37	.23	.55	—			
Personal Responsibility	.24	.29	.27	.36	—		
Self-Confidence	.18	.29	.19	.24	.14	—	
Total	.70	.65	.68	.72	.58	.52	—

It is important for you to answer the questions in your own way, try to answer them as honestly as you can. There is *no right* answer.

Think about each question and circle the answer that seems best to you. Think only of the class that you are in *now*—not any other class.

Administration of the Questionnaire. All of the seventh and eighth grade teachers from six schools participated in the study as part of the motivation project.

Since the teachers themselves did the testing, care was taken to give each teacher instructions that would assure comparability. They were specifically instructed to tell the pupils that the results would be used for research only at the university and neither they nor any other school authorities would see the individual results. Teachers were told to place the finished forms in the folder provided and conspicuously to seal it.

In all, data were obtained from thirty-two trained teachers and twenty-eight untrained teachers. Since class size averaged over thirty, this constituted over 1800 completed questionnaires from which to sample. However, we were not interested in individual responses,[1] but only in the mean for a classroom, i.e., the average perception of that classroom of the teacher. Therefore, we randomly sampled six girls and six boys to obtain two estimates of each classroom. Our sampling unit, then, was classroom (not children), and statistics were computed on two estimates from each classroom, a boys' mean (from six randomly selected boys) and a girls' mean (from six girls).

In the end we compared ten trained and ten untrained teachers in the seventh grade and thirteen trained and thirteen untrained teachers in the eighth grade. The data from twelve protocols from each class (i.e., a total of 552 questionnaires scored) produced forty means for seventh grade (twenty times boys and girls) and fifty-two means for eighth grade.

The Effects of Teacher Training on Pupil Perception

The basic design was a 2 × 2 matrix comparing trained and untrained teachers and within each of these groups boys and girls. The data from the seventh and eighth grades were treated separately statistically. Table 9.2 shows the results in terms of means and variances of total score on the twenty-four items. Figure 9.1 shows the major result graphically in terms of the actual scale value from 1 to 5 or "Never" to "Always" on the questionnaire. Analyses of variance were computed separately for the seventh and eighth grades. In both cases the means for the trained teachers are higher than for the untrained teachers ($p < .01$ in the seventh grade, and $p < .06$ in the eighth grade). Apparently, classrooms of Origin-trained teachers are perceived by the children as encouraging more Origin-type behavior.[2]

The Relationship between Origin Climate and Learning

For each child in the sample an average learning rate was computed (from the Iowa Test of Basic Skills) indicating his gain over the previous year's grade placement scores. If the child gained the equiv-

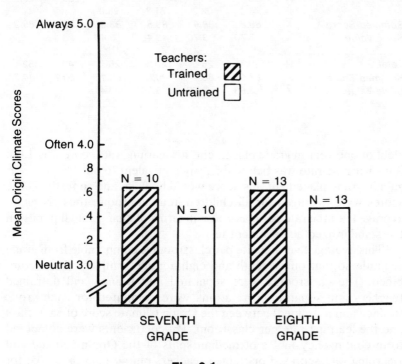

Fig. 9.1

Mean Origin Climate Scores

Table 9.2 — Mean Origin Climate Score for Seventh and Eighth Grade Classrooms

		Classrooms of					
		Origin Trained Teachers		Untrained Teachers		Total	
Sex of Responding Pupil		7th	8th	7th	8th	7th	8th
Boys	N	10	13	10	13	20	26
	s^2	55.2	46.7	52.7	42.8		
Summed Score	$\bar{X}$	85.1	84.0	77.4	83.1	81.3	83.5
Scale Value	$\bar{X}$	3.55	3.50	3.23	3.46		
Girls	N	10	13	10	13	20	26
	s^2	47.1	28.2	61.8	28.0		
Summed Score	$\bar{X}$	88.8	88.8	83.6	83.0	86.2	85.9
Scale Value	$\bar{X}$	3.70	3.70	3.48	3.46		
Total	N	20	26	20	26	40	52
Summed Score	$\bar{X}$	87.0	86.4	80.5	83.1	83.7	84.7
Scale Value	$\bar{X}$	3.63	3.60	3.35	3.46		

alent of one year in grade placement, his learning rate score was 1.00; if his learning rate was below this, say equivalent to only ¾ of a year gain in grade placement, his score would be 0.75, and so forth. These scores were averaged for all children in a classroom, thus giving an average learning rate per classroom in terms of change of all pupils on the standardized achievement test.

This average learning rate per classroom is comparable from grade to grade so that our seventh and eighth grade samples can be combined. The classrooms were separated into trained and untrained teachers and separate correlations were computed for each group (trained and untrained) between the Origin Climate score of each class and the learning rate per classroom. Phi-coefficients were computed from contingency tables of median splits of the Origin Climate and Learning rate scores. For trained teachers phi $= +.45$, $p < .05$; for untrained phi $= +.60$, $p < .01$. The relationships were both significantly positive, indicating that classrooms perceived by the pupils as encouraging Origin behavior also produced increased learning. Evidently, *there is a relationship between how much a teacher is perceived as encouraging Origin behavior and how much learning occurs in her classroom.*

ORIGIN CLASSROOMS ARE DIFFERENT

Both a description of an experimental classroom and data from the children's perceptions of their teacher and classroom give ample evidence that Origin classrooms are different. Not to be overlooked is the important finding that Origin classrooms produce higher learning rates than non-Origin classrooms. This is true for both trained and untrained teachers. For the control classrooms in which the teacher had no motivation training this is very interesting. It indicates that some teachers produce Origin-type perceptions in their pupils without benefit of training and these classrooms have higher learning rates than classrooms where Origin perceptions are not produced.

A very important clarification of the Origin concept, which deserves repeating in summary, resulted from the observations of Mrs. Strong's class. It is a mistake to think that treating pupils as Origins simply means allowing them complete freedom. It is a mistake to think of the Origin-enhancing teacher as a *laissez-faire* leader. What characterizes the Origin classroom is the teacher's warm acceptance of the children along with her firm, consistent rules and high expectations for their behavior. Controls from within the children are enhanced whenever possible, but external controls may be used when clearly designed to promote the good of the children. The goal is to convert external control to control from within.

Notes

1. This measure is not intended as a measure of the individual's own Origin properties. It does not, for instance, discriminate between previously trained and untrained children who are known to score differently on

Plimpton's Origin measure, nor is the Origin-Pawn score correlated with Origin Climate Questionnaire score. The latter was checked in two samples comparing groups classified by median splits on both measures (Self-Contained Classrooms $\phi = +.10$, N = 109, $\chi^2 = 2.23$, $p > .25$; Departmentalized Classrooms, $\phi = +.13$ N = 132, $\chi^2 = 1.09$, $p > .10$).

2. In both samples the girls obtained higher means than the boys. This difference was only statistically significant in the seventh grade. This trend may simply reflect a more positive attitude toward school in general that seems to be characteristic of elementary school girls.

Chapter 10

Personal Responsibility and Ego Development

(Agusto Blasi)[1]

INTRODUCTION

Ego development is a term used by psychologists (Loevinger, 1966; Erikson, 1959) to describe a very general process of evolvement of the mature human being. In the second and third years of the motivation development project we began to see the possibility of developmental changes in the children that might be described as ego development. There were several reasons that we turned to the consideration of ego development. First, we needed a measure of change related to the self. The initial step in motivation development suggested by McClelland (1965) and sought in our training was to engage a person in self-study. In our early attempts (the Real Me Unit) we had not been successful in measuring change. Second, *personal responsibility,* a major aspect of the Origin concept, appeared to be central also to the process of ego development.

The impact of Loevinger's thinking on the project is most clear in three subprojects that became part of the overall design. (*a*) The person perception unit (Collins, see Chapter 5) set out to increase the interpersonal sensitivity and cognitive complexity of the children. These two concepts were seen as central to ego development. (*b*) Blasi

177

(1971) isolated aspects of persònal responsibility from each stage of ego development and studied their manifestations in the behavior of groups of sixth grade non-project children. (*c*) Loevinger's measure of ego development was administered to the project children during their seventh grade year and Coor (1970) and Collins (1973) studied the effects of the project training on that measure.

The effects of the person perception unit on the ego development of the project children (as assessed by the measure to be described below) were minimal, indicating that a few weeks of training in interpersonal sensitivity has little effect in changing ego level. In this chapter, therefore, we shall not report in detail the Collins (1973) and Coor (1970) studies that resulted in this negative finding. Rather, we will concentrate on a more intensive attempt by Blasi (1971) using a group of children that were in the sixth grade when the project children were in the seventh grade. Blasi's data are similar to those of Collins and Coor in showing little training-induced change. Nevertheless, his observations of children at different levels of maturity and his specific use of the concept of personal responsibility led to the integration of developmental concepts with the Origin-Pawn concept which will be presented in the concluding section of this chapter.

THE CONCEPT OF EGO DEVELOPMENT

The term *ego* is most often associated with Freud (1923). As used by Loevinger (1966) and others more recently, it has taken on a distinctive character. The major difference between Freud's use of the term and the way we shall use it (following Loevinger) is the difference between a *thing* and a *process*. Loevinger stresses that the ego is a process; it is not a thing that mediates between the Id and the Superego, for instance. As a process it serves the purpose of maintaining equilibrium of the person as he strives "to master, to integrate, to make sense of experience" (Loevinger, 1969, p. 85). The ego, or self-system, operates to minimize anxiety and to maximize anxiety-free experiences. Development of the ego in the growing child progresses from lower to higher stages, with each advance precipitated by successive developmental crises. Sullivan (1953) and Erikson (1950) have dealt at length with the progression of crises that result from increasing experience of the imposition of other people on the child's freedom. Development from stage to stage is normally very slow, characterized by large individual differences.

In short, the ego cannot be defined like a *thing,* but can be understood by studying the stages that appear in the normal developmental *process.* In this way Loevinger's concept is similar to Sullivan's self-system (1953), Sullivan, Grant and Grant's interpersonal maturity (1957), Isaac's relativity (1956), Kohlberg's moral development (1964), Harvey, Hunt and Schroder's cognitive complexity (1961), and Perry's intellectual and ethical development (1968).

, Loevinger's model has the following major features: (*a*) ego development is hierarchical; (*b*) the order of appearance of stages is invariant, precluding the omission of stages; (*c*) stages are not age-specific, since considerable variation of ego-level may be found at any one chronological age.

The Stages of Ego Development

There are seven major stages of ego development, six of which have been isolated empirically by Loevinger and Wessler (1970). These stages and their distinguishing characteristics may be seen in Table 10.1.

Personal Responsibility and Ego Development

The pivotal role that the development of personal responsibility came to play in our concept of treating students as Origins led Blasi (1971) to analyze each of Loevinger's stages of ego development for its characteristic approach to responsibility. This was done by studying many written statements produced by people known to be at the various developmental stages (for details see Technical Note 10.1). The following descriptions of four of the stages resulted from this analysis.

Self-Protective Stage. There is a dawning concern for the causes of the outcome of one's actions. There is denial of negative responsibility and externalization of blame; externalization may appear in an attempt to disassociate one's body (smile, eyes, mouth) fron oneself. As a result, the self-protective person gets angry if things go wrong, since it is the others' fault, malevolence, etc. Others are attributed bad motives and are seen as impinging on one's absolute freedom. It is not completely clear how the self-protective person sees posi-

Table 10.1 — Stages of Ego Development

Stage	Code	Interpersonal Style	Conscious Preoccupation	Character Development
Impulsive	I-2	Exploitive, dependent. People evaluated on reaction to S's demands (good–bad).	Bodily feelings, especially sexual and aggressive.	Impulse-ridden, fear of retaliation. Physical punishment orientation.
Self-Protective	Delta	Exploitive, manipulative. Zero-Sum game.	Protection of self: Cautiousness, suspiciousness, projection. Simple instrumental hedonism.	Expedient, fear of being caught. Rules are recognized only in the negative effects that their transgression produces.
Conformist	I-3	Reciprocal, superficial. Need for acceptance and approval by authority and group.	Things, appearance, reputation. Stereotyped thinking.	Conformity to external rules. Dichotomization of right and wrong, as based on formulae for behavior and on societal standards. Morality of reciprocity, and of role-taking.
Self-Conscious	I-3/4	Reciprocal, affective. Relationships are described in terms of	Awareness of feelings. The Self as related to the group. Transition	

| Conscientious | I–4 | feelings. Emphasis on limited, closed groups. Intensive, responsible. Mutuality, respect, duty. | from actions to traits (quasi-traits). Differentiated inner feelings. Achievement. Traits. | Internalized rules, guilt. |

Note—Only the stages represented in this study are reported here.

tive responsibility. A passive attitude can be deduced from his insistence on luck and his expectation of getting things.

Conformist Stage. There is a self blame, which may, rarely, assume the general form of wondering what is wrong with oneself. Emphasis, however, is on concrete actions, particularly in relation to obedience and to specific rules. Responsibility for positive outcomes seems to be slower in developing; there is emphasis on luck, on what is given (family, sex, etc.) and on passively receiving (compliments, love, etc.). This dependence is also related to the conformist's passive attitude when he doesn't get what he wants.

Self-conscious Stage. Definitely there is self-blame and a beginning reference to traits or quasi-traits (laziness). The self-conscious person does not focus on action as such but on the person's awareness of the relation between the rule and the action. There is also awareness of the consequences of an action: confession and reparation become important, with the implication that what is done can be changed (not yet change of self). Self-attribution of positive outcomes is finally based on activity and effort. The emphasis seems to be on interpersonal relations (helping, etc.). Though there is no concern as yet with self-change, there begins to be concern with self-control and self-discipline.

Conscientious Stage. There is a clear assumption of responsibility. The emphasis now seems to be on positive rather than on negative outcomes (achievement). The concepts of control, choice and decision are now at the center of concern. Personal traits become important, as does a concern with changing oneself. The orientation toward the active participation in building one's personality is seen in valuing others' recognition only for what one did or accomplishes. There is a clear distinction between abilities and intentions; the latter are decisive for moral responsibility.

These descriptions served as guidelines for the rest of the study. As one can see, no single aspect is emphasized throughout the stages; there appears to be, however, a dominant tone at each level. The sequence could briefly be characterized by changes in the referent to whom one feels responsible: there is no responsibility at the self-protective stage; at the conformist stage responsibility is limited to the authority and specific rules (accountability); at the self-conscious stage the others become the referent; at the conscientious stage the self becomes the focus of responsibility. Very little information was obtained about the impulsive stage, probably because no concept of responsibility is yet present then.

THE RESPONSIBILITY AND EGO
DEVELOPMENT STUDY

There were two main objectives in this effort: (*a*) to study how children, scoring at different stages on Loevinger's Sentence Completion Test, understand different training conditions and react to them; (*b*) to study whether, according to the hierarchical sequence hypothesis, a training in responsibility just above the children's present level of functioning (plus-one training), will be more effective in producing changes than a training representing two developmental steps (plus-two training) above the children's initial stage.

Method

The Sample. One hundred and nine children, 58 girls and 51 boys, served in this experiment. They were all black, lived in a lower to lower-middle class neighborhood and constituted almost the entire population of four sixth-grade classrooms in two different elementary schools. They scored on the Loevinger scale at three stages: the Impulsive stage (17 girls and 10 boys), the Self-protective stage (15 girls and 16 boys), the Conformist stage (29 girls and 27 boys).

Children of each stage were divided into small groups (5 to 8) and randomly assigned to one of three treatment conditions: control or no-training condition, training to the immediately next step (+1), or training to two steps above their present level of functioning (+2).

The Training. For each group, the training consisted of a set of ten stories that the children were to act out and to discuss during one-hour sessions during ten consecutive school days.

Since each ego level was trained under the plus-one and the plus-two conditions, four different sets of stories were devised. The basic principle in the construction and in the presentation of the stories was to challenge the children's present level of functioning by having them deal with contradictions and conflicts. These were introduced by the content of the stories, by confronting the children with their different solutions to different problems, and, most of all, by having them play different and reciprocal roles.

The *Training toward Parent-independent Responsibility* (plus-one for Impulsive children) attempted to deal with two problems that seemed characteristic at this stage: a passive reliance on external punishments and rewards as motivational bases for actions and, therefore, the expectation that parents should "make" children do things; and the tendency to confuse and diffuse one's own actions and intentions against the background of others' actions, of impersonal forces, etc. The reversal of role was mainly done with the parent or with the authority to whom the heroes of the stories transferred their responsibility.

The *Training toward Rule-oriented Responsibility* (plus-one for Self-protective children, plus-two for Impulsive children) had as its objective helping the child to recognize himself as the cause of a negative action and, even more, helping him to accept its consequences. The stories presented heroes who caused an undesirable and negative result, but who, for various reasons (others did the same thing, someone else started, etc.) refused the consequent blame, punishment or repayment. Role reversal was mainly with the authority imposing the sanctions and, occasionally, with the victim of the hero's wrongdoing.

The *Training toward Rule-independent Responsibility* (plus-one for Conformist children, plus-two for Self-protective children) attempted to substitute for a concrete, literal and rigid approach to rules and authorities an understanding of their spirit and function, particularly by contrasting rules with friendship and altruistic concerns. A further objective was to help children to assume responsibility for the negative consequences of acting according to the rules. All the stories presented a double conflict: first, between a rule or an order and a common sense (often altruistic) course of action; second, between the hero's decision to obey and the blame received from the authority precisely for his literal obedience. Reversal of role was performed with the authority.

The *Training toward Self-oriented Responsibility* (plus-two for Conformist children) was less homogeneous than the other training programs in terms of the situations used and of their structure. However, an effort was made to focus the children, at every opportunity, on their own self, both as source of obligation and as referent of accountability. The stories presented heroes who failed to live up to their ideals and principles and who then expressed negative feelings about their inconsistent behavior. Children were asked to make sense of the hero's negative self-evaluations when motives based on obedience, empathy or social reputation were completely absent. This training tried to facilitate the process of self-orientation by using such psychodramatic techniques as having "spectators" comment on the hero as a person, having the hero think out loud about himself, alone or in front of a mirror, and by having another child "play the conscience" while the hero was acting.

An example of how the training was approached is provided by a story taken from the training toward rule-independent responsibility:

> The Joneses and the Smiths were neighbors and had been good friends, but then they had a quarrel and stopped speaking to each other. Mrs. Smith started spreading things about Mrs. Jones. Mr. and Mrs. Jones, therefore, told their daughter Marie not to play or to talk with Kathy Smith any more. Marie didn't like this because Kathy was her best girl friend; but after her parents explained the situation to her, she decided to obey. One day in winter, Kathy was walking just ahead of Marie on the way to school. At one point Kathy slipped on the ice and fell to the ground. Marie didn't know what to do; she felt like helping, but she also wanted to obey her parents (soliloquy). Finally she decided to be obedient, so she walked on to school without stopping.

(Discussion follows.)

> Marie's teacher, however, was driving to school and saw the whole thing. She was surprised that Marie didn't stop to help her friend; so she called Marie's parents and told them what happened. That evening Mr. and Mrs. Jones had a long talk with Marie, criticized her for what she did, and tried to explain to her why they blamed her.

(A soliloquy is followed by role-reversal with one parent or with the friend.)

The Dependent Variables. All children were given, at the beginning of the experiment and at the end of their training, the Sentence Completion Test for Ego Development, which has already been introduced (Technical Note 10.1) as consisting of the completions to 36 stems, each assigned to one of ten levels on the basis of a scoring manual. (For a discussion of scoring see Technical Note 10.2.)

Other measures were based on the children's behavior during the training, as independently seen by the experimenter and by an observer. Ratings on four scales (Involvment, Role Playing Ability, Responsibility Level and Change) were assigned to each child. The Responsibility Level Scale consisted of the description of ten types or combinations of types in responsibility functioning, derived from the basic modes described earlier and from the observations during the training. The investigator and the observers assigned independent scores to each child. There was, between them, agreement in 83% of the cases. Disagreements were discussed and compromised.

In addition, checklists describing children's behavior, verbal and non-verbal, were filled out for each child and each of the ten sessions. The following report of observations is based on all these instruments.

FINDINGS

Responsibility and Ego Development

Statistical analysis indicated no significant change in ego-level of the children as a result of the training. The correlations between the Responsibility Level Scale and Loevinger's Sentence Completion Test were $+.56$ for the boys and $+.54$ for the girls, indicating that ego level was significantly related to responsibility scores ($p < .0001$). Apparently, ego development stages have a meaning that goes beyond verbal behavior and the specific technique of the Sentence Completion Test. The meaning of these quantitative results was made clear by the characteristics that children of each stage displayed in the course of the training.

Impulsive children, independently of their attitudes toward responsibility, seemed to form a special group, different from all the rest of this sample of sixth-graders. They tended to be at the low end of the intelligence continuum. (See Technical Note 10.3 for details.) Their discrimination of feelings was elementary and their insight into motives poor. Consequently, role playing was limited to the representation of actions, was stereotyped and was stripped of details. During the discussion, comments were very literal and focused on secondary matters.

Other general characteristics of Impulsive children were a very short attention span, compulsive and unconsidered laughing and giggling, general restlessness and weak control of impulses, which led these children, in spite of their good intentions and promises, to misbehave and to disrupt the session. There seemed to be a high degree of hostility (or less control over it) towards each other: Impulsive children were alert to any minimal irregularity or deviation in the others and ready to "rat" to the trainer on each other. Though it was usually difficult to get them involved and to obtain comments from them, they became alive as soon as they saw in the issue being discussed an opportunity to attack each other.

In the area of responsibility, Impulsive children seemed to have no difficulty in correctly attributing the cause of negative behavior. This ability seems to develop very early, usually before kindergarten age, as shown by studies attempting to test Heider's typology of causal attribution (Shaw and Sulzer, 1964; Shaw, Briscoe & Garcia-Esteve, 1968). Despite their ability to see themselves as causes of negative behavior, however, they still tried to place the blame outside themselves. The main difference from a similar tendency in Self-protective children consisted in the naiveté and sometimes absurdity of the excuses and justifications that this group resorted to.

As expected, Impulsive children tended to see their behavior as dependent on parents and authorities, particularly on the use of close checks and punishments. A child, they believed, should not be blamed for his misconduct if his parents did not make him behave. As one of them put it, "Just to tell him doesn't do any good; you have to punish." The generality of this orientation towards external control was also suggested by the frequent mention of physical punishments, such as "whipping" and "knocking on the head," and by the extreme exaggeration of physical consequences (going to jail, being shot) as the only deterrent for misconduct.

Self-protective children also recognized correctly the cause-effect relations of their actions. Their main characteristic with regard to responsibility lies in their attitudes towards accountability. Basically, they seemed to look at the world in terms of an everyone-for-himself philosophy; differences in roles were taken into account, but role relations were seen in power terms: one gets as much as one can, within the limits of the others' force and power.

Their role-playing, especially (but not exclusively) of the sneaky opportunistic hero, was frequently very effective. They seemed incapable, however, either of portraying shame or of playing the authority trying to induce shame. What appeared, instead of shame, was sullenness, defiance and rudeness. On the other hand, they tried to arouse shame by yelling and screaming and could not change this approach even when they were aware that they had produced defiance and anger.

The role-playing of sneaky behavior did not differentiate Self-protective children: other children could do it as well. But, while children of other stages disagreed with the behavior portrayed, Self-protective children showed general agreement with their dramatic playing. They were concerned with being found out and with protecting themselves from the authority; sneaky solutions were considered appropriate and even smart. "What's wrong with lying? Everybody lies," said one child, and he explained that his conscience would not bother him if he were not caught. Their philosophy about recognizing one's misdeeds can be formulated in the following manner: the best solution is to lie and to deny one's responsibility, because this is the easiest way to get out of trouble; only if one is actually caught or has no probability of avoiding punishment is it better for him to tell the truth. Then he may not completely avoid trouble, but he will have the punishment cut down. This attitude was so common and pervasive in all the groups at this stage and in all the situations that were discussed that it was given first by almost all the children.

Self-protective children usually manifested contrasting attitudes between what they did as opportunistic heroes, what they expected of the authority and the way they played the authority. As heroes, they approved the satisfaction of their needs as much as possible, but also expected parents and teachers to be "nice," understanding and unendingly forgiving. Otherwise, they became angry and accused the authority of dislike. In the role of the authority, by contrast, they were rigidly authoritarian and punishing. They avoided any dialogue with a subordinate; even when they were explicitly instructed to resort to dialogue and explanations, they kept using such expressions as "you are stupid," "don't talk back." Although the contrast between behavior in the different roles appears a contradiction, it becomes less surprising when we remember that Self-protective children, while recognizing differences in roles, kept them in isolation or related them in terms of power. As the hero, one is right to be sneaky; as the authority, one is also right to punish the hero who lets himself be caught. This tendency to isolate roles was one of the major obstacles to the training.

As expected on the basis of Loevinger's theory, *Conformist children* appeared as the upholders of law-and-order, not only in their choices, but also in the reasons supporting their decisions. They did recognize that rules and laws have a function (which Self-protective children tend not to); more frequently, however, they found a more adequate justification either in the simple presence of a rule or an order, or in such external and non-functional reasons as punishment, the acceptance from the authority, and their love toward the authority.

Their understanding of rules, therefore, tended to be literal and rigid, as suggested by the constant preoccupation with the letter of the law or order and by the lack of recognition of true exceptions. In one of the stories, for instance, the hero, after a squabble between families, was told by her parents not to talk with her girlfriend any longer, but was then faced with the decision of whether to help her girlfriend, who had fallen on the ice. Most Conformist children agreed with the solution of helping but without addressing any word to her. This was a typical attitude.

Moreover, the responsibility in a subordinate was limited to the actual decision of obeying the order. But the evaluation of the order and the consequences of obeying were seen as lying beyond the scope of a subordinate role. "He was just obeying, he wasn't thinking," as a child put it. It is understandable that these children were generally preoccupied with their accountability to the authority ("What will I tell?"); that they tended, as their first solution in cases of conflict, to contact the authority; and that they refused to accept blame after they followed the basic duty to obey. There were practically no exceptions to the last attitude.

It seems, then, that central in the attitudes of Conformist children is the understanding of interpersonal roles and relationships, particularly of the subordinate-authority relationship. From the authority they expected directions and especially consistency, both in the authority's own behavior and in the handling of rules and obedience. Lack of consistency seemed to be a source of anxiety, sometimes expressed as mistrust and frustration. Condoning, and even worse, rewarding an independent interpretation of the rules was seen as an indication of "two-facedness" and indecision ("He can't even make up his mind"). However, anger and hostility toward the authority were rarely, if ever, seen. Rather, Conformist children (in stark contrast with Self-protective children) tended to emphasize reciprocal communication, were aware of the feelings and expectations of the authority and stressed loyalty and love as motives for obedience.

Interpersonal relationships with the authority seemed to be even stronger in the few children of the next level, the *Self-conscious* stage, that were observed. These were even farther removed than Conformist children from the pragmatic and sneaky attitudes of the Self-protective stage, which they openly criticized. The author had the impression in this group of a full internalization of laws based on identification. As a result, Self-conscious children seemed to be even more sensitive than Conformist children to the conflict between independence and obedience and, in a way, even more compliant.

Effects of the Training

On the basis of the instruments with which the children were assessed before and after the training, no change could be measured for any one of the developmental levels in any one of the training conditions. This result is not too surprising considering the rather global characteristics of the instruments, the limited scope of the training and, most of all, the nature of development and of the ego. As suggested by Loevinger (1969) and by others before her one of the basic characteristics of the ego is the tendency to maintain as long as possible its structural properties. In a general sense children's reactions to the training can be viewed as dynamic manifestations of ego stability.

For example, children frequently seemed unable to play certain assigned roles which contrasted with their characteristic way of thinking. In one situation during the training toward parent-independent responsibility Impulsive children were asked to play a responsible girl, one who does not want to watch TV because she has homework to do. The instructions were clear. Nevertheless, one child admitted that she would not study if her mother did not punish her, another refused to watch TV "because we may get in trouble," and all the children, the ones playing the authority as well as the ones playing the hero, seemed to organize their acting around the theme of catching and being caught. As already described Self-protective children were frequently unable to portray shame or to arouse shame in others. The discrepancy between the children's level of thinking and the suggested roles was particularly striking in the training toward self-oriented responsibility. The children role-playing the coach in one of the stories, for example, could not find reasons to convince the hero to practice when external motives were eliminated; the students playing a teacher in another story, contrary to explicit instructions, focused on grades rather than on traits, personality and choices.

A more dramatic and symptomatic (though rarer) phenomenon consisted in the distortion of the facts presented in the stories. In the training toward rule-independent responsibility a child playing the mother blamed the independent rather than the obedient character, as the story demanded. Similarly, several children explained their decision to conform to the coach's ineffective instructions by saying, contrary to the story, that the "coach's way was better." Reinterpretations in the conformist direction were abundant in the training toward self-oriented responsibility. One frequent interpretation for the hero's negative feelings about himself resorted to the parents'

anger and disappointment. An effort made with one group to eliminate that reasoning was all but useless; all the children agreed that the
parents just did not show anger or disappointment, but were really
feeling that way inside.

There was, finally, the children's experience of conflict and their
was of dealing with it. Conflict seemed to be particularly strong during
the training toward rule-independent responsibility, while it was weak
or absent in other training conditions. The children's first reaction,
when presented with the dilemma between obedience and a logical
appearing independence, was to avoid the conflict, often by trying to
eliminate its ground. They looked for contradictions in the story,
deemphasized one element (e.g., friendship or the emergency of the
situation) in order to make the conformist solution more defensible.
As a last resort, they refused to make any decision. When pressed for
a decision, they still tried to avoid the conflict, either by contacting
the authority for instructions or by finding some kind of compromise:
the hero should do part of what the authority desires and part of what
seems reasonable; or, the hero should do what seems reasonable but
observe, at the same time, the letter of the order.

All of the above processes can be interpreted as attempts to adapt
to situations that were difficult to assimilate, but to do so without
changing basic attitudes.

It was hoped that by recording detailed observations in the course
of the training it would be possible to capture both more subtle
changes, to which the pre-post measures would be insensitive, and,
perhaps, the very process of changing. The picture resulting from
such observations, however, though more detailed and interesting, is
not much more optimistic in terms of the effectiveness of the experimental intervention. The following statements provide a fair summary
of the results: (*a*) there was no change of any kind under the trainings
toward parent-independent responsibility, toward rule-oriented
responsibility and toward self-oriented responsibility; (*b*) a definite
impact and some slight change were observed for the training toward
rule-independent responsibility; (*c*) in the latter training, no difference
was observed between Self-protective and Conformist children in the
amount and quality of change.

Starting with the failures, it seems clear that a different explanation is required in each case. Probably the most outstanding flaw in
the training for parent-independent responsibility was its dependence
on abilities and skills that Impulsive children seem to lack. The
training was diffused in several directions, used a variety of techniques, relied on comparing different roles in the same session as well

as different sessions and counted on the children's sensitivity to contradiction. The Impulsive children's lack of interest and lack of ability in discussing issues, their restlessness and short attention span made them particularly unsuited to this approach. As a consequence it is impossible even to suggest why, strictly in terms of responsibility, the training did not work and what could have worked better.

The training toward rule-oriented responsibility dealt with what seems one of the main problems in Self-protective children, the refusal of accountability; these children (in contrast to Impulsive children) did actually face the issue. None of them, however, was judged by the trainer or by the observers to have changed his basic attitude. Even more dramatically, the training did not appear even to touch the children, for instance, by arousing a sense of puzzlement or conflict.

There were at least two reasons for this outcome. One was the inability already described to appreciate the reciprocal nature of different but related roles: the children could not see that if the authority is right in demanding certain behavior of the subordinate, then it is right for the subordinate to comply. Much of the training's effectiveness in producing conflicts relied on the presence of such an understanding. The second reason concerns not a cognitive but a motivational characteristic of Self-protective children, i.e., the need to protect themselves from any negative consequence of their actions. It appears that interventions with children at this stage (as opposed to children of higher stages), in order to be successful, must face squarely what was intentionally avoided in the present attempt, i.e., the self-protective defense system.

Finally, the training toward self-oriented responsibility did not seem to produce changes, because, in spite of the more advanced children's cognitive skills and lack of defensiveness, it presented material and attitudes that were simply too difficult to understand, let alone to assimilate. As one observer put it, "We are too far above their heads." What was intended to generate conflict produced, in general, only puzzlement: the children simply could not understand why anybody should feel bad for not following his own values, when there was no rule about it, and resorted to explanations that were amoral and external in nature, and often seemed absurd. When a self-oriented attitude was clearly presented to them by the experimenter or, very rarely, by another child, they openly and unanimously disagreed and considered that attitude strange.

It seems that the source of the ineffectiveness of this training lies in the children's action orientation, in their looking at people and themselves as a series of actions rather than as centers from which actions proceed. Such an orientation, cognitive in nature, goes beyond the scope of responsibility attitudes. To change it requires broader and more massive developmental processes.

The training toward rule-independent responsibility, by contrast, seemed to be more effective. It attempted to deal with the two main obstacles that children seem to have in their progress toward more independent thinking: their seeing rules and orders in their literal concreteness and their not accepting responsibility for the consequences of their obedience. The first of the two problems was attacked with exercises in role-taking with the authority, in the hope that a child would then reason, step by step, as the authority would. A slightly different exercise dealt specifically with the issue of exceptions. It was relatively easy, at least for some, to understand what the authority really wanted, to realize that the authority could not foresee every possible situation, and even that the authority, in their position, would decide for the independent action. The last step, however, their choosing the independent alternative for themselves, still remained very difficult and was made only occasionally and then very hesitantly.

The second of the two obstacles—the belief that the subordinate is not accountable for the consequences of his obedience—was attacked by facing the children with the contradiction between saying, as some did, that it would be wrong not to choose the independent alternative and saying, as *all* of them did, that the hero could not be blamed for obeying. When this exercise was performed (most of the training time was spent on the preliminary problems), its effectiveness was very limited: some children conceded that both the authority and the subordinate hero should be blamed; more frequently the solution was that the subordinate *does not have to* choose the independent alternative, even when it is the right one; he *could* choose it if he wants to. Similarly, the authority could, but does not have to, praise the hero for his independence. Therefore, there seems to be no obligation outside of the conformist framework.

The training toward rule-independent responsibility was definitely seen by the investigator as having a real impact on the children, at least in the sense of producing subjectively felt conflicts and in forcing the children to deal with them. Change, however, was very limited. Table 10.2 divides the children, at each of the two ego developmental stages to which rule-independent training was offered, into four categories, representing the overall effect of the training: no change, simple consolidation of an independent reasoning based on friendship and empathy, ability to role-take with the authority and to use the distinction words-mind, understanding that the subordinate is accountable for his acts of obedience. The results are eloquent. Moreover, those who could be assigned to category 3 did not seem very stable in their attitude.

Considering the children's reactions to the training toward rule-independent responsibility, it appears that the fundamental problem does not lie in cognitive distinctions, which, when acquired, did not lead to either the unhesitant support of the independent alternative or to the full acceptance of responsibility for obedience. The problem seemed to lie, rather, in the children's understanding of the authority, in their experiential relation with the authority and in their own self-definition relative to the authority. If this hunch is correct, training should follow a quite different route than the present one. Theoretically, the development of responsibility may be different from cognitive development and even from moral development when this is interpreted in purely cognitive terms.

A final comment, clear from Table 10.2, is that the Self-protective and Conformist children who were exposed to this training did not seem to differ in amount or quality of change. This finding, especially when compared with the complete lack of change of Self-protective children during the training toward rule-oriented responsibility (plus-one), was unexpected and seems to contradict directly the hypothesis of hierarchical relations between stages. This conclusion, however, seems premature, because the training toward rule-independent responsibility did not indicate any change among children of either

Table 10.2 — Ratings of Change in the Training for Rule-Independent Responsibility

	Self-protect. Level (N = 12)	Conformist Level (N = 17)
1. No Change	6	9
2. Empathic reasoning	5	5
3. Words-mind distinction	1	2
4. Responsibility for obedience	0	0
5. Ambiguous	0	1
Total	12	17

stage in what appears to be the critical attitude, i.e., accountability for obedience.

Summary of the Study

The outcome of the study can be simply stated: (*a*) there are at least three major and quite different orientations to responsibility observable in sixth grade black children; (*b*) to change these orientations in a short time is difficult if not impossible.

The observations, however, have given us several strong leads that may help us to devise both new ways of developing personal responsibility in children and a model that can be tested in future research.

A MODEL FOR THE DEVELOPMENT OF PERSONAL RESPONSIBILITY

In order to set up a model from what we have learned from Blasi's observations we will accept the basic assumption of most developmental models, i.e., sequentiality of stages. Further we will limit ourselves to the three most common stages according to Blasi's data, namely, Impulsive, Self-protective and Conformist. Next we will assume that at each stage there is a characteristic developmental problem that dominates the child's behavior with regard to personal responsibility. Finally, if we can identify those major problems, we can tentatively suggest techniques for helping the child cope with them.

At the Impulsive stage the primary problem is to learn to defer personal gratification in the face of the demands of others. The major manifestation that the teacher may feel the need to discipline at this stage is conspicuous behavior of all types aimed at attracting attention. The worst instance of this probably arises when the child has learned to settle for attention of a negative sort—seems to court scolding and reprimands. As the research in behavior modification has shown the first and possibly most difficult step here is to stop reinforcing the attention-getting behavior with attention. To tell the teacher "ignore it" is not very helpful, however, unless it is combined with advice of a more positive sort. It would seem that the use of reinforcers such as candy and attention for desired behavior should be uniquely appropriate at this stage for two reasons. Reinforcers can surely be used to bring the child's behavior under control but more importantly they can focus his need for gratification and then, by the use of well-established techniques, they can be used to help him learn to delay gratification. The shift from a "real" reinforcer, such as candy, to a "token" reinforcer to be redeemed later ought to be a significant step for the Impulsive child.

The Self-protective child has learned that he can't have everything he wants immediately precisely because others are so much more powerful than he. His problem is to become powerful and he finds his greatest weapons are cynicism, hostility and, especially, withholding behavior desired by the more powerful agent. He is apt to say, "You can't make me do it." To force him physically involves a power struggle which the teacher can't win. If she succeeds in forcing him, she strengthens his conviction of impotence and his determination to be powerful—he "loses face." If she fails, she is still faced with the immediate problem, a child who difiantly refuses to obey.

At this self-protective stage the concept of saving face is very valuable. Since the major problem for the child is to learn how to be effective and to feel some control of his own, he must be allowed enough freedom of movement to wiggle and save face. If the authority demands exact compliance, the child cannot do this. The teacher can set clear limits, but still give the child some choices and, above all, can get him to initiate the first step rather than push him. The Self-protective child feels smothered by talking and scolding and nagging.

In the long run, however, the child needs to learn to derive his feelings of power from asserting himself in positive ways and from identification with more powerful agents. He can learn to satisfy his power need by identifying with adults and by becoming part of a group of peers that can legitimately have more power than one individual. Thus, his need for personal power can be socialized. As he learns to derive satisfaction from power through identification and association he will learn the importance, i.e., the power, of rules. He will be on his way to the rule-orientation of the Conformist stage.

The Conformist child follows the rules and is little problem to the teacher, but it is probably this stage that is most characteristic of and criticized by American middle-class culture. The conformer is the follower; his problem is to learn to take independent action, to stand up to the group, to have more confidence in himself. The teacher can help the Conformist child by allowing him more and more independence in setting goals and determining his own course of action. By the time he has reached this developmental stage the child's cognitive complexity is such that cognitive techniques of self-study and dilemma resolution are probably appropriate. But as Blasi saw it is very difficult for these children to kick the conforming habit. To begin to rely on self as the standard is quite unnatural to them.

This gives a final clue to one overall theme, i.e., the concept of self at the various stages. Apparently, the concept of self is developing and becoming clear throughout the stages. Though vague at the beginning the very young child assumes that the self is omnipotent. The problems of each stage are imposed from outside, because the child is learning that his self is not the only one that must be considered and that, in fact, he is not very powerful. In the Self-protective stage the self becomes clearer through reduction to a small impotent thing. (The old moral teachings tried to move the child from selfishness to unselfishness.) But once the child has learned to renounce continual gratification (complete selfishness) the self must learn to assert its self apparently first through identification and later through genuine self-consciousness and self-awareness.

This sketch of a model has implications for the Origin concept. One could speculate that at each stage the child is at first a Pawn to the major problem of that stage, but as he learns to deal with it he becomes more of an Origin vis-à-vis that problem. Although he doesn't lose the feeling of being in control of that problem, when the next problem arises he is a Pawn to it, and so on. As he masters each developmental problem the feeling of being an Origin cumulates despite the fact that to the specific next problem he may be a Pawn. There are two implications of this. One leads to a prediction, and the other has potential for helping us to understand our concept of treating a person as an Origin.

First, the prediction. If, as the child passes through the stages of ego development, he becomes an Origin with regard to more and more problems (though he may still feel a Pawn to high-order problems), there ought to be a positive correlation between ego development and the Origin-Pawn measure. Data so far indicate that this may in fact be true, although as yet the number of children on whom we had both measures uncontaminated by any kind of motivation or responsibility training is small ($r = +.24$, $N = 52$, $p < .05$).

Second, our model suggests an important clarification. To treat a person as an Origin is to help him become an Origin with regard to the most important problem he is facing. This is much more specific than simply thinking in terms of "loosening the reins" or giving more freedom. The responsibility problems at each stage suggest specific ways to help the child. In every case there is an element of loosening controls, but the place to do it is suggested by the problem.

Briefly to recapitulate, control is relaxed at the Impulsive stage by not punishing attention-getting behavior but by encouraging greater independence from immediate gratification. Strict control of Self-protective children seems the most natural reaction, but is also the most harmful. The controls must be loosened just enough for the child to initiate some action to save face and then to help him to take responsible action with the group. Our general technique in the Origin training (Chapter VI) of trying to help all children with self-study and goal-setting would seem in retrospect to be most appropriate for the Conformist child.

The model suggests many possibilities, but the acceptance of the stages found in sixth grade black children and of the assumption of sequentiality must be borne in mind. Are characteristics of the stages universal or are they specific to this group? The importance of punishment in the responsibility orientations may be characteristic of this group and less important, say, in a middle-class white culture. Would a different cultural background change everything or just lead to a different "flavor" at each stage? Could the stages be the result of the way former stages were handled? If so, could the Self-protective stage, for instance, disappear if the Impulsive child were given a specific treatment? All of these questions remain to be answered empirically. It is doubtful, however, that all of what we have seen here is situation specific or that the stages could completely reverse their order, for instance.

Notes

1. With introduction and final discussion added by R. deCharms. The research reported in this Chapter was partially supported by National Institute of Mental Health Grant No. MH-05115, Professor Jane Loevinger, Principal Investigator.

Technical Note 10.1
The characteristics of responsibility for each stage were determined empirically from adult responses to the Sentence Completion Test developed by Loevinger and Wessler (1970) to measure ego development. The test consists of thirty-six incomplete sentences or stems which the subject is asked to complete. Fourteen stems whose content seemed to be related to responsibility were selected. For each stem the response categories which seemed to discriminate a particular stage were chosen. All the categories across items which belonged to one stage were then put together to obtain a description of that stage in the area of responsibility. This analysis resulted in the descriptions presented in the text.

Technical Note 10.2
Protocol scores for ego development were obtained by converting the 36 item scores on the sentence completion into a cumulative distribution and by then applying to the same distribution the "ogive rules," a sort of multiple cut-off point procedure. Frequently the stage-score thus obtained is complemented with an impressionistic reading of the protocol. An alternative procedure consists in simply adding the weighted scores of each item.

Technical Note 10.3
A correlation of +.48 was found in this sample between ego development and IQ as measured by the Lorge Thorndike Intelligence Test.

Chapter 11

The Learning of Personal Causation

(R. deCharms)

At the close of a book it is helpful to pose questions at the most general level to help the author and the reader to rise above the welter of specific findings and see the broader implications of what was found. Such questions are often deceptively simple and embarrassingly difficult to answer. Three such questions to which we will address ourselves in this last chapter are: How do our original theoretical ideas about personal causation illuminate the changes produced in the children of the project? What has happened to our concept of the Origin-Pawn variable as a result of the project? What are the implications of the results for teachers and for education in general?

THE LEARNING OF PERSONAL CAUSATION

We started the project with a loosely knit conceptual framework based on the assumption that all men strive to be effective in producing changes in their environment so that they can be in control of their fate and not just buffeted about by the world. The infant human is a helpless victim of the environment if not cared for by an adult. Development and maturation involve not only natural growth but learning how to cope with and overcome the environment. At birth the fate of the child is in the hands of others. The child must convert this external fate control into personal fate control in order to survive. Of course, the baby does not know this in any conscious sense. Apparently he cannot even distinguish his own body from other people or even from physical objects and he only gradually learns about and gains control of his body. During this gradual process he learns what his body can do and what effects he can produce in the people and world around him.

How is this early history, where the importance of the development of personal causation is relatively clear (Hunt, 1971), related to motivation change in grade school children? Such early forms of infant learning are long past in children in late elementary school. The thesis underlying our research is that, although the specific problems faced by the child (and adult) at different ages do differ (Kagan & Klein, 1973), the basic problem remains the same, namely, to cope with external forces in the environment and to convert the fate control held at first by others into personal fate control. Interwoven with the continuing thread of increasing personal causation are the specific problems faced at different ages (or stages of development). These developmental problems, conceived here as similar to but broader than developmental tasks posited by Havighurst (1952), have at their center the development of the conception of self as an active agent.

The self-conception of the child as he enters sixth grade is quite well advance. He is immersed in the basic problem of being a personal cause of effects in other people—the problem of power and influence. He has found himself in a large group of age-mates all competing for attention and recognition. His success in this situation should affect his confidence in his ability to attain his achievement and social goals. Specifically, past success in competition should be related to his level of achievement motivation. More generalized success in reaching both achievement and interpersonal goals should be related to his Origin-Pawn score.

At the same time the cognitive development of the sixth-grader should be progressing apace (Piaget, 1940). According to Piaget, this development through several rather specific stages is closely tied to maturation, follows a definite stage progression and even within the progression is difficult to accelerate (although some data suggest that cognitive development can be accelerated (viz., Gelman, 1969). Intellectual development as shown in academic achievement is also occurring during these preadolescent years of late elementary school. It is probably related to but more specific than cognitive development as discussed by Piaget.

In what follows we shall use our measures in an attempt to penetrate this complex interweaving of motivational and cognitive development. In addition, our data can tell us about "naturally occurring" changes and "training induced" changes. If we divide our measures into more motivationally relevant and more cognitively relevant instruments and look at our data for natural vs. induced changes, we may see an overall pattern of development in persons in middle-childhood. Table 11.1 presents this breakdown of our data.

The thought sample measures of motivation show no change from grades 5 to 7 in the control groups, but in the trained groups we see an increase in the Origin-Pawn score and significantly augmented achievement motivation in boys. Apparently, these two measures of motivation are not naturally changing at this age but can be increased by training. The more behavioral measure of realistic goal-setting was also increased by training. This seems to be the one variable that can be affected with a short-term training unit, since we found that children learn to take more moderate risks in the Spelling Game over a five-week period and the effect was noticeable each week in a monotonically increasing function (see Figure T 5.3.1). Unfortunately, no data were available to test whether this variable was increasing naturally in the control groups.

In sharp contrast to these motivation measures the ego development scores remained essentially unaffected by training. Naturally occurring changes, however, are clear from Coor's (1970) data at least for the period starting with seventh grade and extending to the tenth. A close look at Coor's data indicates that the largest "naturally occurring" increase occurs between seventh and ninth grades. By ninth grade the mean score is at the conformist stage and between ninth and tenth grades it does not increase significantly. Apparently, ego development is difficult (if not impossible) to change by special classroom training, but shows natural growth between seventh and ninth grades.

The ego development measure apparently involves aspects of both motivation and cognition, and has therefore been placed between the purer motivation measures on the left (Origin-Pawn and achievement motivation) and the purer cognitive measures on the right (ego development and academic achievement) in Table 11.1. Although the

Table 11.1 — Summary of Results of Personal Causation Training

	Origin-Pawn Variable	Achievement Motivation	Realistic Goal-Setting	Ego Development	Academic Achievement
Significant Change Induced by Origin-Pawn Training	yes	boys only	yes	no	yes
Significant Change without Training	no	no	no data	yes	yes

academic achievement measure is the most clearly cognitive of the measures, the academic achievement data do not represent a clean "naturally occurring" situation, because, although our training units were not cognitively oriented, the school curriculum is clearly aimed at increasing academic achievement. We can say, then, that academic achievement was increased by the school curriculum and that personal causation training augmented it over and above the change attributable to the curriculum.

If we assume that infants and young children first learn about their world through their affective reactions to it and then very soon begin to find that they can be active in seeking positive states of affect and avoiding negative states (Hunt, 1971), it is clear that the rich affective life of the preverbal period sets the stage for later childhood. The basis for the learning of motives has been laid. The child knows, in general, what kinds of things he wants, and as he grows older, he must learn how to get them in different ways and how to cope with the competition of more and more people as he moves from contact first with mother, then with the rest of the family, then with a few playmates, and finally at school with a whole room full of competitors. By the time the child is in middle to late elementary school *affectivity* per se is not primary. The basic needs and wants are not changing drastically, but the child is learning how to *strive* for his goals. Thus, the affective measures of achievement motivation and the Origin-Pawn variable are not naturally changing very much, but training in *striving*, which stresses active goal seeking and realistic strategies, has an important impact.

As the child develops cognitively it is more and more possible for him to bring his rational faculties to bear on his affective life. Thus, the motivational and cognitive capacities become more and more enmeshed and indistinguishable in the development of the self or ego. Apparently ego development progresses over time and the stages may be linked to prior cognitive development. It is, however, difficult to accelerate by training.

Progress from *affectivity* through *striving* to a mature intertwining of *cognition* and motives adds a middle period to Piaget's sketch in 1940 of what he called the "affective life" from the preverbal period through the dawning of "will" and "moral feelings" to "the personality in the social world of adults." After 1940, Piaget devoted his energies to understanding cognitive development. By so doing he leaves us with a blank between the obvious importance of early affectivity and the mature "will." It is the years between that seem most important for the development of personal causation from initial striving that, because of rudimentary cognitive development, is almost blind to the clear, focused striving that becomes possible with increased cognitive facility. This middle period that seems to be represented by our subjects might be called the period of increasing *conation*. Long ago Plato suggested three faculties of the mind: the affective, the conative and the cognitive. Conation represented action and striving and seems well suited for our concept of personal causation and Piaget's concept of "will."

Placed in this broad context, our results suggest a rich area of research concentrating on conative development during the period after early affectivity and before cognitive maturity. This period should be crucial to the development of personal causation. Guided by the recent advances in cognitive developmental psychology following Piaget, we are led to ask several questions: Is conative development sequential in the sense that Piaget sees cognitive development as sequential? How is conative development linked with early affective development and with later cognitive development? Is it possible to postulate a genetic theory of conation parallel to Piaget's genetic epistemology? Quite obviously our data hold no answers to these questions, but they do raise them and suggest that conation may be thought of developmentally. The data suggest that the period of middle to late elementary school may be the period of most importance for the development of personal causation. Further, if conative development is dependent on the child's increasing interaction and competition with others, then such development is uniquely social. One parameter dictating a potentially sequential but not genetic development is the increasing number of other people that the normal child growing up in our society encounters.

WHAT HAS HAPPENED TO THE ORIGIN-PAWN CONCEPT?

An often overlooked result of attempts to help people change is the effect on the change agent. Such effects are often profound and are clearly evident to us when we think back on our changing conception of the Origin-Pawn concept as the project progressed. Three major shifts in emphasis seem to have been pressed upon us in our interaction with the teachers and students. First, the freedom-constraint dimension, which seemed at first to be the heart of the Origin-Pawn variable, has been replaced by the concept of *striving*. Second, the concept of personal responsibility has taken on even more importance than we at first saw. Third, it has become clear that the terms Origin and Pawn very often lead to misunderstanding. Let us take up each point in order.

Striving Within Constraints Not Complete Freedom from Constraint

Striving within a personally meaningful context has come to be the central core of being an Origin. Thus, striving has supplanted a vague notion of freedom. An Origin sets his goals and determines the actions that he must take to realize the goals. To help a person to be an Origin is not to force him to do anything he wants, to make him a Pawn to the whims of a completely unstructured environment. Rather, it is to free him to do what he must do by structuring, even constraining the situation, so that he makes his own choices based on realistic selection of appropriate action toward selected goals.

A very important clarification of the concept of freedom was forced on us throughout the project. The Pawn feels pushed around by external forces because he has not chosen his own path and charted his course through those forces. The Origin may be no more objectively free of the external forces, but he does not allow them to determine his ultimate goals. *He* determines the goals and within the meaningful context of *his* goals he constantly strives to mold the external forces to help him attain his goals. The difference between an Origin and a Pawn does not lie in a personal feeling of freedom vs. constraint. True, the Pawn feels constrained and complains about it. When asked, the Origin may report equal feelings of constraint, but he is not obsessed with them. What is most important in his life is responsible commitment. He strives to visualize his path through the external constraints to the goals that result from his commitment.

The difference between the Pawn and the Origin is a basic difference in outlook. It is not necessarily conscious in the sense of being reportable by the person when asked. Neither Origins nor Pawns often stand back from themselves to take an "objective look," and if they do, the reported results may be at odds with their ongoing behavior. Immersed in their everyday life they *experience* their actions as different and experience is quite distinct from observation. The Origin experiences his actions as meaningful within the context of what he wants. The Pawn experiences his actions as determined by others and external circumstances.

The Importance of Personal Responsibility

In order for an Origin to concentrate on striving for goals, he must give up the ideal of complete freedom to do anything regardless of the consequences to others; he must learn to take responsibility for the consequences of his actions. This is an early step in developing personal responsibility. It is responsibility to others in the sense of learning to seek self-chosen goals while at the same time promoting (or at the very least avoiding interference with) the goal-seeking of others. The child may take this step in learning personal responsibility by being at first accountable for his actions to an authority. But he must pass beyond accountability to personal responsibility, to a structuring of his world in a manner which makes it meaningful to him to seek his goals in a way that also promotes the goal-seeking of others in his group. Expressed in social-psychological jargon, the development of personal responsibility passes from seeing society as composed of contriently interdependent relations, such as a zero-sum game, to promotively interdependent relations (Deutsch, 1949). In Loevinger's developmental terms the person at the Self-protective stage sees his goals as counterposed (contrient) to those of others. The Conformist has learned that group-set rules can free him from the lonely stand of me against the world. Although the Conformist may look to authority to find the standard of responsible behavior, he is well on his way to internalizing the standards rather then merely being externally accountable to the authority.

We know from project data that fewer than five per cent of the children are above the Conformist stage as they enter seventh grade. Hence, we cannot expect to see fully matured personal responsibility in any of the children. Nevertheless, Blasi's data indicate that the foundation is being laid from which an even more mature responsibility that is beyond accountability could grow. Probably only at the conscientious stage and above, however, does the individual really internalize the idea of personal responsibility in such a way that he can see the real implication of promotively interdependent goals, namely that the most good for the most people is, in fact and in the long run, the most good for me individually.

We can speculate that there is a level at which personal responsibility is completely beyond accountability, a level at which the person is free to do as he must because the responsible striving act is meaningful within his goal-seeking context and no irresponsible act makes sense. At this level a person who has taken responsible action knows he was right no matter what he is told by others, just as someone who has solved a mathematical problem knows he is right. He is not accountable to others, he is personally responsible.

Again the outlook of the Origin is different from that of the Pawn. The Origin is looking to the future to attain his goals within the framework of a constraining world. He seeks means by striving. The Pawn, who has no clear goals or concept of personal striving, sees primarily the constraints.

The types of goals sought (what is thought good) change with development. At first the child has physical needs that he wants ministered to by an adult; having love and having things may be equated (Loevinger's Impulsive stage). As things become more and more important the world is structured as contriently interdependent because desired things are scarce and ownership is exclusive (Self-protective stage). For me to strive for more and more things I must ultimately deprive some other person of those things. For the United States to take fish from South American waters to use as fertilizer may deprive people in South America of food. When scarce physical commodities are the goal, an Origin who strives for his goal without taking others into account may well deprive others and hence treat them as Pawns.

As Maslow (1954) has stressed, however, if physical needs can be satisfied, people can concentrate on social needs. The need for acceptance by others and for warm social interaction (love) introduces a new dimension which is potentially promotive rather than contrient. If I have a warm interpersonal relationship with someone, it is more often than not reciprocal so that my positive feelings for him increase the probability of his having positive feelings for me. Interpersonal warmth, then, is not a scarce commodity that is exclusive of ownership. When goals are interpersonal and promotively interdependent, an Origin can only truly strive for his own goals by promoting others' goals, i.e., by treating them as Origins.

As the Origin-Pawn concept took shape in our thinking we rejected the notion that in order for one person to be an Origin another must be a Pawn. Nevertheless, it seems obvious, at first, that when the goals set by individuals in the group are scarce commodities, competitive striving produces an "if some are Origins then others are Pawns" situation with regard to the objective outcomes of actually attaining the commodities. It is our experience that this is the way some people first understand the Origin-Pawn concept. But this interpretation is based on a superficial concentration on objective outcomes only. After seeing that social goals can be promotively interdependent (an Origin is only truly an Origin when he treats others as Origins), we can see that individuals have both commodity and social goals, and if we concentrate on the striving for both, it is plausible to assume that even when commodities are scarce an Origin striving for his share will fare better in objective commodity outcomes and social acceptance if he plots a course that treats others as Origins whenever possible.

The Misunderstood Origin Concept

The Origin concept is often misunderstood as a mandate for complete lack of restraint. This misunderstanding, as discussed above, can be corrected by defining the Origin as one who concentrates on striving for goals within constraints. A second misunderstanding (that may even grow out of resolving the first) is to assume an Origin-Pawn antagonism in striving, as discussed in the immediately preceding section.

It is striking to consider these misunderstandings in relation to Loevinger's levels of ego development. The first misunderstanding of the Origin concept might be that of a person at Loevinger's Impulsive stage; the second might be that of a person at the Self-protective stage. Such typical misunderstandings give some credence to our sketch (Chapter 10) of the Origin concept at different developmental levels. The problem for the Impulsive person with regard to personal causation is to learn to delay gratification of the desire for attention and physical things in the face of competing demands of others. Perhaps he, at first, grasps the Origin concept as allowing his impulses completely free rein. The problem for the Self-protective person is to learn that not all interactions are zero-sum games, that he does not and cannot stand alone against the world. Again the Origin concept, when misunderstood in the second way, reinforces the Self-protective person's view of the world.

At higher levels of development the Origin concept is sometimes rejected because a conscientious person rejects the self-protective interpretation or is intrigued by, but skeptical about, the possibility that Origins can in fact treat others as Origins. We have heard both reactions from a few students and teachers.

From these speculations about the effects on our thinking of reactions to the Origin-Pawn concept, at least two things are clear. First, we now place even more emphasis on the importance of responsibility and striving and we try to avoid the trap of freedom as license. Second, the Origin concept seems more and more to be bound up with development of the self-concept and thus the concept may be construed quite differently by people at different developmental levels. In retrospect, the importance of the self-concept seems quite reasonable given our initial assumption that personal causation is a core aspect of the self.

EDUCATIONAL IMPLICATIONS OF THE PROJECT

Throughout the project and throughout this book we have tried to avoid telling teachers what they should do in their classrooms. The project was not designed to produce prescriptions for teachers and this last chapter is no place to break our rule. There are, however, some implications that can be drawn for teaching and for education in general. We will confine ourselves to three generalizations and discuss each briefly. First, motivation training for personal causation enhances both motivation and academic achievement when embedded in subject-matter material. Second, developing responsible Origin behavior in children goes beyond (and sheds new light on) the overly simple Autocratic–Democratic–Laissez–faire trichotomy. The trichotomy suggests organizational arrangements without regard for individuals, whereas the Origin concept derives the organizational advantages of the Democratic classroom from individual motivational propensities. The Origin concept is capable of incorporating different leadership styles for different developmental levels. Third, the comparison of personal responsibility with external accountability suggests that school systems that stress competitive achievement in their pupils and base teacher evaluation entirely on the currently popular accountability may be overlooking one of the most important sources of motivation, namely, the feeling of personal causation that derives from internally imposed personal responsibility.

Motivation Training and Academic Achievement

In Chapter 1 we told of the teachers' concern that motivation training was eating up time that should be used for subject-matter study. We related this concern to the educational controversy between those stressing subject-matter learning and those stressing life-adjustment goals in the schools. If the vague concepts of life-adjustment and subject-matter learning are arbitrarily assumed to be independent of each other, they can lead to absurdities. The idea of a pupil who has perfect life-adjustment but has no subject-matter learning after being schooled is absurd. Similarly, since it takes motivation to learn and learning can increase motivation, it is absurd to separate and exclude motivation training from learning. Exclusive concentration on either in the classroom should have adverse effects. The problem is not a simple choice between two alternatives but rather the much more complex question of *how much* of each. The answer to the question "how much?" is partially dependent on the ability of the pupils to assume responsibility. As a result no one who is unacquainted with the pupils can tell a teacher specifically how to pursue the related goals of enhancing motivation and learning, that is, how to promote self-motivated learning in her pupils.

The project data indicate that motivation training enhances academic achievement. Further, the data reveal that training that enhances motivation in the context of academically relevant materials is most effective. Embedding motivational concepts in subject-matter exercises (as was done with the spelling game) was probably the most successful and clearly the best-liked activity of the project.

It seems clear that embedding motivation concepts, especially the connection between striving and goal attainment, into subject-matter lessons has enormous potential for education. The evidence suggests that it is short-sighted of teachers to be so concerned with subject-matter goals that they ignore the motivational implications of their methods.

An Origin Classroom Is Not a Democratic Classroom

As was pointed out in Chapter 9 an Origin teacher is not a *laissez-faire* teacher. To treat children (or anyone) as Origins is to give them the structure, rules, even dictates, that will make it possible for them to develop the capacity to set their own goals and to learn to strive for them. Treating children as Origins is *not* avoiding rules and orders at all cost. To resign from the task of structuring the situation is to give up the major responsibility of being a teacher.

An Origin classroom is not necessarily a democratic classroom either. Treating pupils as Origins is much more difficult than either dictating everything or allowing them to decide everything, even democratically. The teacher is faced with the complex task of deciding how much structure in the classroom will provide an optimum climate for the development of the pupils' own responsibility. This is especially difficult, since in any classroom there will be individual differences in development that will make a climate that is optimum for one child inappropriate for another. The Origin concept does not prescribe the correct classroom procedures but rather is intended to give the teacher a conceptual framework from which to proceed in making decisions about each different class and child that she encounters.

Classroom organization can contribute to motivation enhancement, but it is inadequate if it ignores individual differences. The insight contained in the autocratic-democratic studies is that democratic participation in decision making *often* increases the feeling of enhanced personal causation. *But it doesn't always!* Would you want* to participate in a democratic vote as to whether a doctor should remove your appendix? Can a group of elementary school children be expected to decide democratically everything concerning their lives at school? The answer to the first question is negative, because the decision must be made on the basis of knowledge rather than preference. The answer to the second question is also negative, because children are not developmentally capable of making all decisions for themselves. Classroom organization may be democratic with regard to routine activities, but if the teacher truly has something to teach, she must take the responsibility of determining the best way of encouraging learning. Her goal should be to enhance the children's desire to learn. The specific technique needed to do this may vary from child to child and often may involve rather explicit direction and clear structuring of the situation to help assure the desired outcome for the child.

Beyond Accountability

In educational circles the concept of accountability is presently being hotly discussed. Accountability is seen most simply as "the process of establishing objectives and assessing the degree to which those objectives have been fulfilled" (Marland, 1972, p. 342). The assumption is apparently made that the objectives are externally set and the assessment is made by an external source with power to reward successful attainment of the objectives.[1]

Tempting as it is to enter the debate, we will resist the urge for the same reason that we resist the temptation to prescribe for teachers. Our research cannot be used to damn accountability across the board, nor to urge its universal adoption. The theory of personal causation does suggest that accountability, like democratic organization of a classroom, may affect motivation rather strongly. To be made accountable to an external source may be the first developmental step to becoming personally responsible. Where personal responsibility cannot be assumed, external accountability may be necessary. Where personal responsibility is present already, however, external accountability may well reduce motivation.

The distinction between external accountability and internal personal responsibility symbolizes most clearly our shift from an early emphasis on achievement motivation, with its stress on competition for scarce commodities, to the more generally applicable concept of personal causation of desirable effects in the social as well as the physical environment.

Notes

1. The reader who desires a more detailed presentation of the case for accountability in education may consult Lessinger (1971), Marland (1972) or Perrone and Strandberg (1972), and see Nash and Agne (1972) for a critique.

Appendix A

The Origin-Pawn Scoring Manual

(F. Plimpton)

DEVELOPMENT OF THE MANUAL

The thought-sampling protocols used for the construction of the
scoring manual contains six written cues (adapted from Winterbottom, 1958, and Gall, 1960), each of which is followed by the four
questions: "What is happening?", "What happened before?", "What
is being thought or wanted?", "What will happen?" The subjects
wrote free imaginative stories to each of these six cues.

Out of a random sample of forty protocols, each containing six
stories, approximately one hundred stories were evaluated according
to the following procedure: First, each story was thoroughly read and
absorbed. Next, each was characterized as either an Origin or a Pawn
story. This decision was based upon "personal knowledge," a combination of intuition, training and experience, practice in psychology
with children, personal past experience and a thorough knowledge of
the Origin-Pawn theory, its relating literature and research. Once this
decision was made, the author proceeded to analyze and verbalize her
decision, to justify the classification theoretically, and then to concep-

tualize step by step her reasoning and the factors relating to the initial judgment. After this analysis of the story, a synthesis of the obtained concepts served to reevaluate the initial decision. This procedure was employed for each of the one hundred stories.

In the second step the concepts obtained in the above manner were grouped according to their theoretical and conceptual relationships and proximity.

Thus, at first we obtained seven groups, which in their conception corresponded to deCharms' theory. These seven groups represented the concepts of internal locus of control, internal locus of goal-setting, instrumental activity, reality perception, personal responsibility, self-confidence and self-investment; each forms a scoring category. The empirically obtained factors were retained as subcategories, that is, as operational definitions. These were adopted without any preliminary statistical analysis or support; no frequency counts or similar procedures were used. A set of Pawn categories was developed parallel to the Origin categories.

Following this basic procedure, all the protocols of a total *first sample* of 40 subjects were scored. Again each story was first read and absorbed, but now we proceeded to decide whether a story showed manifestations of any of our seven categories. Each category was defined conceptually and supplemented by specific subcategories. Each category could be scored only once in each story, but one statement could contain more than one category. After conceptual and statistical analysis of these test scores, it was decided to drop the Pawn categories and retain the seven Origin categories only.

A *second sample* of forty protocols was scored according to this coding system. After the analysis of this sample, the seventh category, "self investment," was eliminated, since we found insufficient manifestation of it.

The *third sample* used for the latest refinement of the manual consisted of 175 subjects; for each subject we had three protocols over three consecutive years, totalling 525 protocols, or 3,150 stories. The scoring of this third sample served two purposes, refinement of the manual and exploration of the effects of a two-year Origin-Pawn motivation change project. Before starting to score this sample, the author trained a second scorer in the use of the coding system and an interscorer reliability of 90 per cent was maintained throughout the scoring of the sample. For training purposes we used protocols that were not included in this sample. The reliability of the scorers was calculated by the formula:

$$\frac{2 \times \# \text{ of agreed upon categories}}{(\# \text{ of categories of scorer one}) + (\# \text{ of categories of scorer two})}$$

For the third sample (N = 175) the split-half correlation of the six story cues was .66 (with Spearman Brown correction $r = +.80$). The split-half correlation for the six categories was +.69 (with Spearman Brown correction $r = +.82$).

PROCEDURE FOR SCORING

Before we do any scoring at all, we read the whole story, often several times, until we have grasped the nature of it. We try to project ourselves into the situation, in order to understand the meaning of the plot, feelings, thoughts and behavior, in order to develop a feeling for what the subject is saying and the form in which he says it.

Sometimes we find a clear and strong self-expression in the form of one of the characters involved in the plot. Very often (in the data used here) this character is a child figure. If we find this form of self-expression, we score only for the actions, thoughts and feelings of this one character, and neither for other figures nor for the plot as a whole. In other cases self-expression may take the form of an adult figure; here again we score just for this one figure, and for no other characters or the total plot. We also encounter stories with no single self-expressive figure, but with several characters expressing a trend of thought, sequence of action or compound of feelings. Here we score for several characters. Still a further case is the story where not only several figures reflect the writer's motivational disposition, but where the presentation and perception of the total plot and situation is also a form of his self-expression. Stories in which the subject expresses himself in the whole situation or throughout the entire plot often take the form of a description of a situation, amended by a statement of personal opinion or judgment.

Whenever possible the scorer ought to disguise the identity of the subject. The construction of this manual was based upon scoring without knowledge of the subject's name, sex, age or level of motivation training; the only known factor was the population from which the sample was drawn. We believe that knowledge of the subject's identity is more harmful than useful.

For the scorer each story must present a single unit. He has to read, absorb and score the story completely, and retain the score as definite before proceeding to the next story. The scorer must never read through the entire protocol "in order to get a feel for the subject." Such a preliminary reading will only bias him and make objective scoring difficult. A subject can theoretically write stories ranging in scores from 0 to 6. One story out of six could quite easily influence the scorer's opinion to an extent that the scoring of the whole protocol might be biased and invalid.

Thus the *first rule* is: *deal with each story completely separately.* If one has several protocols to score, the *second rule* is: *score all stories #1 of all protocols, then proceed to scoring all stories #2*, etc. If the number of protocols is large, make bundles of a "manageable" size and proceed with each bundle as just described. We used the word "manageable" on purpose, meaning that the size of such a group depends to a certain extent upon the scorer, upon factors like time required to score one story, time available for continuous scoring, attention span and fatigue. We recommend that persons just getting acquainted with the system choose a group of approximately ten protocols and then proceed to groups of 20. As the scorer gains more experience, he can gradually increase the size of the group of protocols, but we do not recommend exceeding 40. Our experience was that groups of 40 protocols were quite manageable.

With these basic rules in mind we may now proceed to the instructions relating to the actual scoring of the story. Step-by-step instructions for learning to score follow the analyzed stories. As mentioned, the first step is to read and absorb the content, nature and meaning of the story. Next, we make the decision of what we score; we decide whether to score for the thoughts, decisions, actions and feelings of one figure only, of two or more figures, or on the assumption that the whole story expresses the subject's disposition.

Once this decision has been made we proceed to identify the manifestation of our six categories. On the scoring sheet the categories are listed in the order in which we generally identified them. Actual scoring categories may be identified in their conceptual order, Internal Control to Self-confidence, or in order of most to least predominant. Internal Control was usually scored last; the identification of this category is easier to make and is more accurate once we have worked through the whole story and all the other five categories.

The analyses of the sample stories to follow exemplify the natural sequence of our reasoning and decisions for each case. Here we have made an effort to analyze the story by writing down our thoughts in the order that they occurred naturally.

Each category is scored only once in one story, regardless of the number of its manifestations within that story. Thus, the highest possible score for a single story is 6; the highest possible score for one protocol is 36.

A single sentence may contain more than one category and may be scored for more than one category. Different parts of a sentence may be scored under different categories.

Recording the Ratings

The ratings of each story are recorded on a separate sheet; hence one protocol is scored on six scoring sheets. The same scoring sheet may be used for several protocols, but not for different stories. The rating of each category is recorded with an X under the proper category heading. When the analysis of one story has been completed, we add the ratings and record them under "total," proceeding then to the same story number of the next protocol (or the next story and the next scoring sheet). After the ratings of each of the six stories have been recorded in this fashion, it is convenient to record the totals of all stories on a master scoring sheet. Then we add the totals of all six stories in order to arrive at the total score for the protocol.

In summary the rules are:

1. Keep the description of the categories *ALWAYS* at hand.
2. Disguise the identity of the subject.
3. Read each story until its nature is well understood and absorbed.
4. Determine which plot of the story you score.
5. Score each category only *ONCE* in each story (maximum score = 6).
6. One statement may be scored under several categories.
7. Score all stories #1; then proceed to stories #2, etc.
8. Use a separate scoring sheet for each story.
9. The scores, once recorded, must not be changed.
10. Add the total scores of the six stories to obtain the total score for the protocol (maximum score = 36).

DESCRIPTION AND CONCEPTUAL DEFINITIONS OF THE SIX CATEGORIES

(ORIGIN-PAWN CONTENT ANALYSIS SCORING MANUAL)

The following is a description and conceptual definition of our six categories. The list of concepts is supplemented by analyzed sample stories. The reader is strongly urged to study these analyzed stories. The scorer should be aware that we do not score for words or sentences out of context of the total story. Generally a quotation is meaningful and comprehensible as well as scorable only within the context of the whole story. As quotation would only distort our concept and scoring procedure, we make reference to the analyzed stories by identification code; e.g., *E10* for subject #10 and *ss6* for the sixth short story cue of that subject. Thus, *E10ss6*.

Internal Control (IC)

This category is intended to operationalize the concept of "internal locus of causality." Here "internal locus of causality" is a generalized and inclusive concept. It is the individual feeling of being in control of what is happening inside and outside of himself; on the operational level, all thoughts, decisions, activities, perceptions, attempts at problem-solving and their solutions come from within the individual and are internally controlled. The intention, will or decision to behave or not to behave is located within the individual. *Note:* The separate category of IC is not to be confused with the requirement that our other five categories, in order to be scored, must be internally controlled.

Type a: Internal Control of Situation and of Behavior: The individual has complete control over the situation and his behavior is internally controlled. In practice, stories scored for IC of *type a* deal with a decision, goal or desire expressed by the individual, independent of any external factors. The subject creates a situation and deals with it in an independent, internally motivated way. Examples of IC of *type a* are found in *E9ss2, E11ss2, E14ss1, E4ss3, E16ss5.* Some examples where we do *not* score IC are *E4ss1, E10ss1, E5ss3, E9ss1.*

Type b: Internal Control of Reaction: An individual can feel in control of himself and of his environment even when he is in an externally controlled situation; he can still feel internally motivated and behave accordingly. That is, his reaction to an externally controlled or imposed situation can still be totally under internal control. Under this type of IC we also include actions which are "in spite of" external blocks, as in *E9ss6*. The situation is mostly under internal control from the very beginning, but the attempted control imposed upon the person is strong enough, under such conditions, to place IC under the reactive type. Examples for IC of *type b* are *E2ss1*, *E2ss3*, *E4ss2*, *E5ss5*, *E17ss4*.

IC is "Origin-Thema." It is the basic Origin-type behavior that runs through the whole story which is scored. The concept of "Origin-Thema" means that the Origin aspects are manifested throughout the entire story, but not in a form in which we could point to a single word that would represent IC in itself.

As a rule, every-day activities initiated by a physical need (e.g., desire for sleep, hunger, fatigue) or activities compelled by drive states are not scored under IC. If, however, the individual reacts to such a state in an internally controlled way, it is equivalent to IC *type b*, and can be scored as such. Daydreaming is usually not considered an internal type situation; however, a very rare example where daydreaming proves to be constructive planning occurs in *E16ss4*.

A story never receives more than one score for IC even if there seems to be both *type a* and *b* aspects. In the following we refer to GS and IA as being a *type a* or *type b* also. This does *NOT* imply that IC of either type has to be present and scored in order to score GS or IA. It merely means that GS and IA may also be of two types. Again a story may not receive a score of more than one for any of the six categories even if both *type a* and *b* aspects appear.

Goal-Setting (GS)

The decision to behave or act specifically in order to attain a definite goal must be internally caused. The goal-setting is a result of the feeling of being in control of oneself and of one's environment, the result of internal motivation.

Type a: The internally caused decision is entirely independent of any external influences; its origin and source are within the individual. Some examples for GS of *type a* are *E4ss3*, *E5ss3*, *E7ss2*, *E7ss4*, *E9ss2*, *E10ss1*, *E14ss1*.

Type b: The internally caused decision is a reaction to an externally controlled situation. Thus, in its origin it is contingent upon some situation beyond the control of the individual, but the source of the decision itself is still totally within the individual. Examples for GS of *type b* are *E2ss3, E4ss1, E5ss1, E5ss5, E17ss4.*

Goal statements are most often expressed by the use of words like "want" or "decide." But not all statements of "want" are scorable for GS. A statement like "She wants him to hurry" or "He wants him to come home" is not considered to be scorable under GS. In most cases this is a mere statement, a desire, rather than a goal. If such a statement is accompanied by an indication that the subject perceives it as a goal and pursues it as such, then we do score it for GS. Very often such statements are accompanied by an expression of concern for the other, as in *E2ss4, E10ss4* and *E12ss1.* Here the expression of "want" is not scored for GS, but is taken as support for personal responsibility (PR) and the entire statement is scored under that category.

Statements of wishing or hoping are only in very exceptional cases goal statements. Often they are expressions of reality perception as in *E12ss3.*

In order to score GS the *goal must be verbally stated.* We *do not score* under GS for *inferred goals.* We may infer goals in order to understand the plot or in order to score stated *instrumental activity* (IA), but we do not score GS for such an inference.

Goal statements may be either in the past or the present tense. As long as they fulfill the conditions described above, they are scored regardless of temporal reference.

Instrumental Activity (IA)

We define instrumental activity as any internally caused activity which is instrumental to attainment of a goal (GS stated or inferred) of the major plot.

In order to be scored, instrumental activity

1. Must have an internal locus of causality (*type a* or *b*).
2. Must be explicitly stated; again, we do not score inferred instrumental activity.
3. Must be stated in the *present* tense. Past and future instrumental activity are not scored under IA (such statements may be manifestations of some other category).

Some examples of IA *type a* are found in *E3ss1, E4ss3, E5ss3, E9ss2, E10ss1, E11ss2, E13ss3, E14ss1, E16ss5*. IA *type b* examples are *E1ss3, E3ss2, E5ss5, E7ss4*.

Since the cues used in the present protocols contain statements of instrumental activity, the mere exact repetition of the cue in the first sentence is not scored for IA. Examine such a repetitious first sentence very carefully. IA can be scored if the apparent repetition is a significant variation of the cue or if the repetition is further elaborated in the story. Examples of scorable IA are *E12ss1, E3ss2,* and *E9ss2*.

"Thinking" can be instrumental to attainment of the goal in the story, as in *E13ss3* and *E4ss3*. However, beware.

Not all statements of activity are instrumental to goal attainment. *IA is not scored if*

1. The activity is not personal action to attain a goal *(E1ss2, E1ss4, E2ss6)*.
2. The instrumental activity is in the past, future or conditional tense *(E1ss6, E2ss3* and *E17ss4)*.
3. The activity is merely repetition of the story cue *(E2ss1, E8ss2)*.
4. "Thinking" is not instrumental to attaining the goal of the story *(E12ss3* and *E7ss5)*.

Reality Perception

Reality perception is defined as the individual's ability to perceive his position in his environment, his possibilities, strengths and weaknesses. It is the individual's capacity to recognize a problem and to use appropriate means to solve it or to attain a goal. It is often expressed in the ability to recognize "cause and effect" relationships, to perceive environmental problems, the motives of other persons and to adjust appropriately to the situation.

Here more than in any of the other categories, the individual's perceptual environment must be taken into consideration. It is *HIS* reality against which we have to rate him and not *OUR* reality. Since it is often not possible to determine whether a goal is realistic merely from a story, we rely on whether the person in the story is himself questioning its reality by noting blocks and accommodating to them through insights, adjustment, etc.

In the following, we present and discuss the major manifestations of reality perception. These manifestations form subcategories, but they are not separately scored. If any or all appear in a story, the story receives a score of 1 for RP.

(a) *Insight:* The individual has successfully perceived the "cause and effect" relationships involved in his situation. His planning, his actions, hopes and aspirations appear to be based upon an understanding of himself and of his environment and are consequently realizable. Insight may be into the possible reactions of the environment *(E6ss4)*; perception of relationships between personal actions, their interdependence and their consequences in the environment *(E7ss2, E7ss5)*; perception of one's own position in the environment and personal possibilities *(E10ss4, E14ss1)*; or an evaluation of one's own performance. Other examples are *E2ss1, E3ss2, E4ss2, E9ss2.*

(b) *Perception of social interaction:* The individual is capable of perceiving himself as a part of society. He is also capable of insight into and understanding of social interactions and the mutuality of sentiments *(E13ss3)*.

Perceptions of how society functions in the sense of social exchange *(E1ss2)*, of the attribution process *(E2ss1)*, or of the motives of others *(E7ss2)* are also indications of RP.

(c) *Intelligent adjustment:* Adjustment to the inevitable or the insurmountable. It is not equivalent to submission to external forces in a Pawn-like way; e.g., one cannot stop a storm—one can wait until it is over or one can change his plans. Or, one has to go to school by law: one can adjust to that intelligently or never adjust and be a Pawn to the law. Intelligent adjustment can take many forms: the examples below are intended to illustrate a few of them: *E12ss1, E1ss3, E10ss1, E10ss4.*

(d) *Compromise:* Making a compromise is a form of reality perception, closely related to intelligent adjustment but still to be distinguished, since at the same time it is also a form of using appropriate means for goal attainment. Statements of compromises are often found in the last paragraph of a story, as a form of story outcome. In a compromise outcome the manifestation of RP is stronger than that of Self-Confidence (SC) and thus is scored for RP. An example for a compromise is found in *E8ss5.*

(e) *Acceptance of expertness:* A person who perceives reality will inevitably perceive that there are people who are at the moment superior in one field or another. To ask for advice or support from such experts (or from equals) is differentiated here from expecting help in a dependent, passive, escapelike fashion. This aspect manifests itself in the form of the son asking his father for advice, information or help, or perceiving some other person as an expert as in *E3ss2*.

(f) *Obedience:* We need to distinguish two types of obedience: one, the submissive, passive subordination often connected with resignation (Pawnish obedience); the other, more akin to Schiller's concept of freedom, "free is he who makes the law to his own will." Origin obedience is a conscious and rational internalization of social rules. It is a form of adjustment based on sound perception of reality, e.g., "He will think about what his father said and he probably will obey." Obedience sometimes takes the less direct form of wishing to have obeyed, as in *E12ss3*.

(g) *Perception of blocks:* An individual may well perceive blocks within himself or his environment, but find the overcoming of them impossible. Failure to overcome blocks may be due to environmental factors which may be rationally insurmountable, or it may be due to individual weakness.

(h) *Perception of punishment or social sanction:* This subcategory is a combination of subcategories *f, a* and *b*. We see the need to make the distinction between a Pawnish fear of being caught and punished, and the perception of cause-effect relationships in social interaction, which is often accompanied by guilt feelings and consequent activity. An example of the Origin type of perceptiveness is found in *E1ss6*.

(i) *Perception of appropriate means to overcome the block:* This subcategory must be distinguished from the subcategory "overcoming of blocks" under SC. Here we do not refer to the end result of having overcome a block or attained a goal, but rather we rate the ability to *perceive*, or to *discover the appropriate means* to overcome a block (internal or external), or to attain a goal *(E5ss1, E9ss5, E10ss1, E16ss5, E17ss4)*.

(j) *Planning:* Foresight, making provisions for future incidents. These we consider also an essential aspect of reality perception. Manifestations are usually clearly verbalized, as in *E2ss3*.

(k) *Some special cases of reality perception:* In some cases we score *RP instead of PR*. These are generally cases where an apparent PR statement is either externally occasioned, or where the plot of the story makes it evident that the subject is not experiencing or expressing PR, but merely states a perception of some form of RP. Examples for this type of RP are found in *E1ss1* and *E3ss1*. Often we find that a statement of "wishing" or "hoping" expresses reality perception. This might be a perception of any of the RP subcategories, as for example in *E12ss3* or *E1ss5*.

Personal Responsibility

Personal Responsibility is defined as the individual's willingness to assume responsibility for the consequences of his actions, the attainment of his goals, fulfillment of his desires, solution of problems, etc. It is also the willingness to assume "social responsibility" (responsibility for others, the group, community, society). The *feeling* of responsibility is interwoven with the actions, thoughts, feelings and outcomes of a story. There is no single word which we could generally determine to be expressive of personal responsibility; even a word like "worried" may be a mere statement. Below we have listed the major forms in which personal responsibility may manifest itself.

(a) *Responsibility for actions and consequences:* The individual displays a willingness to bear the consequences of his actions, to acknowledge mistakes, and to try to repair damage (of any form) he has done. In many cases this form of PR consists of statements of concern, responsibility or guilt, with subsequent activity; in others, it is only expressed in the way the subject reacts to the situation or context as a whole. Examples of this aspect of PR are found in *E1ss5, E1ss6, E5ss5, E2ss1.*

(b) *Responsibility for goal attainment:* The person does not expect others to fulfill his wishes or to work to attain his goals, but takes the attainment of his goals upon himself. He does not expect *deus ex machina* solutions but makes use of his own resources to get what he wants. Responsibility for goal attainment is also expressed in the decision or desire to assume responsibility for oneself. Persistence in IA and statements of determination are manifestations of responsibility for goal attainment.

(c) *Problem-solving and innovations:* This category is related to the above, but here goal attainment may appear in the form of a specific problem to be solved or overcome, and may be stated in a way which indicates that the subject perceives goal attainment as the solution of a problem. Or the individual has not set himself a goal to be attained, but is faced with a problem and assumes responsibility to solve that problem. We have included in this subcategory *innovation, improvement* and *invention,* since these activities are specific forms of problem solving. Manifestations of PR in the form of the present category are *E5ss3, E9ss1, E9ss2.*

(d) *Social responsibility:* Social responsibility can find expression in many forms. It may be the perception that the individual has responsibilities toward society or vice versa. It may be a feeling or an act of responsibility toward another person, like helping another person. It may also be expressed as respect for others or for the property of others. Examples are found in *E4ss2, E6ss4, E8ss5, E9ss6*.

(e) *Concern for others:* One aspect of social responsibility is concern for another person. We list this as a separate subcategory because concern is not necessarily contingent upon *assuming* responsibility for the other. Concern is often expressed in being "worried" about someone. The mere statement of being worried is not sufficient to be scored PR; it must be supported by either a statement of action concerning the worries, or of the desire or intention to do something about them. These conditions are particularly imperative in *ss4*, where the cue contains the word "worried." Examples: *E2ss4, E3ss4, E7ss3, E7ss4, E10ss4* and *E17ss4*.

(f) *Feeling sorry for or sad for another:* These statements are closely related to the above category. They contain a much stronger affective component than "being worried." For this reason they need no supportive conditions in order to be scorable for PR. *E12ss3* is an example.

(g) *To be friends again:* The decision or desire to be friends *again* or to make up for a fight is a combination of assuming responsibility for one's actions and their consequences and of social responsibility. An example of this subcategory is stated in *E11ss2*.

(h) *Guilt feelings:* An individual who feels personally responsible for his actions and their consequences toward others or society will also have feelings of guilt if he does not live up to his *self-imposed* standards. Manifestations of guilt feelings are thus scored under the category of personal responsibility.

Some examples in which *PR is not scored* are presented and discussed in *E1ss1, E3ss1*.

Self-confidence

Self-confidence is defined as the individual's confidence in his ability to succeed, to effect successful changes in his environment; one's confidence in his personal strength and capability. It is not a striving for power or superiority, but rather a striving for self-actualization and faith in succeeding.

Under this category we also include the individual's faith in a positive outcome, in a positive future and a positive conception of the world.

(a) *Goal attainment:* The goal the person has set himself is successfully attained. SC can only be scored goal attainment if the person succeeded by his own efforts. Such goal attainment is present in *E2ss3, E9ss2, E9ss3*.

(b) *Overcoming of blocks (internal or external):* Often an individual has not set a specific goal, but is dealing with a problem, an internal or external block. Or there is a block between himself (or within himself) and the goal he has set. The successful overcoming of a block or the solution of a problem is a manifestation of self-confidence. Examples are found in *E1ss3, E1ss5, E1ss6, E5ss1, E11ss2, E5ss5, E9ss5, E9ss6, E13ss3, E16ss5, E17ss4*.

(c) *Positive outcome:* Here we deal with stories which are not centered around a specific goal statement, or block to overcome, although both of these aspects may be present. If the outcome of such a story is positive we score for SC, provided the story is not a mere narrative and the positive ending does not fall under any of the nonscorable outcomes. Some examples of positive outcomes scored for SC are *E1ss4, E5ss3, E14ss1*.

(d) *Confidence in goal attainment or positive outcome:* Outcomes that are stated in the future tense but clearly imply attainment of the goal aspired to in the story are scored under SC for confidence in goal attainment, as exemplified in *E4ss3*. Confidence of positive ending occurs under the same conditions as "positive outcome," only it is stated in the future tense, as in *E9ss1*.

(e) *Affect:* Affect is scored under Self-confidence. The theoretical rationale behind this decision is not very strong, nor is it satisfactory. Statements of affect are so rare that we could not see a necessity for establishing a special category, although such a rare category might be the really discriminative one. Thus the decision to score them under SC is arbitrary. At the present time, all statements of affect, except feeling sorry or sad for someone, which are scored under PR, are scored under SC. Our recommendation: in case of doubt, do not score it.

Cases where Self-confidence is NOT Scored
1. If the outcome is *conditional, uncertain, undetermined (E3ss1)*.
2. If a positive ending is unrelated to the scored plot *(E2ss4, E3ss4, E7ss3)*.
3. If positive outcome is a *deus ex machina* solution *(E12ss3)*.
4. If the outcome is a *mere wish fulfillment (E6ss1)*.
5. If *others attain the goal* for the person *(E10ss1)*.

6. If positive outcome is a *completely detached, mere state of narrative fact (E2ss6)*.

7. *If the ultimate outcome is negative (E7ss2, E7ss4)*.

Scoring Rules Specific to Particular Cues Only

Cue ss1   *"A father and son talking about something important."*

The general rule that an exact repetition of the cue is not to be scored for IA applies also to this cue. If the cue is varied to "The son is talking to his father," and his talking is instrumental to attainment of a stated or inferred goal, we do score this statement under IA.

Cue ss2   *"Two men working at a machine."*

The repetition of this cue may be IA only if it is a significant variation of the cue or further elaborated in the story.

Cue ss3   *"A boy with his head resting on his hands."*

This cue often calls for stories dealing with physical drive states (being tired), daydreaming or fantasies. Such stories are scored only if the person expresses an attempt, desire or decision to overcome this state of physical need, or perceives ways to overcome it. Such stories are rarely scorable for IC. An exception is a response of the type in *E16ss5*.

Cue ss4   *"A mother and her child look worried."*

Being "worried" in this story is scored for PR only if it is supported by consequent activity, statement of desire or decision to deal with the worries or further aspects of PR. Examples are listed in subcategory (e) under RP.

Cue ss5   *"A young person sitting at a desk."*

This cue when presented to children of school age often produces stories about school situations. Going to school, in our society, is imposed upon any child; each child is forced into that situation. School therefore is an important part of a child's world and, although externally imposed, we must not a priori discard plots involving school or teachers as Pawnish. A child can react in an Origin way to school or to any imposed situation as well as in a Pawnish way. We believe it is essential to keep this in mind.

    Cue ss6   *"Brothers and sisters are playing—one is a little ahead."*

In this story the statement "He (she, they) *wants to win*" is *not scored for GS*. "Wanting to win" is so common that GS, if scored for this, in *ss6* becomes a completely meaningless score. This statement appears to be a response elicited by the cue of the story, and the third question (what is being thought or wanted), and thus lacks the requirements placed upon Goal Setting. Statements of elaboration, "wanting to pass," "to get ahead," "to catch up," as well as other goal statements fulfilling the conditions of GS are scorable. Two further aspects of this cue pose difficulties for the scorers. We often find outcomes of the nonscorable type of SC and responses to this cue are very often noninvolved answers to the four questions listed. Study the examples and discussions of responses to cue *ss6* carefully.

ANALYZED SAMPLE STORIES

    The stories and their corresponding analyses are ordered according to consecutive numbers assigned for identification within this manual; they are not the original ones used in the research project. The stories appear in the same order as they do in the test protocols, that is, from 1 to 6. In many cases all six stories are not present, but the order is the same. In each case we present the authentic copy of the story out of the protocol, followed by our analysis of that story.

Elss1

    The son has broken a window by accident an ran. his best friend to the lady that he threw the rock. The father went over to talk to the lady about the window.
    The two boys had a fight and are mad at each other. His friend wants to get him in trouble.

He wished that he had never met his friend and to beat him up.

His father will make him pay for the window with his money.

E1ss1 Discussion

No score can be given for the son. He ran away after having broken the window; his best friend tells the lady who broke the window; his friend wants to get him in trouble; he wants to beat him up: these are all indications of externalization.

His father will make him pay for the window with his own money: here also the control is external to the subject, but the perception of having to assume responsibility for his actions, even though expressed through the father, can be scored. Because of the initial lack of responsibility, the several expressions of externalization, and the fact that the father "will make him pay," it cannot be scored under PR but merely under RP; the subject perceives that this is the "normal" or usual solution. Total score is 1 (RP).

E1ss2

They are making cars and one man has a problem about their boss.

He caught his boss going into a bar and not coming out for some time.

The other man wanted no part in his partners problem.

Both men forgot about the problem and kept on working.

E1ss2 Discussion

This story is scored for RP: the other man wanted no part in his partner's problem. RP here takes the form of perception of one's own position in one's environment and of the environment itself. Not wanting to take part in the partner's problem is not lack of responsibility but rather keeping out of something that is not of his concern, something which might bring him into difficulties. IA is not scored, as making cars is not connected with the plot.

The whole story does not show much self-involvement (both men forgot about the problem and kept on working) and could be classified as what we call "descriptive." The total score is 1 (RP).

E1ss3

The boy is thinking about the school picnic. They are going to Holiday Hill.

The last year they went a boy fell off the roller coaster. He also broke his leg.

He is thinking that the same thing will happen to him this year.

The boy will go but he will not get on the roller coaster or other dangerous rides.

E1ss3 Discussion

The subject is going to the picnic, which can be taken as an inferred goal object. Thinking about whether or not to go and about what might happen is instrumental to goal attainment or rejection (IA).

"The boy will go" is scored under SC for positive outcome, and overcoming of blocks (danger, past experience). "But he will not get on the roller coaster or other dangerous rides," is scored for RP: perception of the blocks and intelligent adjustment to reality, which is composed of the personal desire to go to the picnic, the possibility of an accident, the wish to prevent an accident and the consequent avoidance of situations in which an accident might occur. The total score is 3 (IA, RP, SC).

E1ss4

Their brother was kidnapped and the police are looking for him.

The kidnapper said he was going to drive the boy home when getting out of school that day.

The mother thought whoever the kidnapper is he will let him go.

The police found the boy in an alley tied up.

E1ss4 Discussion

"Their brother was kidnapped and the police are looking for him" is not personal action and therefore not scored for IA. We may infer that the police had been alarmed, which is scorable for intelligent adjustment under RP. A further indication of perception of a situation is the second statement, which we can only take as support for RP. In itself it is not scorable for RP, since it is the descriptive and not self-involved part of the story.

The mother's thoughts indicate a faith in a positive outcome, but for the lack of realism and also the lack of any further involvement or action from her part we do not score this for SC, but merely regard it as support for any stronger statement of SC.

"The police found the boy" can be scored for positive outcome under SC; "in an alley tied up" is a further aspect of RP. Total score is 2 (RP, SC).

E1ss5

He just received notice that he did not pass this year.

He didn't do nay work this year and played hookie many times.

He wished that he was like the rest of the kids and not played hookie as much.

He will go the school term over but never played hookie that next year.

E1ss5 Discussion

This story expresses a clear perception of "cause and effect" relationship: The boy didn't do any work, played hookie, didn't pass, wishes he had not played hookie as much, so he will do the term over, never playing hookie. Sentences 1 and 2 combined, the last part of sentence 3 and sentence 4 could all be scored RP. We score the last part of sentence 3 for RP, as the most direct and self-involved indication.

"He will do the school term over" is scored under SC for positive outcome, overcoming of blocks (failing before) and standard of excellence (doing better than before, which is also expressed in the second part of the sentence). "But never played hookie that next year" is scored under PR for willingness to accept responsibility for his actions and their consequences. The total score is 3 (RP, PR, SC).

E1ss6

They are playing a game that they just bought in the store and the girl is leading.

The game was knocked over and the girl purposely put her button ahead.

She was afraid someone would catch her and no one will play with her again.

She put her button back and the game was on.

E1ss6 Discussion

The inferred goal of the girl is apparently to win the game but it does not play the central role in this story. The activity instrumental to that goal (purposely put her button ahead) is not scored, since we do not score past IA.

The central plot concerns the girl's feelings and consequent reactions after she has cheated. Sentence 3 is scored under RP for perception of punishment (social sanction) and perception of her momentary situation in her environment. The last sentence is scored under SC for overcoming of blocks (the desire to win by all means; fear of social sanction) and under PR for assuming responsibility for one's action and making up for it.

The overall story is scored under IC for the strong internal decision to win, the action to attain that goal, the consequent conflict and successful solution. Total score is 4 (IC, RP, PR, SC).

E2ss1

The boys father is talking to him about important
The boy broke their lawn mower
His father said, "since it was an accident, he wouldn't punnish him."
The boy said since he broke it he will pay for it to be fixed out of his allowance.

E2ss1 Discussion

In the first two sentences one gets the impression that the boy is entirely subject to external control. It is the father who talks to him and he broke the lawn mower. In the third sentence the subject expresses, through the father, the perception of an attribution process as it functions in social interaction. This insight we score under RP for perception of Cause and Effect relationships.

In the last sentence the boy assumes responsibility for the consequence of his actions by offering to pay for the lawn mower to be fixed out of his allowance. This we score for PR.

In spite of external factors (father talking to his son; broken lawn mower), the overall story is scored also under IC *type b* for the subject's definitely internally controlled reaction to the situation and handling the problem objectively and responsibly. Total score is 3 (IC, RP, PR).

E2ss3

A boy is tired from raking leaves.
his mother told him seh wasn't going to give him any more money. His said he would work for his money. Because it is hot and he wants an ice-cream cone.
   After he finishes the man gives him a dollar. The boy buys his ice-cream and saves the rest for tomorrow.

E2ss3 Discussion

This story centers around the definite decision to attain a goal in spite of blocks.
   "Because it is hot and he wants an ice-cream cone," is the stated goal and is scored under GS *(type b)*. The second and third sentences we score under PR for assuming responsibility for the attainment of the goal by working for his own money. He finishes his work and gets his money; this is scored under SC for overcoming of blocks (mother doesn't give him money; tired from raking leaves) and goal attainment (getting one dollar). He buys the ice-cream and saves the rest for tomorrow; the latter is scored under RP for foresight and planning.
   The overall story is scored under IC for the strongly internally controlled decisions, overcoming of blocks, and solving the problems posed by the situation. The total score is 5 (IC, GS, RP, PR, SC).

E2ss4

A mother an her doughter is waiting for John to come home.
   John was hit by a car after work.
   They want him to hurry home so they'll know he's alright.
   15 min. later, John, comes home. He went to buy some groceries.

E2ss4 Discussion

Story 4 appears to be a cue that by its nature has a pull for PR in the form of true concern for others. Often it is difficult to determine whether the figures in the story are truly concerned, feel responsible for some other person. For that reason the story must contain either a statement of IA, affect expressing concern, or a goal-statement expressing either concern or is in some form beneficial to the other person. With this cue we often find a form of goal statement that we do not score for GS: statements such as "They want him to hurry" is not a goal that can be set. If no further statements are made in connection with this one, it cannot be scored at all. Or "They want him to get well soon" is also not scorable under GS, but to want someone to get well can be expressing concern for the other person and can be scored under PR. These are further examples that not every expression of "want" can be scored for GS.

In the present story the third sentence is scorable. Wanting to know that he is all right expresses concern for the other person and is scored for PR. The positive ending of the story cannot be scored for SC, since it is independent of the main plot, the two persons being worried. The total score is 1 (PR).

E2ss6

They are seeing who can work the puzzles quick
All of them finished the same time
They will a prize to the winner
The youngest, Susan, wins.

E2ss6 Discussion

This story is an example of the noninvolved, descriptive type which is often found in Cue 6. The goal here apparently is to win, but "seeing" cannot be regarded as IA, nor can "They will [give] a prize" (future tense). "The youngest, Susan, wins" is a positive statement, but for lack of a decision to attain that goal, and for activity instrumental to goal attainment, it is regarded as a mere statement not scored under SC. The total score is 0.

E3ss1

The son is asking his father can he have the car
When the son took the car before he had an accident
The boy is thinking and hopeing that his father will give in.
The father will probly give his son the car on certain conditions. He will be responsible for any damage.

E3ss1 Discussion

The inferred goal here is to get the car. Asking for the car can be scored as IA. On the other hand in this case "thinking" is not scorable for IA. "The father will probly give his son the car" is an example of a conditional or uncertain outcome which is not scored for SC.

The statement "on certain conditions. He will be responsible for any damage" is scored under RP for insight and perception of his position in his environment. In spite of the statement of having to assume responsibility for any damage, we cannot score it under PR, as the statement is made by the father and is external to the boy; for the lack of internal involvement we merely score it for RP. The total score is 2 (IA, RP).

E3ss2

The men are tring to fix the machine but one of them doesn't kno much about it because he just started working.

His friend that work with him knew all about the machine and he home sick in the bed

The man is wanting his friend to get well so that he can return to work.

In about two weeks of the work of a new comer his friend will get well and return.

E3ss2 Discussion

To fix the machine is scored as IA to the inferred goal—to get the machine fixed. "One of them doesn't know much about it because he just started working" plus the second sentence is scored under RP for perception of the situation, insight into one's own position in reality and as an indication for acceptance of expertness, which all go under RP.

The third sentence is not scorable for PR (concern), since the purpose of wanting him well is so he can return to work. It is furthermore an example for "wanting" which is not GS. Wanting his friend to be well and back at work appears to be instrumental to the goal of fixing the machine but cannot be scored for IA, since it is not real activity that could lead to goal attainment.

The last sentence is a positive outcome unrelated to the plot of fixing the machine and is not scored under SC. The total score is 2 (IA, RP).

E3ss4

The mother an child is worried because they can seem to contact her husben at the office.
Her husben had to work late and they were worried
The mother and child is wanting him to come home right away
The father will get in about 12:00 and the mother and child will be sleep.

E3ss4 Discussion

From the first sentence we may infer that the mother and child have tried to contact the father. They seem to be worried for a good reason; they cannot seem to contact him. This chain of sentiments and activities we can score under PR for concern for another person. The third sentence is a statement of wanting that cannot be regarded as GS, but we may take it as a further support for PR.

The positive ending is a factual statement in direct connection with the main plot, concern for the father, and is thus not scored under SC. The total score is 1 (PR).

E4ss1

The son is asking the to spend more time with him
The son was eggnored on father and son day
The son wanted a little attention
The father and son will be the champion of fathers and son day in most contests.

E4ss1 Discussion

We find here a clear goal statement in reaction to the situation: "The son wanted a little attention" and also a consequent activity aimed at attaining this goal: "asking his father." The former we can score for GS, the latter for IA.

The last sentence contains a strong connotation of wish fulfillment, although with one realistic aspect expressed in "in most contests." Even though the son wants more attention, the affective involvement seems rather secondary, not strong enough to be scored for SC. The total score is 2 (GS, IA).

E4ss2

The boss comes and says he must lay one man off one month.
Business was going great he hired two men to do most his work.
One man will have to be layed off now one man this is his only job.
The man who has two other jobs has vollonted.

E4ss2 Discussion

This story expresses an accurate perception of reality and is permeated by a sense of social responsibility. We can score RP for the sequence: business was going great, he hired two men, now that business slows down he has to lay off one man for one month and "one man this is his only job." This latter sentence also expresses a perception of social responsibility which is even stronger in the last sentence: "The man who has two other jobs has vollonted" (assuming: to be layed off). These we score for PR.

The story is also scored under IC, for the internal decision to be layed off instead of the other man, for the internally controlled assumption of personal responsibility, and the generally positive internally controlled approach in a rather externally controlled, hopeless (or Pawnish) situation. The total score is 3 (IC, RP, PR).

E4ss3

The boy is thinking of a present to get his mother
The boy got three job no matter how long and hard to get the money
he wants her the best present for her.
He will get her something very meanful and lovely to her.

E4ss3 Discussion

The goal is stated in sentence 3 and is scored for GS; the decision is internal and definite, as is apparent from the rest of the story.

Thinking in the first sentence is connected with taking three jobs and can thus be scored as IA leading to goal attainment. The second sentence is scored under RP for perception of blocks (no money), for perceiving the realistic solution and overcoming of the block. This sentence also expresses PR in assuming responsibility for attaining his goal, and for the persistence ("no matter how long and hard to get the money"). Concern for others is expressed in "he wants her the best present for her" and in "He will get her something very meanful and lovely to her." The confidence that he will reach his goal is expressed in the last sentence and is scored for SC.

The overall story is scored under IC for completely internally motivated decision, approach and solution to the problem. Total score is 6 (IC, GS, IA, RP, PR, SC).

E5ss1

The father is telling the son about driving.
The son complained that all his friends can drive now.
The knowledge to drive.
The son will learn to drive.

E5ss1 Discussion

The plot of this story is developed around the desire of the son to learn to drive. This goal is stated in the third sentence and is scored for GS. The first statement leads us to assume that the son approached his father with his problem, and is scored under RP for acceptance of expertness. A further support for RP is contained in the third sentence; the son wants the knowledge to drive.

The last sentence is a statement of goal attainment, containing instrumental activity (will learn) and is scored under SC for positive outcome and overcoming of blocks (the lack of knowledge is overcome by learning). The total score is 3 (GS, RP, SC).

E5ss3

The boy is trying to figure out a way to make money.
He saw a model airplane he wanted at the store
The boy wants money
The boy will get the money.

E5ss3 Discussion

The central theme of this story is getting money. In most stories "wanting money" is contingent upon some sort of physical need or external circumstances and thus cannot be scored for GS, since the concept of GS (like the other categories) is based upon internal control. In this case, wanting money is based upon the goal of getting a model airplane, which appears to be an internally motivated goal, thus either of these could be scored for GS *(type a)*. Since sentence 3 contains the more immediate goal, we score this under GS.

The first sentence is scored for instrumental activity (IA) as well as for assuming responsibility for goal attainment and problem-solving under PR ("trying to figure out a way").

The last sentence is scored under SC for positive outcome, since the story contains enough self-involvement to justify this score. The total score is 4 (GS, IA, PR, SC).

E5ss5

This person is doing difficult math.
This flunked math and now wants to do better.
A thourough knowledge of math.
Gradually they will understand math.

E5ss5 Discussion

The theme of this story is the reaction to an externally controlled incident: "This [person] flunked math." The reaction to this is an internally controlled decision: to do better, and to acquire a thorough knowledge of math. Either of these statements can be scored for GS. We scored the more immediate "A thourough knowledge of math" for GS. Wanting to do better is scored under PR for assuming responsibility for the consequences of one's actions, which here (although passive) is flunking math. Instrumental to goal attainment is doing difficult math stated in the first sentence, and is scored under IA. The last sentence contains an overcoming of blocks scored under SC. It also contains perception of reality, "gradually," which is scored under RP.

In spite of the external control occasioning the sequence of thoughts and actions, the story is scored under IC for the independent, positive, responsible and realistic approach to the situation. The total score is 6 (IC, GS, IA, RP, PR, SC).

E6ss1

The father will not let the son go skating so the boy started to cry

last time he asked his father would not not give him the
money to go. so he started to cry and went to his room
     The father thought he had been a little selfish
     So the father gave his son the money to go skating with

E6ss1 Discussion

In previous stories we had examples of internally controlled,
Origin-type reactions to an externally controlled situation. This story
is an example of a Pawnish reaction to an externally controlled
situation. The whole story expresses a Pawnish, dependent, externally led attitude toward the environment.
     The inferred goal is to go skating. The father neither lets him go
nor gives him the money. The reaction is to cry, which we regard as
an expression of helplessness, resignation, uncontrolled emotions—a
Pawnish reaction. The last two lines are a positive ending of the wish
fulfillment or *deus ex machina* type and is not scorable. The total
score is 0.

E6ss4

The dont have any food in the hous to eat and they are
starving
     last time they dind have any food on christmas the people
collected money to buy them food
     The mother wish there was some way for them to eat
because her little girl was hungry
     Maybe they will get their food so they will not starve or the
neighbors will feed them.

E6ss4 Discussion

This story faces us with two alternatives. The mother is the
helpless or even resigned subject of an external situation. She
expresses concern for her little girl, but since the condition for PR in
story 4 is either some kind of instrumental activity, expressed self-
involvement or affect, this concern can at its best be scored under RP
for perception of blocks, the necessity of food for the little girl. If we
assume that the subject expresses himself in the figure of the mother,
the story is a "Pawn story," scored for RP, the total score being 1.
     The other alternative is to assume that the subject expresses
himself in the whole situation; the plot expresses his disposition to
view the world. This assumption may find support in the last state-

ment. He does not want the people to starve, but he only has a conditional outcome. Under this assumption both the second and the last sentences are expressions of social responsibility and scored under PR. Also the perception of reality is now stronger, finding expression in the insight into the mother's situation and insight into the possible reactions of her environment, both scored under RP. We decided for the second alternative. The total score is 2 (RP, PR).

E7ss2

Joe and Harry argue about another job they say working in a beer factory isn't good.
they were content and liked the job because they got free beer but they now want to quit.
they want to get out of the factory and get a good job
they get what they want and were not satisfied because they come late every morning and get fired.

E7ss2 Discussion

This story is a narrative of the type in which the subject describes the situation with all its figures and circumstances, and then amends the story with a personal remark.

Goal-setting is expressed twice, in "but they now want to quit" and then in "they want to get out of the factory and get a good job," and is scored under GS. The apparent goal attainment stated at the beginning of the last sentence cannot be scored under SC, since ultimately the two men get fired again.

The subject seems to express a somewhat ironical or cynical perception of reality in both the second and the last sentence. Even though cynical, it is a keen perception of another's possible motives and of a relationship between personal activities and consequences in the environment (the men are late and are fired) and is scored for that under RP. The total score is 2 (GS, RP).

E7ss3

tom was sad because his mother wass ill, so he went to the church to say a prayer.
everything was allright before but when tom stopped going to church and fighting and skipping school his mother became ill.

toms mother wanted him to do right and kept after tom
until he decided to do right

his mother became well and tom did better and was not
ever going

E7ss3 Discussion

This story is governed by the external power of superstition,
expressed in the second paragraph, and the external control executed
by the mother, expressed in the third paragraph. The mother ultimately becomes well and Tom does better, but both of these outcomes are unrelated to an internal decision or internally guided
activity and thus not scorable for SC. Although subject to the external
power represented by a deity, the fact that the boy is sad and does go
to church expresses a concern for his mother which we score under
PR. The total score is 1 (PR).

E7ss4

the father hasn't come home and the mother is so upset she
calls the police

he had been drinking and got drunk drove in his car and
didn't come back

she wishes he would stop drinking and the son wants the
father to spend more time with him.

the father gives up drinking but doesn't pay any attention to
his son he goes out with other women

E7ss4 Discussion

It appears that there are three goals involved in this story. One is
for the father to come home, the second, for him to stop drinking, and
the third, for him to spend more time with the son. The latter two
seem to be the immediate ones. We find a direct goal statement in the
sentence, "and the son wants the father to spend more time with
him," which we can score for GS. The theme of spending more time
with the son is taken up in the last sentence again. The concern about
the father's drinking is even more elaborated, appearing in the second, third and fourth paragraphs, but since the goal statement is not
direct, we cannot score it as such. The goal to have father come home
is elaborated, since the mother gets so upset that she calls the police.

The decision to make is whether to choose one goal-determined
plot or whether we can take the whole story as a unity, containing
several goals and consequently several different behaviors contingent

upon each goal. We have decided for the latter; hence the fact that the mother calls the police is scored for IA. The mother appears to be truly concerned about the father's absence and expresses concern for his drinking; this is scored under PR. The ending is at first positive, but then takes a negative turn, so that we cannot score it for SC. Total score is 3 (GS, IA, PR).

E7ss5

John had done a math test and is wondering whether or not he passed.

he studied for the test he just didn't seem to be getting anything out of it so he sat up and daydreamed.

he wishes he had studied more and is hoping he made a grade good enough to pass.

he made a passing grade but because he did, instead of studing to make it better he played.

E7ss5 Discussion

Here we find a further example where thinking or wondering cannot be regarded as IA. Although the goal is to pass the test, wondering whether he passed it after (or before) he has taken the test is not instrumental to goal attainment.

He had studied for the test, now he wishes he'd studied more, and finally instead of studying he plays. All are perceptions of the interdependence of behavior and its consequences and are scored for that under RP. Total score is 1 (RP).

E8ss2

Two men are working at a machine.

The machine conked out.

Onlooker wants the machine to be fixed so he can buy a candy bar. The two men wish the man would get lost.

The two men will fix the machine and say about the onlooker, "One crackpot like that is enough."

E8ss2 Discussion

The first sentence is an exact repetition of the cue, not to be scored as IA. The reason for fixing the machine is contingent upon the external factor of the machine having broken. Later we find the statement of the onlooker, which is independent of the situation of the two men, and thus not scored for GS. Finally the two men fix the machine and make a remark about the onlooker.

The story appears to be narrative, with little or no self-investment. Total score is 0.

E8ss5

A young lad that just had his 18th birthday has got a job as a typist. He is sitting at his desk now.

The young lad had a lot of trouble finding a job.

The boss is thinking that the lad should be in school getting more learning. The lad wants to be in school.

The boss will tell the lad that he is firing him for his own good. The lad feels very sad.

E8ss5 Discussion

The situation consists of two figures, equally involved; we decided *in dubio pro rero* and score the goal statement of the boy for GS. The concern of the boss for the boy and his consequent action we score under PR for social responsibility and concern for others. The outcome is ambiguous; the boy is being fired after having difficulty finding the job, but as he is being fired for his own good, it is a compromise which we score for that under RP. Total score is 3 (GS, RP, PR).

E9ss1

A man is talking to his son about the rent and bills that was over due.

Befor that the man could aford the mony but his wife died and all the money went to the hosipitle.

The man thought gettin a job will be the best thing to solve their problems.

The man will get a job and everything will work out fine.

E9ss1 Discussion

The concern is with obtaining the money to pay the bills. The subject perceives his environment well; the hospital bills took all the money, and getting a job might be the way to pay the bills; this is scored under RP. "The man will get a job." The man assumes responsibility to take the problem's solution upon himself and is scored under PR. "And everything will work out fine" expresses the subject's confidence that problems can be solved by personal will and action and is scored under SC. Even though all these categories are present, they are not strong enough to rate the overall story IC. Total score is 3 (RP, PR, SC).

E9ss2

The men is working at a new machine that will do all the work.

Befor the men had to work hard and work late at night.

The men wanted to no if the new machine would really do all the work.

The men found out the machine can do the work just by pushing button.

E9ss2 Discussion

The first sentence is a significant variation of the cue, since the men are actually inventing a machine, and is scored for IA. At the same time inventing or innovation is a subcategory of PR and is scored for that. The goal is to know whether the machine is really doing all the work, as well as making the machine. Wanting to know is scored for GS. "Befor the men had to work hard and work late at night" and now they want to do something about it, is perception of blocks with consequent instrumental activity, scored under RP. The last sentence is scored for goal attainment and overcoming of blocks under SC. The overall story is also scored under IC. Total score is 6 (IC, GS, IA, RP, PR, SC).

E9ss3

A boy is thinking about the test he had to take the next morning.

Before that he didn't take any time to study.

The boy thought if he study that it may be a chance that he could past the test.

The next morning the boy pass the test just by studing and thinking.

E9ss3 Discussion

The boy is concerned about passing the test. "The boy thought if he study that it may be a chance that he could past the test" is scored under RP. Apparently he does study and the next morning he passes the test, which is scored under SC for goal attainment or mastery. Total score is 2 (RP, SC).

E9ss5

The girl is sitting at the desk after school doing her work.
Before that she could work very fast and had no problems at all.
The girl though if she study hard like she use to it would do her some good.
the girl didn't have to stay after school.

E9ss5 Discussion

Here we have the theme of *ss3*. In *ss3* the boy didn't take any time to study; here the girl could work very fast before and had no problems. There the boy thought he ought to study, and that may give him a chance to pass; here the girl thinks that if she studied hard like she used to, it would do her some good, which is scored for RP. She didn't have to stay after school; by studying hard and doing her work, implies that she has overcome the block and is scored under SC. Total score is 2 (RP, SC).

Such comparisons within a protocol we can only make if we have just one protocol to score, or in retrospect, since we must strictly adhere to the procedure of scoring one story for all protocols, before proceeding to the next story. A protocol like the present gives a good example of the advantages of our procedure; it saves us from becoming biased, negatively or positively, from becoming bored or emotionally involved. The single-story scoring method is not only recommended for reliability and validity of the data, but also for the scorer's own benefit. It is much easier to score objectively if one can avoid knowledge of the subject's identity, even sex, and if one strictly avoids looking either at previously scored or unscored stories in a subject's protocol. A scorer can put himself into much conflict and can make his data biased by thinking "that is X, I know him," or "I had him before."

E9ss6

The children are play ball. one is ahead in playing.
they thought that he would never be able to hit a ball.

The children thought if they spent time helping his he would do better.

he learn how to play ball and was a little ahead of them

E9ss6 Discussion

The story is about a boy whose peers (social environment) think he will never be able to perform a certain task. At the same time, these children think if they spent some time helping him, he would do better, which we score under PR for assuming social responsibility and helping others. His learning how to play ball is scored under SC for overcoming of blocks, and the overall story is scored under IC for its social aspect, for overcoming of blocks in spite of adverse expectations. Total score is 3 (IC, PR, SC).

E10ss1

John and his father are talking about getting John a job. One that he could do after school. And on Sat. days. John had asked his father if he could have a bicycle his father didn't have enough money So John had to get a job. John wanted to get a job so that he can bicycle. John's father will get him the job and he will buy the bicycle he wants.

E10ss1 Discussion

The boy wants a bicycle but his father did not have the money, so he had to get a job. This adjustment to the real situation we score under RP. Wanting the job is an "in order to" goal; but the decision to get the bicycle appears to be internal, so we can score this goal under GS *(type a)*. It is not John himself, but his father who gets the job for him. Thus we cannot score for PR. Even though the father is ultimately instrumental for goal attainment, the fact that it is John who talks to his father can be scored as instrumental for goal attainment under IA. But since it is the father who gets him the job, we do not score for SC. The total score is 3 (GS, IA, RP).

E10ss4

Father and son was expected to be home at 4:00 clock and it is now 5:30 p.m.

Once when father was that late he was in an accident.

The mother and her child want their fathers to come home safely.

They will call the job to ask if they were still at work.

E10ss4 Discussion

The third sentence is another example of an apparent goal statement that is not scored for GS. But since the statement is amended with the one word "safely" we can score it under PR for concern for others. Furthermore, PR is expressed in that they will call the job to see if he is still at work. While this is supportive for PR, it is also a correct perception of the personal possibilities to do something about father and an immediate adjustment to the circumstances, and is scored under RP. Total score is 2 (RP, PR).

E11ss2

Mr. Bill & Mr. Evans is working together at a machine talking and appologizing to each other.

At first they had had a fight up in the bosses office about something that didn't matter.

So Mr. Evans thinks that they should make up for it.

Mr. Bill & Mr. Evans a verry good friends agin now there talking together.

E11ss2 Discussion

The inferred goal is "making up for the fight;" instrumental to attaining that goal is "talking and appologizing," which is scored under IA. We score the third sentence under PR for the subcategory being friends again. In the second sentence the subject expresses insight into a realistic situation, where people fight about unimportant matters. This is scored under RP. The two men overcome the block, which we score under SC. The overall story is scored under IC for the completely internally controlled and independent way of thinking, deciding and acting. Total score is 5 (IC, IA, RP, PR, SC).

E12ss1

The father is talking to his son about getting a job.

Before, he had a job but he didn't keep it long because he was never ontime

The father is wanting his son to be something in life.

The boy makes up his mind that he is not going to be like his brother. He's going to get up in time to go to work. And he's going to work harder on his job.

E12ss1 Discussion

The first question concerning us is whether to view the plot as the son being subject to the external control of the father (thus being a Pawn), or whether to score for the writer and not for one specific figure. In the figure of the father we find PR and IA expressed; in the boy we find an intelligent adjustment to reality and a firm decision in the form of making up his mind. These factors speak against viewing the writer as submitting totally to external control; we may assume that he expresses himself throughout the story.

It appears that the son has behaved in an irresponsible way. The father wants his son to be something in life; this statement of "want" cannot be scored for GS, but it is an assumption of responsibility for the other and is scored under PR. Talking to his son about a job is instrumental to making something out of his life and is scored under IA. The son makes up his mind to work harder. This is not a completely internal decision, but is contingent upon his father's initiative and thus is scored under RP for intelligent adjustment. Total score is 3 (IA, RP, PR).

E12ss3

A boy is thinking about his dog. It has just been ran over by a car.

His mother told him not to take the dog out for a walk without a chain.

The boy is wishing he had obeyed his mother.

His mother & father is feeling sad for him. So for his birthday, they buy him a puppy german sheperd dog that he's always wanted.

E12ss3 Discussion

Wishing to have done or not done something can be an expression of insight or perception of reality. Obedience which is more a form of intelligent adjustment than submissive resignation to external powers is also a form of RP, especially for children. In the present story we find these two forms of reality perception combined in the sentence "The boy is wishing he had obeyed his mother," and score it for that under RP. The final paragraph appears to be a *deux ex machina* solution and is not scored for SC. But we do find the statement, "His mother and father is feeling sad for him," which is scored under PR. Total score is 2 (RP, PR).

E13ss3

Gary is sitting at his desk at school and is thinking about something.

At first he was just sitting down running his mouth to his classmates.

He is thinking that maybe if he were nicer he would be liked by more of his classmates and he'd love that to become true.

So he will start acting nicer and being more friendly around his friends in his class with him, and gain friendship.

E13ss3 Discussion

The inferred goal in this story is to be better liked by classmates. The boy "is thinking about something," which we later discover is how to be better liked. Here we score thinking as IA. If he were nicer he might be better liked is insight into social interaction, the mutuality of sentiments and social exchange. We can score under RP. The last sentence further supports RP and can be scored for SC for overcoming a personal block. At the same time, the fact that he does act friendlier expresses responsibility to attain his goal and is scored for PR. Total score is 4 (IA, RP, SC, PR).

E14ss1

The son is talking about a loan. And why he won't get a job.

He wanted it to help buy a car. Instead getting a job.

They both think that he won't have the money to pay back.

He wont get the loan and instead he gets a job.

E14ss1 Discussion

The immediate goal is stated in the second paragraph, in the form of an explanation of paragraph one. He wants a loan; this we score for GS. The son seems to be the initiator of the conversation and talking about the possibilities, advantages and disadvantages of taking up a loan is instrumental to applying for and getting one, and is scored under IA. He wants the loan instead of a job, and talks about why he does not want to take a job—both are aspects of insight into one's own position and into one's personal reality, but since there is not sufficient elaboration of these statements, they are in themselves not expressions of RP. The third sentence appears to be the result of their mutual evaluation of the son's possibilities, and this we score under RP. The same sentence also expresses a perception and willingness to assume responsibility for the consequences of one's actions and is scored for PR.

Deciding to take a job is scored under SC for positive outcome with self-investment. The overall story is scored for IC for the self-determined approach and solution to the problem. Total score is 6 (IC, GS, IA, RP, PR, SC).

E16ss5

The person is daydreaming of the future. He wants to be a great scientist.

While day-dreaming he found that he must work hard in school to become a scientist in later years.

The person wants to study as hard as possible but fears he will not succeed.

He sets a goal to reach. And studies and tries to reach this goal.

E16ss5 Discussion

Stories about daydreaming as a rule are not scorable, since in most cases it is an expression of escape from reality, externalizing causation and responsibility, or of wishful thinking.

The present story is an example of an exception to the rule. We find here a form of constructive daydreaming of an internally controlled person where daydreaming is synonymous to indulgence in a sequence or trend of thoughts which lead to goal attainment and self-fulfillment.

The first and third sentences contains goals scored under GS. He discovers that he must work hard in school to attain his goal, an expression of perception of the appropriate means for goal attainment, but he "fears he will not succeed," a perception of blocks; both of these are scored under RP. "He sets a goal to reach," is a further perception of reality, but at the same time is instrumental to reaching the ultimate goal and is scored under IA. Then he does study, assuming personal responsibility to reach his goal (scored under PR) and tries to reach his goal. This last statement is an overcoming of the fear that he might not succeed, which is an overcoming of a block (although no direct positive outcome). We score this under SC. The overall story is scored for IC for the independent, self-determined attitude, approach and problem solving. Total score is 6 (IC, GS, IA, RP, PR, SC).

E17ss4

The mother and child or in the hospital worrying about the father.
The father was in a car accident and they doctor said he was in serious condition.
The mother want to know is there anything she could do. The child is thinking he is going to die.
The mother would give father some of her blood and a few more of her friends will, too. He will live.

E17ss4 Discussion

This story is one of those rare cases (in this population) where the concept of personal responsibility is very explicit and carried through, governing the theme of the plot. PR is expressed in her being worried and is accentuated by the required support of wanting to know what she can do, and also in that she would give her blood to save her husband. This we score under PR for concern for others, for decision and attempt to solve the problem (problem-solving), for assumption of responsibility to attain the goal. Perception of blocks, in the form of the accident and the father's serious condition, and the perception of how to overcome the blocks in the form of blood donation by the mother and friends are scored under RP. To want to know what she can do is an internal reaction to external forces, and as such we score it under GS. The story ends with a simple statement expressing a confidence in one's capability to overcome blocks, to cope with external forces and is scored under SC.

The overall story is rated IC for the completely internally controlled, responsible, realistic and confident reaction to an externally imposed situation. (IA cannot be scored, although expressed in "The mother would give father some of her blood," since we only score IA stated in the present tense.) Total score is 5 (IC, GS, RP, PR, SC).

PROCEDURE FOR TRAINING ORIGIN-PAWN SCORERS

1. Read the manual carefully, making notes.

2. Take a scoring sheet and start scoring the analyzed stories as you read. Cover each discussion with a piece of paper until you have decided how you would score the story. Then read the discussion and check your reliability. At first it may seem impossible but the sooner you *actively* try to score, the sooner you will begin to catch on. You will never learn by *passively* reading the manual and discussion. Check each story for every category and go back to the manual description of the categories *often,* especially when in doubt.

3. Now—make yourself a *prompter sheet.* Design it yourself to include all categories and brief notes on *one page only* so you can check it at a glance as you score. Leave room for further notes.

4. Go back to the analyzed stories and score all Cue #1 Stories for subjects *E1* to *5* on a new score sheet without referring at all to the discussion. Check your reliability and read the discussion for all discrepancies.

5. Score Cue #1 Stories only for subjects *E6* to *17*. Then check your reliability and note reasons for discrepancies.

6. Score Cue #2 Stories for subjects *E1* to *5* without consulting the discussion. Check your reliability and read the discussion for all discrepancies.

7. Score Cue #2 Stories only for Subjects *E6* to *17*. Check reliability and note reasons for discrepancies. Repeat the process of steps 6 and 7 for Cues #3, 4, 5, 6.

8. Now check your reliability *by category* actually figure the percentage of agreement for *E1* to *17* by each category. Plot reliabilities on graph paper.

9. Starting with the category of lowest reliability, choose at least 10 stories where the category is in question, including all where you disagreed with the manual and some where you agreed. Rescore them for that category only, without reference to correct scores. Check your reliability. Repeat for the next lowest reliability category and so on for all categories.

10. Now sit down with the manual and write out in your own words qualifications and clarifications to help you. Use examples from stories.

11. Select 20 new protocols (that have been scored by an expert,

if possible). If no expert scoring is available, work with a partner, scoring separately, checking agreement and discussing each decision at length.

   12. Warm up on Cue #1 for as many stories as you need from the analyzed stories.

   13. Score all Cue #1 in the new set and check your reliability with expert and/or partner.

   14. Warm up on Cue #2 from manual. Then score all Cue #2 in new set and check your reliability.

   15. Repeat warm up and scoring for Cues 3–6.

   16. Now check your reliability *by category* and rescore by category from lowest to highest reliability as in Steps 5 to 10. (Plot reliabilities. Are they in the 80's yet?)

   17. Select another set of 20 protocols and repeat Steps 11 to 16.

   18. Repeat with as many sets of 20 protocols as it takes to reach 90% agreement in reliabilities.

   NOTE: it helps to keep a card file after Step 16 of crucial stories that gave you trouble, and easy ones too. Sort them by Cue # and warm up on them after the manual is old hat, adding new stories with each batch. Keep your *prompter sheet* in front of you at all times when scoring. When in doubt reread the manual. As you progress past the first set of nonmanual protocols, feel free to reword the manual to help you remember, always recalling the theory.

   19. When two scorers have 90% agreement with an expert and between themselves, then, and only then, can they score new data!

Appendix B

The Origin Climate Questionnaire

(Sharon S. Koenigs & Robert J. Hess)

The Origin Climate Questionnaire contains the following seven items:

1. I.C.—Internal Control
2. G.S.—Goal Setting
3. I.A.—Instrumental Activity
4. R.P.—Reality Perception
5. P.R.—Personal Responsibility
6. S.C.—Self Confidence
7. W.—Warmth

For each category there are two negative items and two positive items, indicated by the plus (+) and the minus (−) signs. For positive items "always" received a score of 5, "often" 4, "seldom" 2, and "never" 1. The reverse was true for negative items, i.e., "always" received 1 and "never" received 5. These scores could then simply be totaled for the scale score. Note that the total Origin Climate Score did not include the "Warmth" items.

DIRECTIONS FOR GIVING THE QUESTIONNAIRE

1) Give the questionnaire after the short story exercise,
either the same period or in another period. It should
take about 20-30 minutes.

2) This exercise consists of 25 statements on 3 pages and one
page of directions.

3) Pass out one set to each child.

4) Tell the children that the questionnaire will be used for
research purposes only at Washington University and that
you will not look at them.

5) Ask the children first to put their first and last names on
the paper at the top of the first page, and to fill in their
school, grade, teacher, and birthdate.

6) Tell the children you are going to read the directions on
the first page out loud and ask them to pay attention and
read the directions silently with you.
       a) Read the direction aloud.
       b) Answer any questions.

7) Read the first item on page 1 aloud, ask them to think
about it and circle the most appropriate alternative of
Always, Often, Seldom, Never.

8) Let them work silently reading each item and circling one
choice for each at their own speed. Encourage them to
work quickly.

9) As each child finishes, pick up his paper and put it
immediately into the folder.

The Origin Climate Questionnaire

NAME_____   Circle one: MALE   FEMALE

SCHOOL_____   GRADE_____

HOMEROOM OR BLOCK TEACHER_____

BIRTHDATE _____ _____ _____
            mo.   day   year

QUESTIONNAIRE INSTRUCTIONS

THIS QUESTIONNAIRE WILL HELP US TO UNDERSTAND HOW YOU FEEL ABOUT YOUR CLASS. IT IS NOT A TEST AND WILL NOT COUNT AS PART OF YOUR SCHOOL WORK.

IT IS IMPORTANT FOR YOU TO ANSWER THE QUESTIONS IN YOUR OWN WAY. TRY TO ANSWER THEM AS HONESTLY AS YOU CAN. THERE IS NO RIGHT ANSWER.

THINK ABOUT EACH QUESTION AND CIRCLE THE ANSWER THAT SEEMS BEST TO YOU. THINK ONLY OF THE CLASS THAT YOU ARE IN NOW--NOT ANY OTHER CLASS.

1.	We get to decide what we do in this class	+I.C.	ALWAYS	OFTEN	SELDOM	NEVER
2.	The teacher lets good students help those who are not doing so well	+P.R.	ALWAYS	OFTEN	SELDOM	NEVER
3.	The teacher gives us many things to do that I am not good at	-S.C.	ALWAYS	OFTEN	SELDOM	NEVER
4.	I think the teacher likes us	+W.	ALWAYS	OFTEN	SELDOM	NEVER
5.	The teacher gets into a bad mood	-W.	ALWAYS	OFTEN	SELDOM	NEVER
6.	The class rules are made just to help the teacher	-R.P.	ALWAYS	OFTEN	SELDOM	NEVER
7.	In this class I can decide how to use the extra time	+G.S.	ALWAYS	OFTEN	SELDOM	NEVER
8.	The teacher gets angry when we work ahead in our lessons	-I.A.	ALWAYS	OFTEN	SELDOM	NEVER
9.	I like to ask the teacher for help when I have a problem	+R.P.	ALWAYS	OFTEN	SELDOM	NEVER
10.	The teacher likes to help us when we have questions	+W.	ALWAYS	OFTEN	SELDOM	NEVER
11.	The teacher lets us try new ways of doing things	+I.A.	ALWAYS	OFTEN	SELDOM	NEVER
12.	The teacher gives us the answer to a problem when we ask her.	-P.R.	ALWAYS	OFTEN	SELDOM	NEVER

13.	The teacher makes our assignments too hard	-S.C.	ALWAYS	OFTEN	SELDOM	NEVER
14.	The teacher tells us how to use our extra time	-I.C.	ALWAYS	OFTEN	SELDOM	NEVER
15.	The teacher gets upset when we try new things	-I.A.	ALWAYS	OFTEN	SELDOM	NEVER
16.	The rules we have in this class are made to help the students	+R.P.	ALWAYS	OFTEN	SELDOM	NEVER
17.	The teacher gets angry with us	-W.	ALWAYS	OFTEN	SELDOM	NEVER
18.	The teacher lets us do things our own way	+I.C.	ALWAYS	OFTEN	SELDOM	NEVER
19.	In this class I get to do things that I want to do	+G.S.	ALWAYS	OFTEN	SELDOM	NEVER
20.	The teacher makes us do what she wants us to do	-G.S.	ALWAYS	OFTEN	SELDOM	NEVER
21.	The teacher gets angry when students try to help each other	-P.R.	ALWAYS	OFTEN	SELDOM	NEVER
22.	I can do even the hardest work in this class if I try	+S.C.	ALWAYS	OFTEN	SELDOM	NEVER
23.	In this class we can work at our own speeds	+I.A.	ALWAYS	OFTEN	SELDOM	NEVER
24.	We must try to do a problem ourselves before the teacher will help us	+P.R.	ALWAYS	OFTEN	SELDOM	NEVER
25.	We do many things in this class that I can do well	+S.C.	ALWAYS	OFTEN	SELDOM	NEVER

26.	The teacher decides what I should do when I finish my work early	G.S.	ALWAYS	OFTEN	SELDOM	NEVER
27.	The teacher makes me feel dumb when I ask for help	R.P.	ALWAYS	OFTEN	SELDOM	NEVER
28.	The teacher gets upset when we don't do things her way	I.C.	ALWAYS	OFTEN	SELDOM	NEVER

References

Adorno, T. W., Frenkel-Brunswick, E., Levinson, D., & Sanford, R. N. *The authoritarian personality.* New York: Harper & Row, 1950.

Alschuler, A., Tabor, D., & McIntyre, J. *10 thoughts.* Middletown, Conn.: Education Ventures, Inc., 1969.

————*Teaching achievement motivation.* Middletown, Conn.: Education Ventures, Inc., 1970.

Anderson, H. H. Domination and integration in the social behavior of young children in an experimental play situation. *Genetic Psychological Monograph,* 1937, *19,* 341–408.

————The measurement of domination and of socially integrative behavior in teachers' contacts with children. *Child Development,* 1939, *10,* 73–89.

Anderson, R. C. Learning in discussion: A resumé of the authoritarian-democratic studies. *Harvard Educational Review,* 1959, *29,* 201–215.

Atkinson, J. W. (Ed.) *Motives in fantasy, action and society.* Princeton, New Jersey: Van Nostrand, 1958.

Atkinson, J. W. & Litwin, G. H. Achievement motive and test anxiety conceived as motive to approach success and avoid failure. *Journal of Abnormal and Social Psychology,* 1960, *60,* 52–63.

Babbitt, I. *Literature and the American college; essays in defense of the humanities.* Boston and New York: Houghton Mifflin Co., 1908.

Battle, E. The relationship of social class and ethnic group to the attitude of internal versus external control of reinforcement in children. Unpublished master's thesis, Ohio State University, 1962.

Battle, E. & Rotter, J. B. Children's feelings of personal control as related to social class and ethnic group. *Journal of Personality,* 1963, *31,* 482–490.

Bestor, A. *The restoration of learning.* New York: Knopf, 1955.

Blasi, A. A developmental approach to responsibility training. Unpublished doctoral dissertation, Washington University, 1971.

Bridgman, P. W. *The logic of modern physics*. New York: Mac-Millan, 1927.

———*The way things are*. Cambridge, Massachusetts: Harvard University Press, 1959.

Brown, W. Some experimental results in the correlation of mental abilities. *British Journal of Psychology*, 1910, *3*, 296–322.

Callahan, R. E. *An introduction to education in American society*. New York: Knopf, 1960.

Campbell, D. T. & Fiske, D. W. Convergent and discriminant validation by the Multitrait-Multimethod matrix. *Psychological Bulletin*, 1959, *56*, 81–105.

Campbell, D. T. & Stanley, J. C. Experimental and quasi-experimental designs for research on teaching. In N. L. Gage (ed.), *Handbook of research on teaching*. Chicago: Rand McNally & Co., 1963, 171–246.

Carnap, R. Psychology in physical language. *Erkenntnis,* III (1932–1933). Reprinted in A. J. Ayer (ed.), *Logical positivism*. Glencoe: Free Press, 1959.

Carpenter, Virginia. Motivational components of achievement in culturally disadvantaged Negro children. Unpublished doctoral dissertation, Washington University, 1967.

Coleman, J. S., Campbell, E., Mood, A., Weinfeld, E., Hobson, C., York, R., & McPartland, J. Equality of educational opportunity. U.S. Department of Health, Education, and Welfare. Washington, D.C.: U.S. Government Printing Office, 1966.

Collins, J. Person perception training unit. Unpublished doctoral dissertation, Washington University, 1973.

Cooley, C. H. *Human nature and the social self*. New York: Charles Scribner's Sons, 1902.

Coor, I. F. The effects of grade level and motivation training on ego development. Unpublished doctoral dissertation, Washington University, 1970.

deCharms, R. *Personal causation*. New York: Academic Press, 1968.

———Personal causation training in the schools. *Journal of Applied Social Psychology,* 1972, *2*, 95–113.

——— & Carpenter, V. Measuring motivation in culturally disadvantaged school children. In H. J. Klausmeier & G. T. O'Hearn (eds.), *Research and development toward the improvement of education*. Madison, Wisconsin: Dembar Educational Research Services, Inc., 1968.

————Carpenter, V. & Kuperman, A. The "origin-pawn" variable in person perception. *Sociometry,* 1965, *28,* 241–258.

Deutsch, M. A theory of cooperation and competition. *Human Relations,* 1949, *2,* 129–152.

Dewey, J. Plan of organization of the university primary school. Unpublished, 1895. Copy in the William Rainey Harper Library, University of Chicago.

————Experience and education. New York: The Macmillan Co., 1938.

Erikson, E. H. *Childhood and society.* New York: W. W. Norton & Co., 1950.

————Identity and the life cycle. In *Psychological Issues,* 1959, *1,* 1 (Monograph 1). New York: New York International Universities Press, Inc.

————*Identity, youth and crisis.* New York: W. W. Norton & Co., 1968.

French, E. G. & Lesser, G. S. Some characteristics of the achievement motive in women. *Journal of Abnormal and Social Psychology,* 1964, *68,* 119–128.

French, J. R. P. & Raven, B. The bases of social power. In D. Cartwright & A. Zander (eds.), *Group dynamics: Research and theory,* (2nd ed.). Evanston, Illinois: Row, Peterson & Co., 1960.

Freud, S. *The ego and the id.* London: Hogarth Press, 1961, Standard Edition, 19, 3–66.

Future Planning Manual, Behavioral Science Center, 1967. (mimeographed booklet)

Gall, H. S. *The development of affiliation motivation.* (Doctoral dissertation, University of North Carolina), Ann Arbor, Michigan: University Microfilms, 1960. No. 60-4837.

Gardner, J. W. *Excellence: Can we be equal and excellent too?* New York: Harper, 1961.

Gelman, R. Conservation acquisition: A problem of learning to attend to relevant attributes. *Journal of Experimental Child Psychology,* 1969, *7,* 169–187.

Ginsburg, H. *The myth of the deprived child: Poor children's intellect and education.* Englewood Cliffs, New Jersey: Prentice-Hall, Inc., 1972.

Glasser, W. *Schools without failure.* New York: Harper and Row, 1969.

Harvey, O. J. (ed.), *Motivation and social interaction.* New York: Ronald, 1963.

Harvey, O. J., Hunt, D. E., & Schroder, H. M. *Conceptual systems and personality organization.* New York: John Wiley & Sons, Inc., 1961.

Havighurst, R. J. *Developmental tasks and education.* New York: Longmans, 1952.

Heider, F. *The psychology of interpersonal relations.* New York: Wiley, 1958a.

————Consciousness, the perceptual world, and communications with others. In Renato Tagiuri & Luigi Petrullo (eds.), *Person perception and interpersonal behavior.* Palo Alto, California: Stanford University Press, 1958b.

Hunt, J. McV. Intrinsic motivation and psychological development. In H. M. Schroder & P. Suedfeld (eds.), *Personality theory and information processing.* New York: Ronald Press, 1971, 85–177.

Isaac, K. S. Relatability, a proposed construct and an approach to its validation. Unpublished doctoral dissertation, University of Chicago, 1956.

James, William. *The principles of psychology,* Vol. 2. New York: Henry Holt & Company, 1890.

Jensen, A. R. How much can we boost IQ and scholastic achievement? *Harvard Educational Review,* 1969, *39,* 1–123.

Kagan, J. & Klein, R. E. Cross-cultural perspectives on early development. *American psychologist,* 1973, *28,* 947–961.

Katz, I. Academic motivation and equal opportunity. *Harvard Educational Review,* 1968, *38,* 57–65.

Kelley, H. H. Attribution theory in social psychology. In D. Levine (ed.), *Nebraska symposium on motivation.* Lincoln: University of Nebraska Press, 1967, 192–240.

Kelly, G. A. *The psychology of personal constructs.* New York: Norton, 1955.

Koch, S. Behavior as "intrinsically" regulated: Work note towards a pre-theory of phenomena called "motivational." in M. R. Jones (ed.), *Nebraska symposium on motivation.* Lincoln: University of Nebraska Press, 1956.

Kohlberg, L. The development of moral character and moral ideology. In M. L. Hoffman & L. W. Hoffman (eds.), *Review of child development,* Vol. II. New York: Russell Sage Foundation, 1964, 383–431.

Kuperman, A. Relations between differential constraints, affect, and the origin-pawn variable. Unpublished doctoral dissertation, Washington University, St. Louis, 1967.

Labov, W., Cohen, P., Robins, C., & Lewis, J. A study of the nonstandard English of Negro and Puerto Rican speakers in New York City. Final Report, U.S. Office of Education Cooperative Research Project No. 3288. New York: Columbia University, 1968.

Lessinger, L. Teachers in an age of accountability. *Instructor,* June/July, 1971.

Lewin, K., Dembo, T., Festinger, L., & Sears, P. A. Level of aspiration. In J. McV. Hunt (ed.), *Personality and the behavior disorders.* New York: Ronald Press, 1944, 333–378.

——Lippitt, R., & White, R. Patterns of aggressive behavior in experimentally created "social climates." *Journal of Social Psychology,* 1939, *10,* 271–299.

Likert, R. A. A technique for the measurement of attitudes. *Archives of Psychology,* 1932, *140,* 44–53.

Lindquist, E. F. & Hieronymous, A. N. Iowa test of basic skills. Boston: Houghton-Mifflin, 1955.

——Iowa test of basic skills: Teacher's manual (-66062). New York: Houghton-Mifflin, 1964.

Litwin, G. H. & Ciarlo, J. A. Achievement motivation and risk taking in a business setting. Technical Report, The Behavioral Research Service, General Electric Company, New York City, 1959.

Loevinger, J. The meaning and measurement of ego development. *American Psychologist,* 1966, *21,* 195–206.

——Theories of ego development. In L. Breger (ed.), *Clinical-cognitive psychology: Models and integrations.* Englewood Cliffs, New Jersey: Prentice-Hall, 1969, 83–135.

—— Wessler, R. *Measuring ego development: 1. Construction and use of a sentence completion test.* San Francisco: Jassey-Bass, Inc., 1970.

Malcolm H. Behaviorism as a philosophy of psychology. In T. W. Wann (ed.), *Behaviorism and phenomenology.* Chicago: University of Chicago Press, 1964, 141— 155.

Margenau, H. *The nature of physical reality.* New York: McGraw-Hill, 1950.

Marland, S. P., Jr. Accountability in education. *Teachers College Record,* Feb. 1972, *73,* 3, 339–345.

Maslow, A. H. *Motivation and personality.* New York: Harper, 1954.

McClelland, D. C. Toward a theory of motive acquisition. *American Psychologist,* 1965, *20,* 321–333.

——Longitudinal trends in the relation of thought to action. *Journal of Consulting Psychology,* 1966, *30,* 479–483.

—— & Alschuler, A. S. Achievement motivation development project. Final Report, Project #7-1231, Grant #0-8-071231-1746, U.S. Office of Education, Bureau of Research, 1971.

——, Atkinson, J. W., Clark, R. A., & Lowell, E. L. *The achievement motive*. New York: Appleton-Century-Crofts, 1953.

——, Davis, W. N., Kalin, R., & Wanner, E. *The drinking man*. New York: The Free Press, 1972.

—— & Steele, R. S. *Motivation workshops: A student workbook for experiential learning in human motivation*. New York: General Learning Press, 1972.

—— & Winter, D. G. *Motivating economic achievement*. New York: Free Press, 1969.

Murray, H. A. *Thematic apperception test manual*. Cambridge, Mass.: Harvard University Press, 1943.

Nash, R. J. & Agne, R. M. The ethos of accountability: A critique. *Teachers College Record,* Feb. 1972, *73,* 3, 357–370.

Neill, A. S. *Summerhill*. New York: Hart Publishing Co., 1960.

Osgood, C. E., Suci, G. J., Tannenbaum, P. H. *The measurement of meaning*. Urbana, Illinois: University of Illinois Press, 1957.

Perrone, V. & Strandberg, W. A perspective on accountability. *Teachers College Record,* Feb. 1972, *73,* 3, 347–355.

Perry, W. G., Jr. *Forms of intellectual and ethical development in the college years: A scheme*. New York: Holt, Rinehart & Winston, Inc., 1968.

Piaget, Jean. The mental development of the child. In David Elkind (ed.), *Six psychological studies*. New York: Vintage Books, 1968, 3–73. (Originally published in *Juventus Helvetica,* 1940.)

Plimpton, F. H. Origin-Pawn manual: A content analysis coding system designed to assess the Origin syndrome. Unpublished manual, Washington University, 1969.

—— The effects of motivation training upon the Origin syndrome. Unpublished doctoral dissertation, Washington University, 1970.

Polanyi, M. *Personal knowledge*. Chicago: University of Chicago Press, 1958.

Prosser, C. A. *Life adjustment education for every youth*. Office of Education *Bulletin,* 1951, No. 22, Washington, 1951.

Redl, F. & Wineman, D. *Controls from within*. New York: Free Press, 1952.

Roethlisberger, F. J. & Dickson, W. J. *Management and the worker*. Cambridge, Mass.: Harvard University Press, 1939.

Rogers, C. R. *Freedom to learn.* Columbus, Ohio: Charles E. Merrill, 1969.

Rothenberg, P. T. Locus of control, social class and risk taking in Negro boys. Unpublished doctoral dissertation, Washington University, 1968.

Rotter, J. B. Generalized expectancies for internal versus external control of reinforcement. *Psychological Monographs,* 1966, *80* (1, Whole No. 609).

Rosen, B. C. & D'Andrade, R. G. The psychological origins of achievement motivation. *Sociometry,* 1959, *22,* 185–218.

Ryals, K. Achievement motivation training for average ability underachieving eighth and tenth grade boys. Unpublished doctoral dissertation, Washington University, 1969.

Saint-Exupery, A. *A sense of life.* New York: Funk & Wagnalls, 1965.

Scheffé, H. *The analysis of variance.* New York: Wiley, 1959.

Scott, W. A. Measures of test homogeneity. *Educational and Psychological Measurement.* 1960, 20, 4, 751–757.

Shaw, M. E., Briscoe, M. E., & Garcia-Esteve, J. A cross-cultural study of attribution of responsibility. *International Journal of Psychology,* 1968, *1,* 51–60.

———& Sulzer, J. L. An empirical test of Heider's levels in attribution of responsibility. *Journal of Abnormal and Social Psychology,* 1964, *69,* 39–46.

Shea, D. J. The effects of achievement motivation training on motivational and behavioral variables. Unpublished doctoral dissertation, Washington University, 1969.

Skinner, B. F. *The behavior of organisms.* New York: Appleton-Century-Crofts, 1938.

Smith, L. M. & Geoffrey, W. *The complexities of an urban classroom: An analysis toward a general theory of teaching.* New York: Holt, Rinehart & Winston, Inc., 1968.

Sommer, R. Hawthorne dogma. *Psychological Bulletin,* 1968, *70,* 6, 592–595.

Spearman, C. Correlation calculated from faulty data. *British Journal of Psychology,* 1910, 3, 271–295.

Stevens, S. S. Psychology and the science of science. *Psychological Bulletin,* 1939, *36,* 221–263.

Sullivan, C., Grant, M. Q., & Grant, J. D. The development of interpersonal maturity: Applications to delinquency. *Psychiatry,* 1957, *20,* 373–385.

Sullivan, H. S. *The interpersonal theory of psychiatry.* New York: W. W. Norton & Company, Inc., 1953.

Thelen, H. A. *Education & the human quest.* New York: Harper & Row, 1960.

U.S. Commission on Civil Rights, *Racial Isolation in the Public Schools,* Vol. I, Washington, D. C.: U.S. Government Printing Office, 1967.

Veroff, J. Social comparison and the development of achievement motivation. In C. P. Smith (ed.), *Achievement-related motives in children.* New York: Russell Sage Foundation, 1969.

Warner, W. L., Meeker, M., & Eels, K. *Social class in America.* New York: Harper & Row, 1960.

Weiner, B. *Theories of motivation: From mechanism to cognition.* Chicago: Markham Publishing Company, 1972.

White, R. & Lippitt, R. Leader behavior and member reaction in three "social climates." In D. Cartwright & A. Zander (eds.), *Group dynamics: Research and theory.* (2nd Ed.), Evanston, Illinois: Row, Peterson & Co., 1960.

White, R. W. Motivation reconsidered: The concept of competence. *Psychological Review,* 1959, *66,* 297–333.

Winer, B. J. *Statistical principles in experimental design.* New York: McGraw-Hill, 1962.

Winter, D. G. A revised scoring system for the need for power. Unpublished manual, Wesleyan University, 1968.

Winterbottom, M. R. The relation of need for achievement to learning experiences in independence and mastery. In J. W. Atkinson (ed.), *Motives in fantasy, action and society.* Princeton, New Jersey: Van Nostrand, 1958.

Wirth, A. G. *John Dewey as educator: His design for work in education (1894–1904).* New York: John Wiley & Sons, Inc. 1966.

Wolfenstein, M., Laites, N. *Movies: A psychological Study.* Glencoe, Ill.: Free Press, 1950.

AUTHOR INDEX

271

SUBJECT INDEX

Academic achievement
  classroom groups compared, 158–159
  effect of motivation training on, 141–160, 173, 202, 204
  ego development related to, 154
  goal realism measure related to, 102–104, 153–154
  origin concept as mediator of, 154–157
  risk taking measure related to, 153–154
  self concept measure related to, 153
Acceptance of expertness
  Origin-Pawn behavior category, 224–225
Accountability, 212
  achievement motivation and, 8, 17_n, 213
  contrasted with personal responsibility, 15, 182, 187, 207–208, 210, 212–213
Achievement
  motive for, 8
  as need, 68, 96
  scoring for, 50
  themes in teachers' stories, 50
  words, 69–70, 86
Achievement motivation
  attrition, effects on, 106–107
  categories for, 68–69, 96–97
  compared to Origin-Pawn, 131–133
  defined, 8, 96
  different from personal causation, 8, 67–68
  emphasis of motivation training, 23, 30, 63, 67–70, 96, 97
  goal of, 8, 17_n, 96
  measures, 122–126
  teachers and, 21, 50–51, 56
  theory of and motivation training, 8–10, 17_n, 67–68
  training for businessmen, 8, 67–68
  see also Thought samples
Achievement motivation measure, 122–126, 131–133
  thought sampling, 48, 50–51, 94–99
Achievement motivation scores, effects of motivation training on, 94–99, 104, 106–108, 202
Achievement motivation unit, 20, 23, 67–70, 96, 97

Adjustment, intelligent
  Origin-Pawn behavior category, 224
Affectivity
  development of, 204
  scoring for, 228
Affiliation, 56
Arithmetic scores, 142–145, 147–150, 153–154
Attendance, affected by motivation training, 150
Attribution theory, 10
Attrition, effect on scores, 106–107, 135
Authority
  ego development and, 179–196 passim., 201
  Origin-Pawn behavior and, 13–14, 207–208
  see also Accountability; Leadership; Leadership style

Battle's Measure of Locus of Control (Children's Picture Test) 99, 101, 104
  scoring of, 108–111
  validation for origin measure, 131, 133–134
Behavior
  motivated, components, 54–55, 56
  physicalism, 119–120
  relationship to personal concepts, 4, 5–6, 119–123
  see also Origin behavior; Pawn behavior
Behaviorism, 5–6, 119–120
Blindfold Game (Input #8), 51–52, 58
Block Stacking Game (Input #5), 48, 67, 68
Brainstorming (Input #18)
  person-perception technique, 79, 81
  teachers' workshop activity, 60
Business Game, 62_n

Causation, personal, see Personal causation
Cause, 7
Chicago Laboratory School, 11
Children
  academic skills and, 38
  background of, 19–23, 33–36, 39
  as described by interview data, 36–38

273